ENDORSEMENTS

We've all dealt with tragedies in our lives. Dr. Lessing's tour of the Book of Jeremiah shows us how to do this in the most constructive manner: by pointing us to Jeremiah's reliance on God and the prophet's words that point us to the real "man of sorrows"—Jesus. Lessing skillfully guides his readers through the longest of the Old Testament's prophetic books while also demonstrating its continuing message for Christians who are seeking comfort in the midst of life's griefs and heartbreaks.

—Dr. Andrew E. Steinmann, Distinguished Professor
of Theology and Hebrew, Concordia University Chicago

Reed Lessing delivers a meaningful, scholarly, authentic, and heart-penetrating message in *Overcoming Life's Sorrows: Learning from Jeremiah*. For anyone who has struggled with anything, this is the book you need. Woven with relevant facts, refreshing humor, practical application, and keen insight, Lessing's narrative pours the refreshing water of life into parched and thirsty souls. Timely words call us to a narrative beyond the moment, beyond the latest woes of the culture, and beyond fear of complete loss, always upward to a faithful Savior, who bestows eternal hope.

—Rev. Michael Newman, president, Texas District, LCMS,
and author of *Getting Through Grief: Eight Biblical Gifts for Living with Loss*

When we are in pain, we see our world through a lens clouded with sorrow. We need a Savior who knows our name and draws us to Him. Pastor Lessing has given us a book that is both compelling and genuine. Each chapter walks us through the prophet Jeremiah's life circumstances, leaving God's comforting Word lingering in our hearts. In these chapters, we see that God's Word is relevant to every aspect of our lives, especially our pain.

—Dr. Kim Marxhausen, speaker, instructor, consultant,
and author of *Weary Joy: The Caregiver's Journey*

Known as an exegete, pastor, speaker, and professor par excellence, Reed Lessing expands his significant theological portfolio as he combines textual mastery, deep theological insight, and edifying practical application of lived experiences to inspire readers. He uses the weeping prophet as a "God-given example [for us] of how to overcome massive setbacks" in an engaging and personally applicable manner. Lessing searches the life of a prophet "obsessed with God's Word" in the hope that the reader will be similarly obsessed and, through the answer, Jesus Christ, overcome life's traumas and know the One who gives "a future and a hope."

—Rev. Dr. Brian L. Friedrich, president, Concordia University, St. Paul

Reed Lessing has composed a faithful and inviting way to overcome life's sorrows. By drawing upon passages from the prophet Jeremiah in twenty areas, such as "Overcoming through God's Word," "Overcoming through Hope," "Overcoming through Shalom," and "Overcoming through the New David," Lessing provides the reader with practical guidance that is theologically sound. Meaningful contemporary and historical examples enhance the book's capacity to guide the reader to scriptural resources. Lessing illumines a great truth, namely, "Jeremiah presents himself as a God-given example of how to overcome massive setbacks."

—Rev. Dr. Dean O. Wenthe, president, Concordia University System

"No one is immune to chaos and confusion." Reed Lessing's theological and, as always, thought-provoking insights from the Book of Jeremiah make *Overcoming Life's Sorrows* a uniquely personal text. Lessing offers the reader compassion, connection, and empathy while grounding the reader in the hope of God's Word and the narrative of hope of God's people through the storms and tumults of life. With fascinating biblical commentary and meaty scriptural application, interwoven with stories of both humor and sorrow, *Overcoming Life's Sorrows* will meet any reader right where God's Word needs to speak into both the heart and mind.

—Heidi Goehmann, licensed clinical social worker and mental health provider, deaconess, writer, and speaker

As Kansas, Iowa, and Nebraska are sometimes called "flyover country," Dr. Lessing laments that the Book of Jeremiah, with its jungle of judgment and sorrow, can sometimes become a "flyover book." Instead of flying over life's sorrows, Lessing leads us through life's sorrows, learning from Jeremiah that "the worst parts of life are the gateways to the best parts of life," conforming us to the character of Christ (Romans 8:28–29). For anyone who has experienced a major setback in life, Dr. Lessing is a blessing.

—Rev. Dr. David Coe, assistant professor of theology and philosophy, Concordia University, Nebraska

The Book of Jeremiah is "a survivor's guide for exiles living in despair," writes Dr. Reed Lessing. So is this book, with its masterful portrayal of how pain is not pointless when it points us to Christ. Striking a balance between personal and professorial, Lessing draws parallels between the experiences of the Old Testament prophet and our own, making this a remarkably relevant book for anyone seeking hope amid suffering. It is a beautiful book of shalom.

—Jane Wilke, author and communications strategist

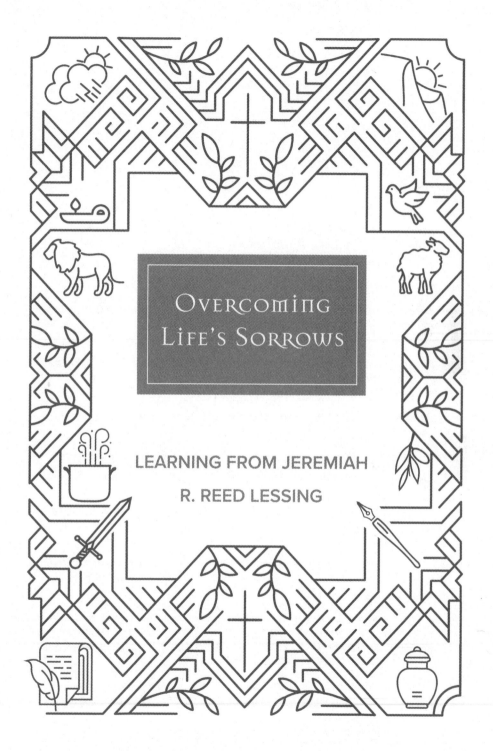

Overcoming Life's Sorrows

LEARNING FROM JEREMIAH

R. REED LESSING

CONCORDIA PUBLISHING HOUSE • SAINT LOUIS

Published by Concordia Publishing House
3558 S. Jefferson Avenue, St. Louis, MO 63118-3968
1-800-325-3040 • cph.org

Manufactured in the United States of America

2 3 4 5 6 7 8 9 10   30 29 28 27 26 25 24 23 22

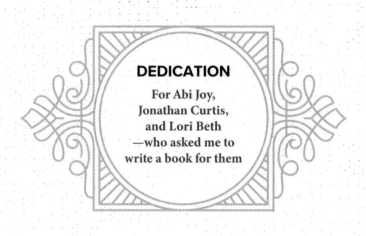

DEDICATION

For Abi Joy,
Jonathan Curtis,
and Lori Beth
—who asked me to
write a book for them

TABLE OF CONTENTS

INTRODUCTION

I taught at Concordia Seminary in St. Louis, Missouri, from 1999 to 2013. During those years, I went to annual meetings of the Society of Biblical Literature, where I frequently attended presentations on Jeremiah. I learned to treasure the book from scholars such as Kathleen O'Connor, Walter Brueggemann, Louis Stulman, Terence Fretheim, and others. Their insights, as well as my own personal sorrows, prompted me to write this book.

This isn't a commentary; neither is it a book of devotional reflections on Jeremiah. Instead, it's a combination of the two, based upon one of the prophet's major themes—surviving life's sorrows. I'd liken this contribution to an application commentary. I apply biblical truths, especially for people who have experienced a major setback in life.

If you've gone through a difficult time, you're left with questions—questions like these:

- Can I experience sorrow and not be destroyed?
- Can I keep my heart from turning to stone when it's been wounded and broken?
- Is there a road map that takes me from death to life so I can live again?

Jeremiah answers yes, yes, and yes. There is hope! The prophet composed his book for Judeans who endured Babylonian invasions in the late seventh and early sixth centuries BC. These people lived through warfare, death, and starvation. Then the Babylonians deported them to a foreign land. Almost every passage in Jeremiah foresees these times of sorrow, defines them, or looks for ways to cope with their painful realities.

Anyone who serves as a pastor, counselor, chaplain, or missionary; anyone who works as a doctor or nurse, or on a fire or police department; anyone who has dealt with homelessness or victims of domestic violence—you have all encountered horrific trauma. Within the rough-and-tumble of family life, parents and spouses also witness their fair share of sorrows. No one is immune to chaos and confusion.

What should we say to someone whose life has just been crushed? What can we do? How can we avoid glossing over the depth of their pain? How can we not be traumatized ourselves when reaching out to help? And how do sorrows—personal and public—fit into our Christian beliefs that God is merciful, kind, and just?

This book provides concrete answers to these urgent questions. I've written it for a broad audience—caregivers and counselors, as well as anyone who has been broken by life's cruel events. It's for those who have buried their head in tears and wept into the night. It's for people who have seen a sunny, cloudless day suddenly change into a storm, lightning, and tempest. A granddaughter was born with cystic fibrosis. A mother died of dementia. A childhood was filled with the anguish of alcoholic parents. The fear of failure refuses to lessen its death grip. A sister once decided to break all ties with you.

Often authors share these kinds of lists in an attempt to relate to people's sorrows. That isn't this list. This list is personal. From the cystic fibrosis to the spurning sister. Yes, this list is all me.

With lists like this, it's easy to get lost in despair. Trust me. I know. *I really know.* I haven't written this book from the perspective of an expert who has it all together. I'm looking to overcome my own sorrows and setbacks—just like you.

I invite you to take a journey through Jeremiah with me. I promise not to offer hollow hope or simplistic bumper-sticker quotes. And rest assured, I will repeatedly point you to Jesus.

When all seemed lost, King Zedekiah asked the prophet, "Is there any word from the LORD?" (Jeremiah 37:17). What is God's answer? He gives us the Book of Jeremiah.

CHRONOLOGY

JEREMIAH

Jeremiah's Birth
[655 BC]

Jeremiah's Call
[626]

Jeremiah Taken to Egypt
[582]

Jeremiah Dies in Egypt
[570]

JUDEAN KINGS

Amon's Reign
[642–640 BC]

Manasseh's Death
[642]

Josiah's Reign
[640–609]

Josiah Begins Reforms
[621]

Jehoahaz's Reign
[609]

Jehoiakim's Reign
[609–598]

Jehoiachin's Reign
[598–597]

Zedekiah's Reign
[597–587]

EVENTS

Assyria Loses Control
of Judah
[629–620 BC]

Scroll of the Law of Moses
Found
[622]

Assyria Falls to Babylon
[612]

Egypt Controls Judah
[609–605]

Nebuchadnezzar Becomes
King of Babylon
[605]

First Babylonian Exile
[597]

Jerusalem Destroyed and
Second Babylonian Exile
[587]

Third Babylonian Exile
[582]

The Assyrians deported people from Galilee and Transjordan as early as 733 BC. They crushed Syria in 732 BC. God permitted Assyria finally to destroy idolatrous Israel in 722 BC. Much of the Israelite population was deported and assimilated into upper Mesopotamia (2Ki 15:8–17:23). Assyria resettled other peoples in Israel (2Ki 17:24–41).

Nebuchadnezzar became king of Babylon in 605 BC. He deported Jehoiachin of Judah and others in 597 BC after Jerusalem was destroyed (2Ki 25:1–25; 2Ch 36:11–21). Other Judeans escaped to Egypt after further unrest (2Ki 25:22–26, which resulted in a further deportation ca. 582 BC. The Judeans lived in refugee colonies in the vicinity of Babylon.

1

MEET JEREMIAH

"The words of Jeremiah, the son of Hilkiah,
one of the priests who were in Anathoth in the land of Benjamin."

(Jeremiah 1:1)

On January 17, 2004, a sixty-ton whale died and was beached on the southwestern coast of Taiwan. Two weeks later, authorities decided to haul the dead whale to a laboratory where they could do an autopsy. It took fifty men and three lifting cranes thirteen hours to hoist the whale onto a flatbed trailer truck. People poured into the streets of a local city to watch the spectacle of a whale carcass pass through their town.

And then it happened! As the truck crawled through the city, with crowds looking on, the whale exploded. That's right, the whale exploded. The insides of the whale splattered cars, people, and local shops. Traffic stopped for hours. The smell was unbearable. Betcha no one saw that coming!

Isn't that just like life? We're going about our business and a whale explodes. We're left stunned with lots of questions that begin with this word: *Why?* Why did she leave me? Why did he have to die so young? Why did we lose so much money? Why does our daughter continue to cause us so much pain? Why? Why? *Why?*

Exploding whales come in all shapes and sizes. Hurricanes, earthquakes, floods, forest fires, and tornadoes. There are also financial, relational, emotional, marital, and spiritual disasters. And we can't forget military disasters, public health disasters, political disasters, and, increasingly, environmental disasters. Disasters come in all shapes and sizes. They turn our lives upside down and inside out.

What do we do when a whale explodes? The great temptation is to fake it; to say that everything is "just fine"; to put on a face and put on a smile and say, "Ignore the torpedoes, full speed ahead!" Exploding whales are unpleasant, messy, and ugly, and they smell to high holy heaven! It's better to ignore them and pretend they don't exist.

Denial, however, only lasts so long. Eventually we come to the realization that there is something incredibly wrong and painful going on. We don't know what to do next. Everything seems so fuzzy. Some people can't work. Others can't get out of bed. Still others don't feel like eating. *Sorrows bring with them more sorrows.* The ripple effect might mean our finances will never be the same—nor will our health, our job, or our family. This snowballing effect devastates us. We self-medicate through too much food, work, exercise—you name it and we can overdo it. This, in turn, creates deeper and more painful sorrows.

Perhaps there comes a day—shortly after the sorrow—when we feel like we've turned the corner, moved through it, and come out on the other side. This is an illusion. The smallest sight, smell, sound, or touch triggers the memories and we're back where we started. Recollections of the catastrophe hit us right between the eyes. We're retraumatized. We feel lifeless. We have no language to describe our pain. To survive, we shut down. To keep going, we turn off our emotions. Questions plague us. When will I stop being possessed by my past? When will I stop recycling my brokenness and passing it on to others?

There are things that happened to us as children. There are things that happened to us as teenagers. There are things that happened to us as adults. What happens if we don't address these things? We develop anxieties, anger, and fear. We become negative, cynical, and sarcastic. Increasingly, we isolate ourselves from everyone and everything.

Disaster specialists encourage us to stock up on axes and flashlights, along with a "grab-and-run kit" that includes enough food and water for seventy-two hours. We also should have a portable shelter and plenty of first-aid supplies. Add to our list of survival "must-haves" a book called Jeremiah.

Jeremiah describes life as it is, not life as he hoped it would be, not life as it should be. Jeremiah begins with life as it is—exploding whales, experiences that exceed our ability to cope and carry on. Every poem, narrative, or sermon in his book relates to Babylonian-inflicted sorrows of the late seventh and early sixth centuries BC. The prophet either announces them, explains them, or offers hope for living through them.

More Than a Bullfrog

You may remember a group called Three Dog Night. In one of their songs, "Joy to the World," they sing, "Jeremiah was a bullfrog." The Jeremiah of the Bible was a mighty prophet in word and deed. He was hardly a bullfrog!

The biblical Jeremiah is the most complex and developed character in the Old Testament. In fact, the book gives us one of the best portraits of any person in the ancient world. Jeremiah was a poet of grace and a preacher par excellence who knew the bittersweet experience of loving God and loving people. Jeremiah stays hard as a rock while being torn apart on the inside. He is anything but shy and reserved. The prophet frequently wears his heart on his sleeve.

Jeremiah was born in Anathoth (modern 'Anata), a town three miles north of Jerusalem. His father, Hilkiah, was a priest after the order of Abiathar whom Solomon expelled to the small village of Anathoth (1 Kings 2:26–27). Jeremiah's historical references (e.g., Jeremiah 1:1–3; 25:1–3; 36:1–2) indicate that his public influence lasted over forty years.

God calls Jeremiah in 627 BC, a time of national grandeur and power. However, things quickly begin spinning out of control. Jeremiah lives through Judah's rapid decline and the country's end in August of 587 BC, which brought death, broken families, and massive deportations. The prophet's ministry ends several years later with his deportation to Egypt (Jeremiah 42–44). He probably died in the land of the Nile.

That's a broad outline of Jeremiah's life and times. Let's look at some details.

Judah's political landscape began to change with the fall of Assyria and the destruction of its capital city, Nineveh (612 BC). Assyria was down, but not out. In a fight of heavyweights—Assyria and Babylon—the Judean king Josiah sided with the Babylonians. This was a fatal mistake. Josiah was killed at the Battle of Megiddo (609 BC). It was the beginning of the end for Judah. Jeremiah sensed that, so he uttered a lament for the slain king (2 Chronicles 35:25).

Next up? The Battle of Carchemish in 605 BC, where Babylon defeated an Egyptian-Assyrian coalition. Jeremiah was witnessing changes of historic proportions, led by the meteoric rise of Babylon under its founding king, Nabopolassar, and his famous son Nebuchadnezzar. Babylonian success led to Judah's downfall, the burning of God's holy city, the destruction of the temple, the loss of the land, and multiple deportations.

Jeremiah lived through the halcyon days of Josiah through Judah's last gasp and eventual death under Babylon's vacillating vassal Zedekiah. Through it all, the prophet is bold, authentic, unintimidated, and direct. Jeremiah is an overcomer.

An Overcomer

Most of the time, Old Testament prophets are eclipsed by their oracles. Isaiah is mentioned by name 17 times in his book and Ezekiel just twice. What about Jeremiah? He's mentioned a whopping 125 times. Jeremiah participates fully in the events he describes. Judah suffers and Jeremiah suffers. Judah loses hope and, at times, so does Jeremiah. Judah is exiled and, in the end, so is Jeremiah—to Egypt. By combining his life with his message, Jeremiah is unique among prophets. He doesn't merely tell us about what happens. He shows us what happens through his own experiences. Jeremiah doesn't want us only to understand the events of the Babylonian captivity. He wants us to live and feel them.

To say, therefore, that we know more about Jeremiah than any other prophet vastly understates the evidence. Amos was a successful cattle rancher. Hosea was married to Gomer and had a painful family life. Isaiah, for his part, was also married and had at least two sons that we know of. Ezekiel was married and one day his wife died suddenly.

On the other hand, Jeremiah presents his book in a completely different way. He paints a full portrait of his life, from times before he was born to his ignominious exile to Egypt. Jeremiah gives us vivid accounts of his spiritual life, including his ongoing wrestling with God.

Why does the prophet give so much information about himself? We all instinctively know that when we read about someone else's life, it leads us to reflect on our own life. By giving us what is close to an autobiography, Jeremiah invites us to consider our losses in light of his—and to see that God's promises for him are for us as well.

What did Jeremiah do that caused him to suffer so much? We can answer that question with two words: radical threat. The prophet rejects an accommodated, tamed, safe approach to the issues of his day. In short order, Jeremiah's enemies become legion. They include his fellow townspeople from Anathoth (Jeremiah 11:23), members of his own family (Jeremiah 12:6), the monarchy (Jeremiah 22:13–30; 36:1–32), and his prophetic counterparts (Jeremiah 27–28). In fact, Jeremiah 8:8–13 depicts the prophet in conflict with every element of Judean society. Even the public taunts him, saying, "Where is the word of the LORD? Let it come!" (Jeremiah 17:15). People call Jeremiah names like "Terror on Every Side" (Jeremiah 20:10). Jerusalem's leaders go so far as to label him a Babylonian sympathizer, a spy aiding and abetting the enemy. The prophet was considered a traitor—an ancient Benedict Arnold.

Jeremiah's enemies threaten to kill him (Jeremiah 11:18–23). They plot against him (Jeremiah 18:18–23) and dig holes to trap him (Jeremiah 18:22). Officials bar him from the temple (Jeremiah 36:5) and arrest and imprison him—not once but twice (Jeremiah 20:1–6; 37:11–16). King Zedekiah finally consigns Jeremiah to death in a mud pit (Jeremiah 38:4–6). It comes as little surprise that the prophet would rather die than keep facing such hostile opposition (Jeremiah 20:14–18).

Miraculously, though, Jeremiah lives to tell us about it. Like the proverbial cat, he has nine lives! Like a Hollywood movie hero who repeatedly dodges death, Jeremiah does so over and over. He has numerous narrow escapes, often though threats appear seemingly out of nowhere.

Let me count the ways.

Jeremiah's first imprisonment occurs in Jerusalem's temple, a place we would think he would be welcome. Instead, a priest named Pashhur strikes the prophet and puts him in stocks (Jeremiah 20:1–6). The next morning, for no stated reason, Pashhur releases the prophet.

Then, after a sermon, a mob attacks Jeremiah and self-righteously tells him, "You shall die!" (Jeremiah 26:8). That's a pretty tough congregation to preach to! Then, without explanation, Ahikam son of Shaphan rescues the prophet, "so that he was not given over to the people to be put to death" (Jeremiah 26:24).

When Jeremiah and his scribe, Baruch, create a scroll containing the prophet's words, Jeremiah almost gets killed again. Banned from the temple by the government, Jeremiah sends Baruch to read the scroll there in his stead. Following the public reading, allies tell Jeremiah and Baruch to hide from the king's wrath: "Let no one know where you are" (Jeremiah 36:19). Both the prophet and scribe escape unscathed.

Years later, during the Babylonian siege against Jerusalem, the enemy army withdraws. Jeremiah takes the opportunity to visit the area of Benjamin, when suddenly a guard accuses him of desertion (Jeremiah 37:11–21). Despite his denial of treason, officials arrest, beat, and imprison the prophet. King Zedekiah intervenes and orders the captors to free Jeremiah and even give him a daily ration of food. He survives still another near-death experience.

Soon afterward, Judean officials seize Jeremiah again. King Zedekiah, who had so recently saved Jeremiah from prison and starvation, gives the order that Jeremiah should die (Jeremiah 38:1–6). State officials lower the prophet into a muddy cistern. Surely, this time the prophet's luck has run out. Yet unexpectedly, an Ethiopian named Ebed-melech saves Jeremiah from the pit. Against all expectations, he survives once more (Jeremiah 39:11–18).

At the book's beginning, God promises Jeremiah that he will overcome every enemy: "I make you this day a fortified city, an iron pillar, and bronze walls, against the whole land. . . . They will fight against you, but they shall not prevail against you" (Jeremiah 1:18–19). Jeremiah suffers greatly, but he survives. No one is able to silence him. He keeps on preaching into Judah's darkness.

JULY 587 BC

Put yourself in the shoes of someone living in Jerusalem in July 587 BC. The noise of military operations is enough to raise your anxiety level off the charts. But that has been going on now for two years. What's new is that Babylonian army engineers are building siegeworks right outside your window. You have no idea what to do. Your spouse and children look dumbstruck. You're all trapped; there's no way out. Your neighbors know this. That's why they've entered panic mode and have started screaming.

The battering rams are enough to give you a splitting headache. *Bam! Bam! Bam!* If only your father were here. He would be such a source of strength right now—but alas, the Babylonians killed him when they attacked Jerusalem ten years ago. He was bludgeoned to death with a sword.

That was then. This is now.

As the city walls are shattered, you hear women and children crying. Animals are going berserk. Everyone and everything is shouting at the top of their lungs. Once the enemy soldiers breach the wall, you begin to hear foreign words. It must be Akkadian, you reason—the language of the invaders. Once inside the city, the captors begin barking out orders.

Thousands of your fellow citizens fall in line. Babylonians drag those who resist to the middle of the city square and execute them on the spot.

Within the next few days, the conquerors surround the temple, confiscate its liturgical vessels, and set the building on fire. You can't believe your eyes. The temple. Solomon's temple. Up in smoke! Those barbaric Babylonians begin splattering the blood of dead priests on sacred places! Where is God in all of this?

After a month, Jerusalem, the city of David, is unrecognizable. Houses, streets, markets—the entire infrastructure is ruined. Surveying the damage, you see the unspeakable: unburied corpses of people and animals. You cover your eyes, then your nose. The stench is unbearable.

You're hungry. So is your family. That's why you keep walking through the city—or what's left of it. With each passing day, hunger turns into an obsession. If you don't eat soon, you'll die. On top of everything, you start hearing rumors of young girls being raped while others are rounded up and deported to Babylon.

Babylon! That's a seven-hundred-mile journey. You've heard how prisoners are treated—like cattle, threatened with insults and whips. You know if your fellow Judeans survive the death march around the Fertile Crescent they'll be forced to work in the fields—the killing fields along the Euphrates River.

What you see next brings you back in the moment. It's beyond description. The occupiers mutilate Judean officials with swords and clubs. Enemy soldiers treat it all like a game.

You knew all along that the ragtag Judean army would succumb to Babylon, but it's so much worse than you ever imagined. You can barely talk about it, much less describe your pain. None of it makes sense. You begin to feel as though you're going crazy, caught in a vortex of forces beyond your control. Deep from within your heart you cry out, "How in the world did I get *here*?"

ISRAEL'S SLOW DEATH

Israel's history was like a downhill train ride in the Rocky Mountains—alternating between mountains of faithfulness and valleys of apostasy. It was a steady decline from faith to idolatry to finally exile. Faith at the Red Sea with Moses. Idolatry in the Promised Land with its seducing Canaanite gods and goddesses. Exile to Babylon.

After leaving Egypt and inheriting the Promised Land, Israel got off to a rocky start. Even though many of the judges, like Deborah and Gideon, were heroic figures, the nation needed a king (Judges 17:6; 21:25). Israel finally arrived when the monarchy began to take shape. With David and Solomon, the nation had everything going for it—the promises to the patriarchs and matriarchs, the gift of the land, and the temple in Jerusalem.

Then everything began to fall apart. The liberated slaves from Egypt began to enslave one another (1 Kings 4:6; 5:13; 9:15). The oppressed in Egypt became the oppressors in the Promised Land. God's people neglected orphans, widows, and foreigners. Jerusalem became the new Egypt, and everything was undone.

Psalm 106 reviews this slow death. God's people mixed with the nations and served their idols. They sacrificed their sons and their daughters to demons, shedding innocent blood. They were rebellious, stubborn, and unbelieving. The result? A monstrous reality showed up like a fire-breathing dragon, ripping apart everything.

Jeremiah frequently describes the horror with the words "sword," "famine," and "pestilence" (e.g., Jeremiah 14:12, 16; 15:2). "Sword" appears over seventy times in the book; "famine," more than thirty times; and "pestilence," over twenty times. On several occasions, the prophet even says the dead were dishonored by not being given proper burial (Jeremiah 7:33; 8:1–3; 9:22; 16:4; 19:7; 34:20). Who was responsible for all the gory and ghastly suffering? Babylon.

THE BABYLONIAN EMPIRE

The Babylonian Empire—centered in present-day Iraq—was an

alliance of two people groups, the Medes in the Zagros Mountains to the east and the Chaldeans in southern Mesopotamia. The kingdom began with Nabopolassar's ascension to the throne in 626 BC and became a superpower when its army overthrew the Assyrians at the Battle of Nineveh in 612 BC. Babylon's moment in the sun, however, was fleeting. The empire barely outlasted its greatest king, Nebuchadnezzar II, and came crashing down when the Persian king Cyrus the Great conquered the city in October of 539 BC.

While Babylon and Assyria controlled roughly the same region, their military strategies were vastly different. Assyrians repopulated lands they defeated. The goal was to establish economically productive provinces. On the other hand, Babylon's policy was "slash and burn." Marauding armies destroyed buildings, vineyards, crops, and vegetation. Once a nation was subdued, the demographic movement was one way—to Babylon. Babylonians didn't invest time and effort to create productive provinces. Instead, they engaged in military campaigns to secure wealth that supported life in their urban centers along the Euphrates River.

It's not surprising, therefore, that after the Babylonians defeated Jerusalem, the city's population declined by 90 percent, while that in the land of Judah fell by 70 percent. During the Persian era (539–333 BC), Jerusalem's population was about three thousand, or 12 percent of the population of the city and its suburbs on the eve of the destruction in 587 BC.

The Napoleon Bonaparte of his day, Nebuchadnezzar, Babylon's king from 605 to 562 BC, was a military genius. In his native language of Akkadian, his name means "May Nabu [a Babylonian god] protect the boundary." Babylonian boundaries were not only protected, they expanded greatly—especially after Nebuchadnezzar's defeat of Pharaoh Necho at the Battle of Carchemish in 605 BC. The victory catapulted him to sole control over the ancient Near East. Jeremiah describes Nebuchadnezzar's powerful military machine:

- "He comes up like clouds; his chariots like the whirlwind; his horses are swifter than eagles." (Jeremiah 4:13)

- "At the noise of horseman and archer every city takes to flight; they enter thickets; they climb among rocks; all the cities are forsaken, and no man dwells in them." (Jeremiah 4:29)
- "Their quiver is like an open tomb; they are all mighty warriors." (Jeremiah 5:16)
- "They shall eat up your harvest and your food; they shall eat up your sons and your daughters; they shall eat up your flocks and your herds; they shall eat up your vines and your fig trees; your fortified cities in which you trust they shall beat down with the sword." (Jeremiah 5:17)
- "They lay hold on bow and javelin; they are cruel and have no mercy." (Jeremiah 6:23)

The prophet tells us that this fierce enemy is from the north (e.g., Jeremiah 1:13; 4:6; 6:1). In Jeremiah 20:4, however, the prophet states the adversary's name—Babylon. Then, from Jeremiah 20:4 to the end of his book, Jeremiah mentions Babylon over 180 times. The nation is God's agent to judge His people Judah.

- "I will give all Judah into the hand of the king of Babylon." (Jeremiah 20:4)
- "To Babylon you shall go." (Jeremiah 20:6)
- "I will give Zedekiah king of Judah and his servants and the people in this city who survive the pestilence, sword, and famine into the hand of Nebuchadnezzar king of Babylon." (Jeremiah 21:7)
- "I am giving this city into the hands of the Chaldeans and into the hand of Nebuchadnezzar king of Babylon." (Jeremiah 32:28)
- "Thus says the LORD: This city shall surely be given into the hand of the army of the king of Babylon." (Jeremiah 38:3)

BABYLON ATTACKS

While King Josiah (640–609 BC) sat on Judah's throne, everything came up roses. Freedom was in the air. A weakened Assyrian Empire allowed Josiah to reverse the pro-Assyrian policies of his father, Manasseh. In 622 BC, Josiah even led one of the greatest reformations in the Bible (2 Kings 22–23 = 2 Chronicles 34–35). While carpenters and masons were repairing the temple, Hilkiah the high priest found "the Book of the Law" (2 Kings 22:8). This led to sweeping religious renewal throughout the land. It was a time of optimism and national autonomy.

It was also the calm before the storm.

Josiah died in 609 BC while fighting Egyptians at the Battle of Megiddo. The king was trying to prevent Egyptians from siding with Assyrians who were contending with Babylonians for supremacy in the ancient Near East (2 Kings 23:29–30 = 2 Chronicles 35:20–24). King Josiah's death led to a four-year Egyptian occupation of Judah (609–605 BC). The land of the Nile also captured Jehoahaz, Josiah's successor, and placed Eliakim upon the throne, renaming him Jehoiakim.

It was then Babylon's turn to set up a puppet government in Judah. Nebuchadnezzar shackled Jehoiakim in chains and deported him. Judah's third-to-last king died in Babylon. His son, Jehoiachin (also known as Jechoniah), became king in 597 BC—but not for long. After three months, Jehoiachin, the queen mother, government leaders, and many skilled workers were exiled to Babylon (2 Kings 24:6–15). This deportation included the prophet Ezekiel.

With the newly minted Judean king Jehoiachin locked away in prison, Nebuchadnezzar installed Mattaniah, Jehoiachin's uncle, upon the throne, changing his name to Zedekiah—the last king of the Davidic dynasty. Still another a puppet king. What an insult! Ezekiel refused to acknowledge Zedekiah, dating his oracles according to the years of the exiled King Jehoiachin (Ezekiel 1:2).

Most Judeans believed this was all a temporary setback. Egypt would rise again, defeat Babylon, and free Judah from Nebuchadnezzar's rule. The spiritually astute, however, saw things differently. For them, the yet-to-come dismantling in 587 BC was appearing on the horizon. Example A? The ever-vacillating King Zedekiah continued to withhold tribute from Babylon. He was playing a game of Russian roulette.

Things completely fell apart in Zedekiah's eleventh year (2 Kings 24:17–20). Nebuchadnezzar moved to blockade Jerusalem. The city stood its ground for almost two years. Food and water became scarce. Diseases ran rampant. Egypt played to type. Promising everything. Delivering nothing. Hoped-for help from the pharaoh never arrived. Zedekiah experienced Babylon's iron fist. The empire struck back in all its fury (2 Kings 25:1–21).

THE END

The coup de grâce came on August 28, 587 BC—the darkest day in Judah's history. Babylon finally decided to destroy the "rebellious city, hurtful to kings and provinces" (Ezra 4:15). This is "why this city was laid waste" (Ezra 4:15). Nebuchadnezzar toppled the city's walls and torched Jerusalem's temple. Soon everything—the monarchy, the priesthood, the storied history in the Promised Land—all went up in smoke. The city of David was reduced to ruins (Jeremiah 39:1–10; 52:4–30). Babylon's army also incinerated a number of Judean cities—including Lachish, Azekah, Beth-Shemesh, Bethel, and Ein Gedi.

Judah's collapse brought unspeakable suffering. Many died in battle. Some resorted to cannibalism (Jeremiah 19:9). Women were violated and raped. The empire deported the nation's brightest and best and occupied Judah for almost fifty years. Nebuzaradan, the commander of the Babylonian imperial guard, put it this way: "The LORD your God pronounced this disaster against this place. The LORD has brought it about, and has done as He said. Because you sinned against the LORD and did not listen His voice" (Jeremiah 40:2–3). It was a catastrophe of historic proportions.

As for Zedekiah? He witnessed his sons' execution and then the Babylonians blinded him, leading him into exile (2 Kings 25:7). Nebuchadnezzar then appointed Gedaliah as governor; he ruled from Mizpah, as Jerusalem had been reduced to rubble. The peace didn't last long. A small band of freedom fighters, led by a certain Ishmael, assassinated Gedaliah at the provincial capital (Jeremiah 41:1–3). Under the leadership of Johanan, a remnant of Judeans, fearing Babylonian reprisal, fled to Egypt—forcing Jeremiah to go with them (2 Kings 25:22–26; Jeremiah 43).

If all this sounds confusing, imagine living through it!

In all, Babylon inflicted four deportations upon Judah: (1) 605 BC, the third year of Jehoiakim (Daniel 1:1–7); (2) 597 BC, during the reign of Jehoiachin (2 Kings 24:10–17); (3) 587 BC, during the rule of Zedekiah (2 Kings 25:1–21); and (4) 582 BC (Jeremiah 52:30). These forced population movements inflicted a mammoth rupture in Judah's life, unleashing untold misery and mayhem.

According to Jeremiah 52:30, the total number of Babylonian deportees was 4,600. This probably denotes only men. Adding women and children brings the aggregate number to around 15,000. Others estimate the total number to be between 20,000 and 100,000. Whatever the exact figure was, Babylon left Jerusalem like a ghost town (2 Chronicles 36:21). Judah was ravaged in four significant ways.

The monarchy. Had not God promised an everlasting kingdom to David and his descendants? Zedekiah is now blinded, captured, and exiled. And Jehoiachin? Where is he now? Sitting in a Babylonian prison.

The land. Had not God given the land to Abraham, Isaac, and Jacob and their descendants forever? Had not Israel lived in Canaan since 1401 BC? Now Babylon controls the land. And the empire had the audacity to slash and burn, pillage and destroy trees, crops, and farms.

The covenant. The relationship God established with Israel at Sinai was now broken (Jeremiah 31:32). God unleashed the covenant curses Moses spelled out in Leviticus 26 and Deuteronomy 28—full bore.

The priesthood. The Babylonian butcher Nebuzaradan executed Seriah, the high priest. And the temple? The domain of Judah's priests? Trashed. Burned. Dust in the wind.

What does the future hold? Nothing. Less than nothing. "Nebuchadnezzar the king of Babylon has devoured me; he has crushed me; he has made me an empty vessel; he has swallowed me like a monster" (Jeremiah 51:34).

Exile

Jeremiah 1:3 concludes with the expression "until the captivity of Jerusalem." The book ends describing this disaster (Jeremiah 52:27–34). This literary envelope signals Jeremiah's singular focus—exile.

The word denotes forced population movements, refugee camps, prisoners of war, uncertainty, brutalization, displacement, and post-traumatic stress disorder. Exile implies a total loss. Judeans in Babylon had no recognizable landscape and no familiar tastes, smells, or sounds. Nothing gave them a sense of belonging. They were captive to the grip of despair. "We looked for peace, but no good came; for a time of healing, but behold, terror" (Jeremiah 14:19).

A myriad of emotions assault us when we feel like we've lost everything. We become angry. We protest and blame. We want revenge. The next day, we conclude that we're beyond repair, that things are irreversible, that nothing will ever make sense again.

Exile. Much of what we loved and worked for is now gone. We doubt both God's compassion and His power to deliver. We're tempted to believe in nothing and hope for nothing. That's what exile does.

Judeans, for their part, were paralyzed, unable to move forward. Babylon had fractured their world beyond recognition. Cultural givens and cherished institutions had vanished into thin air. Everything near and dear was shattered into a million pieces. "Judah has gone into exile because of affliction and hard servitude; she dwells now among the nations, but finds no resting place; her pursuers have all overtaken her in the midst of her distress" (Lamentations 1:3).

Judean deportees to Babylon wondered, "Does God care about us? How can we believe in Him anymore? Why not instead worship Babylonian gods? After all, their armies are more powerful than ours. What does our future hold?" The loss appeared unending.

Life wasn't what it used to be. The "new normal" wasn't close to normal at all. The past was over. Done. Finished. The temptation was to disappear into the woodwork. To live counter to the Babylonian culture was too demanding and costly. It was so much easier to go along. After all, when in Rome, do as the Romans do. In this case, the Babylonians.

Jeremiah pushes back against this defeatist mind-set. He offers exiles a counter-identity located in God's mercy. The prophet refuses to serve as a chaplain for the establishment or as a guardian on behalf of the status quo. Instead, he gives exiles spine and courage so they trust God's unlimited power and unending compassion. The prophet imparts a holy defiance that refuses to accommodate to Babylonian truth claims. Exile doesn't negate God's promises.

Jeremiah comes to the aid of all who despair—of all times and all places. The prophet empowers us to become unintimidated by pain and loss. No, he doesn't promise a return to the past. Instead, he offers a new reality fulfilled in Jesus. God's grace in Jesus is the only solution for the twin demons that accompany times of sorrow: conformity and hopelessness. Christ's love raises us to new life. Jesus leads us on a journey to "a watered garden" where we will "languish no more" (Jeremiah 31:12). To get there, though, we must go through barren deserts, godless wastelands, and places of terror, grief, and shattered trust. Is the journey worth it? It was for Judean exiles. It is for us.

Longing for Home

For most people, the word *home* evokes feelings of love and laughter, security and serenity, warmth and welcome. Home means Mom and Dad, fun and games, good food and deep sleep. "Home, home on the range." "When Johnny comes marching home again." A little girl from Kansas says it best: "There's no place like home."

For Judean exiles, Zion is a distant, fading memory. They're stuck in a land of canals and ziggurats, the Tigris and Euphrates Rivers, the Ishtar Gate, and the detestable statue of Marduk, the empire's chief god. Babylon has replaced Judah, Jerusalem, and the Jordan with the building projects of Nabopolassar (the empire's founder) and his famous son Nebuchadnezzar. The new arrivals from Judah have no Davidic king, no temple, no royal city, no land, no liturgy, no sacrifice, no hope, and no future. They have no song to sing.

By the rivers of Babylon, they sit and weep, reminiscing about the good old days when they worshiped in the splendor of Solomon's temple, worked and shopped in the city of David, and saw the Mount of Olives from a distance. But now? They're exiled in a foreign land. "There's no place like home!"

Judeans lament in Psalm 137: "On the willows there we hung up our lyres" (Psalm 137:2). They cry out, "For there our captors required of us songs, and our tormentors, mirth, saying, 'Sing us one of the songs of Zion!'" (Psalm 137:3). Babylonians mock the exiles.

Jeremiah writes his book for these people living through the angst expressed in Psalm 137. Their lives were split in two: before Babylon and after Babylon. The past was gone and the future lacked clarity. Well-known support systems had vanished. Families were scattered all over the Fertile Crescent. Everyone felt like leftovers.

Who Loves Leftovers?

Who loves leftovers? Not me. After our last child, Lori Beth, left for college, it became difficult to fix a meal that didn't leave us with leftovers. For almost twenty years, we enjoyed meals that included our three children. After they abandoned ship, our refrigerator became filled with loads of leftovers!

One time we fixed chicken. I love chicken. Then I had chicken sandwiches, chicken soup, and chicken casserole. Soon our chicken was in soufflés, sauces, snacks, and salads. I began having nightmares where a six-hundred-pound chicken was after me!

Judean exiles in Babylon felt like leftovers. Has-beens. Marginalized. Left out. Rejected. Forgotten in the back of the refrigerator. At the bottom of the barrel.

Whether our sorrow was caused by a catastrophic hurricane, a massive earthquake, or something much more personal and private, now we feel like a leftover. Part of us has become dead to the world. We've turned off our emotions just so we can keep going. Warfare, violence, rejection, rape, and abuse exact a tremendous toll. After the initial shock, these experiences linger like unwanted guests, often impacting future generations in our family.

There's a word for this. *Traumatized.*

"Trauma"—originally a Greek word—appears in the New Testament. It's often translated "wound." The Good Samaritan binds up the wounds of the man who fell among robbers (Luke 10:34). One of the messengers sent by the master is wounded by the vineyard's workers and then cast aside (Luke 20:12). The seven sons of Sceva are wounded by a man with an evil spirit to the point that they run away naked (Acts 19:16). Put these three texts together, and what do we have? *Trauma* refers to sudden and unexpected assaults—physical or emotional. Try as we might, we can't erase traumatic memories. We can't forget them or run from them. Our ghosts from the past return repeatedly. That's what makes us feel like leftovers. We've been traumatized.

Sometimes trauma is so painful that we cry out, "There are no words!" What happened was so catastrophic that language fails us. We become mute. Disconnected. Unable to talk about our wounds. Life continues, but only robotically. We do the right things. Show up at the right time. But inside? Something is terribly wrong. It feels like we've eaten glass. The glass won't go away no matter how often we try to spit it out.

Life has become increasingly less interesting. What used to thrill us thrills us no more, be it sports, hobbies, or our work. We're just trying to keep a semblance of life going. Most of the time, a deadening hopelessness hovers over us.

There is something worse.

Trauma can sabotage our trust in Christ. We can feel alone and abandoned by the Savior. We say to ourselves, "God promised to protect me. God said He would answer my prayers. But nothing. Nothing!" Everything in the Bible that used to give us joy can look joyless. Without a process that walks us through the pain of trauma, we live a kind of half-life in a barren, affectless landscape—feeling like one huge unwanted leftover.

ANOTHER LEFTOVER

The Judean exiles in Babylon lost more than their land, life, and liberty. They also lost their will to live. "Death shall be preferred to life" (Jeremiah 8:3). The Babylonian army left an indelible memory and a shameful reality. Refugees didn't know how to work through their trauma. They needed a map, a compass, and a trusty guide. They needed the Book of Jeremiah.

At the heart of the prophet's book lies another leftover—make that *the* Leftover. His name is Jesus. On Good Friday, Jesus was paraded outside Jerusalem and taken to a place called Golgotha where criminals were intentionally bent and broken, maimed and mauled, shoved down the garbage disposal, ground up, and thrown away. Jesus was betrayed, denied, mocked, accused, scourged, pierced, cursed, and forsaken as He hung on a cross, lifeless and limp. Jesus endured it all. Why? He deeply loves leftovers.

Jesus delights to baptize us, teach us, counsel us, instruct us, heal us, hold us, and forgive us. Jesus gives His true body and blood in His Holy Supper. Jesus also gives us the Book of Jeremiah—a survivor's manual for anyone who has ever felt like a leftover.

Jeremiah's Book

It happened when I was seven years old. I was with my family at a place called Elitches, an amusement park in Denver, Colorado. My dad talked me into going on a roller coaster. We began slowly, making our way up a steep incline. Off to one side, we could see Denver's skyline. On the other side, we could see Pike's Peak. Soon we could see downtown Kansas City! Then we got to the top. Suddenly everything changed. Within a few seconds, we went from a ride that was calm and enjoyable to one that was frantic, unsettling, and very loud.

Life is a lot like a roller coaster ride. How many times have we been on easy street? "I just got a raise!" "Look at the inheritance Uncle Ralph gave us!" "Wow, Carson made the honor roll!" It's smooth sailing. Then a car bill shows up. An illness appears out nowhere. A child has a major meltdown. Within minutes, we go from a ride that was calm and enjoyable to one that is frantic, unsettling, and very, very loud.

Jeremiah's book is a lot like a roller coaster ride. It's not a smooth journey. The book is not coherent literature—at least not according to what we're used to. Jeremiah reads like it was written by a committee that couldn't make up its mind. So much appears to be random. Jeremiah taxes our interpretive skills at every turn, whether the issues are literary, historical, or theological.

Poems and narratives stand by each other, and often they aren't thematically connected. Images of destruction and hope compete with each other for prominence. Most notably, the book has three endings—chapters 45, 51, and 52.

Twenty-eight times Jeremiah lists specific dates connected to his ministry. This doesn't mean, however, that he organizes his book in chronological order. Nor does he make points in a linear fashion. If you've ever seen what happens when first graders are given scissors, colored paper, crayons, paint, and glue, and are told to make something, then you're on the right track with Jeremiah.

Why is Jeremiah's book in such disarray? Why didn't he give it more of an even flow? What are we to make of this mishmash of metaphors and poems, laments and symbolic actions? Why do we have to wait until chapters 39 and 52 for the actual historical account of 587 BC and Jerusalem's demise?

What was the prophet thinking?

Jeremiah presents a fragmented, disassembled book because that's what life looks like during deep sorrow. It's anything but neat and tidy; that's why Jeremiah gives us a helter-skelter book that matches our helter-skelter lives. The prophet leaves us with a hodgepodge of a book because that's the nature of life after loss. The literary shapelessness of Jeremiah mirrors the fragmentary nature of our sorrow. The book is messy because it wants to reflect the messiness of a life beset by deep sadness.

To insist on straightforward recovery is to insist that the world is flat, that pigs fly, that chocolate is the new health food. Restoration occurs in fits and starts. We re-enter the pain, grieve deeply, and relive the nightmare. Then we do it again the next day. Normally, God extracts pain's poison very slowly.

NAVIGATING OUR WAY THROUGH JEREMIAH

Jeremiah is more of a musical composer than an orderly architect. He states his main theme of Law and Gospel in Jeremiah 1:10, then repeats and develops it throughout the book. These twin doctrines hold the book together. Along the way, he includes a number of subthemes. They also appear and disappear, then, unexpectedly, reappear in dramatic fashion. Jeremiah explores each motif through poems, narratives, and laments. The book meanders, shifts, turns, and changes.

While the Book of Jeremiah is notoriously complex, all is not lost. The prophet leaves several important literary markers. For instance, Jeremiah presents the death of one world (chapters 1–25) in order to prepare for the resurrection of another (chapters 26–52). Put another way, chapters 1–25 uproot, tear down, destroy, and overthrow, while chapters 26–52 build and plant. Moreover, Jeremiah's inner life is on display in the first half of the book and his public life is in full view in the second half.

There are additional signposts. Chapters 2–20 are almost entirely lacking in historical specificity, as are chapters 30–31. Conversely, the prophet adds considerably more dates beginning in chapter 24 (e.g., Jeremiah 24:1; 25:1–3; 26:1; 27:1), while narrating the cataclysmic event of 587 BC in Jeremiah 39:1–10 and 52:1–30. Several words and phrases connect chapters 1 and 25—for example, "the thirteenth year of Josiah" (Jeremiah 1:2; 25:3) and "the tribes of the north" (Jeremiah 1:15; 25:9). Jeremiah 25 serves as the book's hinge, holding together its two major sections.

The prophet employs framing devices in other places as well. For instance, the question "What do you see?" (Jeremiah 1:11; 24:3) links together the first twenty-four chapters. A subsection comes in Jeremiah 11:1–17:27. The unit begins with a prose sermon and ends with one. Both begin with similar words: "Hear the words of this covenant, and speak to the men of Judah and the inhabitants of Jerusalem" (Jeremiah 11:2). "Hear the word of the LORD, you kings of Judah, and all Judah, and all the inhabitants of Jerusalem, who enter by these gates" (Jeremiah 17:20). The prophet signals still another subsection with the phrase "In the fourth year of Jehoiakim" (Jeremiah 36:1; 45:1). This is the so-called "Baruch Narrative," where Baruch, Jeremiah's secretary, plays a key role.

JEREMIAH AND WORDS

The world is a perilous place to live. We can suffer indescribable pain and heart-stopping adversity. These experiences sometimes steal our speech. We lose the capacity to talk about what happened. We're reduced to groaning, crying, and weeping. Words? They aren't there. What we've been through is beyond words. Clichés make us nauseous. Even when we find the right words, once spoken, they seem grossly inadequate.

The Book of Lamentations—likely composed by Jeremiah after 587 BC—describes this utter despair. The book's cries are visceral. The expressions are raw. Are there any words to describe these dark moments?

- "My eyes are spent with weeping; my stomach churns." (Lamentations 2:11)
- "Panic and pitfall have come upon us." (Lamentations 3:47)
- "We are weary; we are given no rest." (Lamentations 5:5)
- "The joy of our hearts has ceased; our dancing has been turned to mourning." (Lamentations 5:15)

We need words like these when we're caught in the clutches of sorrow. We need language that helps us express how we feel. We need images and symbols that help us describe our deep brokenness. What Jeremiah does in Lamentations he does throughout the book that bears his name. He presents a mosaic, a collage, a kaleidoscope of words that parallel what we're going through.

Most people are unable to confront trauma directly, head-on. That's why Jeremiah mostly takes an indirect approach. If we looked straight at our sorrow, most of us would be blinded by the horror of it all. With traumatized people, delicate is the order of the day. Life's painful events need to be reframed, told in less "in-your-face" ways.

Jeremiah is skilled and savvy with slant. Although he's from Anathoth and therefore outside of Jerusalem's elite class, the prophet learned the power of language and the capacity of words to evoke comfort and courage. While Jeremiah was at home in the Israelite tradition, he reshapes and recasts it to give us words—words to describe our loss, our hopelessness, our pain. Jeremiah is divinely ordained to bring words, God's Word. He does it with authority, power, freshness, creativity, boldness, persistence, and deep compassion.

The Babylonian exile was so dire that Jeremiah couldn't use conventional language. Stock phrases wouldn't get a hearing. People would ignore safe and predictable expressions. Faced with exiles who had been traumatized by deportation, the death of loved ones, destruction, and utter chaos, Jeremiah had to break from the routine. His book has all of the characteristics of a person doing whatever it takes to give his audience words—words to describe their sorrow. Jeremiah's words cut through hollow euphemisms. In doing so, they give us speech to talk about our nightmare, and about our pain, rage, anger, indignation, bewilderment, and shame that come with it.

Jeremiah is living as an exile in Egypt when he completes his book. Babylon has taken everything away from him—everything, that is, but words, God's words. Words that point forward to the Word made flesh—Jesus Christ, our Lord. Jeremiah's inspired and inerrant words restore to us the joy of our salvation. We don't have to see our world only through the eyes of anxiety, brutality, and dead ends. Jeremiah sets forth a different, counterintuitive, and countercultural way to order life after a season of painful disappointment. The prophet invites us into a different ending—one that is true and lasting, one that reverberates and overflows because of God's Word made sure and certain in Jesus Christ.

LEARNING FROM JEREMIAH

Is your heart broken? Perhaps the wound is old. A father abused you. A coach ignored you. A spouse disowned you. A business partner turned on you. Maybe the wound is fresh. The boss who hired you with promise of promotion has forgotten how to pronounce your last name. Your friends escaped on a weekend getaway, and you weren't invited. Your adult son forgot your birthday—*again*. You're hurt, deeply. It feels like "game over."

Why read the Book of Jeremiah only to watch the prophet go through unthinkable tragedies? Cities are torched. The temple is destroyed. People's lives are dismantled. Babylon is behind it all. How can an Old Testament prophet heal my heart and bind up my wounds?

Jeremiah presents himself as a God-given example of how to overcome massive setbacks. The prophet survives rejection, public humiliation, mockery, conspiracies, death threats, captivities, depression, times of doubt, imprisonments, and forced exile. He speaks about this darkness, writes a book, and provides hope.

You still have questions. Does Jeremiah speak to me? Can the prophet, rooted in ancient events and culture, address my pain? Can he generate hope and reignite my faith? Is it worth my while to invest time and energy in an Old Testament spokesman?

No doubt, Jeremiah stands at a distance from us. My! He lived over 2,500 years ago! I still invite you to take the plunge. Roll up your sleeves. Dig in. I promise Jeremiah will become a trusted companion. His book will become a lantern, lighting the way through your darkest valleys. Jeremiah will help you make sense out of life's nonsense.

What makes the prophet so relevant? He repeatedly points us to Jesus. Jeremiah directs us to Christ's suffering, but also to the empty tomb. That's where we see a new day dawning—for Jesus and for us. Sure, the path to recovery is uneven. It's often one step forward and two steps back. Yet as we study Jeremiah, by God's grace, we will make progress. Through the prophet's alarming poetry, jarring narratives, and multiple near-misses with death, our hope will be born anew. Let's get started!

2

OVERCOMING THROUGH GOD'S WORD

"You are my hiding place and my shield; I hope in Your Word."

(Psalm 119:114)

We all know about injustice, interminable suffering, and the failure of love—not only on a broad historical level but also in deeply personal and intimate ways. The fabric of life includes threads of betrayal, abandonment, cruelty, and sometimes utter grief and angst. Jeremiah doesn't dodge or deny any of this. However, he insists that it's not the last word. The prophet gives us promises rooted in God's Word.

Let's look at Jeremiah 1. This chapter summarizes the entire book. It's a microcosm of everything the prophet says. It is very important, then, for us to pay close attention to these nineteen verses.

Endurance

In 1959 Alfred Lansing wrote a book called *Endurance*. It's the story of Sir Ernest Shackleton's attempt to cross the continent of Antarctica in 1914 and the struggle for survival endured by his twenty-eight-man crew.

The plan was risky, to say the least.

Jeremiah also set out on a risky and hazardous journey. The prophet served through the reigns of Josiah, the reformer; Jehoahaz, the fleeting (he only reigned for three months; therefore, the prophet doesn't mention him); Jehoiakim, the tyrant; Jehoiachin, the exiled king; and Zedekiah, the great vacillator. The warm sunshine of Josiah's righteous reign turned into a blustery autumn wind. It all ended like a dark, cold, cheerless winter day—"the captivity of Jerusalem in the fifth month" (Jeremiah 1:3). What sustained the prophet? God's Word. God's Word, which calls us by name.

God Knows Our Name

If you're like most people, your mail is often impersonal. Your mailbox regularly has letters addressed to former residents, catalogs with your name misspelled, and advertisement flyers labeled "Resident." Although one of my daughters, Abi Joy, has been out of the house for years, and her married last name is now Eaton, she still receives mail at my home addressed to "Abi Joy Lessing."

The Book of Jeremiah isn't impersonal. It isn't addressed to "Resident." It begins with a personal name—*Jeremiah*, meaning "the Lord lifts up." Eight more personal names are listed in the book's first three verses: Hilkiah, Benjamin, "the Lord" (Yahweh), Josiah, Amon, Judah, Jehoiakim, and Zedekiah (Jeremiah 1:1–3).

It's telling that Jeremiah begins his book with so many names. He is the most personal prophet of them all. In fact, Jeremiah names over fifty people in his book. Names matter to Jeremiah. Names matter to God.

On July 21, 2007, I preached to a crowd of thirty thousand people in Orlando, Florida. It was my denomination's national youth gathering. Before things got started, sound, stage, and light technicians surrounded me to make sure everything was ready. Just then, a teenager from the gathering walked up and asked me, "Are you somebody important?" I've often asked that question. We've all asked that question, "Am I somebody important?"

That's because it's easy to feel like "Resident"—just another person in the crowd. It's natural to feel unimportant when teenagers take all your money, when your job takes all your energy, when your depression takes all your joy, and when old age takes away all your dignity.

"Am I somebody important?" God says we are. He knows our name! In Holy Baptism, God doesn't number us. God doesn't classify us according to our race. He doesn't label us as a compound of chemicals. He doesn't assess us for our economic potential. God says, "Fear not, for I have redeemed you; I have called you by name, you are Mine" (Isaiah 43:1).

We may call ourselves "Alone," "Widower," "Retired," "Divorcee," "Empty Nester," or "Messed-Up." God calls us "Beloved," "Chosen," "Elected," "Forgiven." God says, "You are Mine."

Having highlighted God's personal concern for us—by name (Jeremiah 1:1–3)—the prophet does an about-face. He takes us to a time before the world began (Jeremiah 1:5). That's when God planned Jeremiah's life. That's when God planned our lives as well.

God Knows Us before Birth

Instead of telling us about his parents, his childhood in Anathoth, or his extended family, Jeremiah tells us about God. He tells us about God, who says, "Before I formed you in the womb I knew you" (Jeremiah 1:5). Before Jeremiah knew God, God knew Jeremiah. David puts it this way: "In Your book were written, every one of them, the days that were formed for me, when as yet there was none of them" (Psalm 139:16).

God's purposes go back before our birth and before our conception. Long before we thought that God might be important, God singled us out as important. "He chose us in [Christ] before the foundation of the world" (Ephesians 1:4). Just as Jeremiah entered the world as ancient history, so do we.

Jeremiah employs the word *formed* not only to describe God making him but also to describe a potter forming a vessel from clay (Jeremiah 18:6). Moses uses the same the term to describe God's creation of Adam from the dirt (Genesis 2:7). What a God! There He is, getting His hands dirty sculpting and creating Adam. This isn't a distant or aloof God. This is a "hands-on" God—literally. He forms and shapes us while we are still in our mother's womb, using plans He designed before He made the world.

God Sets Us Apart for Service

"Before you were born I consecrated you" (Jeremiah 1:5). The word *consecrated* means "set apart for God's service." Or, more colloquially, chosen to be on God's side.

Growing up with a big sister and older cousins, except for my cousin Paula—I was proudly one month older than her—I was usually the last person chosen for a game of basketball or football. Several times, when everyone had been chosen, I was left standing in the middle between the two teams. My cousin captains argued over who was going to have to choose me. As the argument continued between them, the hard truth began to sink in. Having me on the team was no one's preferred option.

But not with God! Before I was born, God decided I was on His team. My place in His kingdom didn't depend on how well I did on the entrance examination or multiple-choice test or final essay. I'm in. Consecrated. Chosen. On the team.

So are you. You were set apart to be on God's team—the winning side. That's what Holy Baptism is all about. We need this truth to go deep down in our "insidest inside." Why? You know. Random events, bad decisions, and unmet expectations often make us feel like losers. Jeremiah felt like that. Government officials rejected him. His fellow citizens ignored him. And Babylon attacked him and his country. None of this, however, was the last word.

What about us? Sin doesn't have the last word. Neither does selfishness or Satan. We are baptized, consecrated, chosen, elected, and selected to belong to God's kingdom—forevermore!

God Gives Us to the Nations

God not only knew Jeremiah by name before he was born, God not only formed the prophet and consecrated him, God also appointed him to be a prophet to the nations (Jeremiah 1:5). Behind the word *appointed* is the Hebrew word *nathan*—"gave." God "nathaned" Jeremiah. God gave Jeremiah away. Before the prophet ever got it together, he was given away to the nations. Note that the prophet employs the plural word *nations*, not the singular word *nation*. Yes, God is chiefly concerned about His people Judah. They are the "apple of His eye" (Zechariah 2:8). But God also cares for the nations. At the end of his book, Jeremiah includes oracles concerning Egypt, Philistia, Moab, Ammon, Edom, and Babylon (Jeremiah 46–51).

God, the great Giver, gave Jeremiah away to the nations. I can hear Jeremiah objecting, "Wait a minute, God. Don't be so quick to give me away! I've got something to say about this! I can make my own decisions! I've got inalienable rights!" Imagine God's response. "Sorry, but I gave you away before you were born. It's already done!"

God also gave Jesus away. God didn't keep Jesus on display. God didn't preserve Jesus in a museum. God didn't show Jesus off as a trophy. "For God so loved the world that He gave His one and only Son, that whoever believes in Him shall not perish but have eternal life" (John 3:16). God gives. God gives forgiveness and God gives life. God gives mercy and God gives grace.

Can God really be that generous? that loving? that giving? Yes. Yes. And yes! Jesus doesn't say, "Everyone who achieves" or "everyone who succeeds" or "everyone who is on the board of trustees." Jesus says everyone who believes will not perish. Giving is woven into the very fabric of God's heart.

Jeremiah's life is for others. So is Christ's. So is ours. "He died for all, that those who live might no longer live for themselves" (2 Corinthians 5:15).

The most important events in our lives happened before we were born.

God knew us; therefore, we are no accident. God chose us; therefore, we aren't a zero. God gave us; therefore, we have purpose and dignity. These three anchors keep us from drifting and drowning when fear and anxiety overwhelm us.

Excuses

When we're scared we make excuses, just like Jeremiah. "Ah, Lord GOD! Behold, I do not know how to speak, for I am only a youth" (Jeremiah 1:6). Jeremiah is only twelve or thirteen years old. This was roughly Samuel's age when God called him to be a prophet (1 Samuel 3:1–18). Samuel didn't make excuses. Why does Jeremiah?

I once came across this list of excuses. "Billy was late for school today because his little brother replaced the milk in his cereal with Crazy Glue. Billy's mouth stuck together and we needed to melt the glue." "A Vaseline truck crashed on the highway and cars were sliding all over the place." "I put my uniform in the microwave to dry it and it caught on fire." "My false teeth flew out of the window while I was driving on the highway."

Everyone has a list of excuses. "I couldn't find the right tools." "I threw out my back bowling." "I'm too busy, too tired, and too old." How can we overcome all of our sorry alibis? God gives us His Word.

God's Word

"You have my word!" It's easy to become skeptical when someone says that—when they give us their word. Why is that? We live in a world of empty words. Hollow promises. Vows made, later ignored. Pledges guaranteed, then forgotten.

People speak words with great fanfare. "I'll always love you." "We're BFF—best friends for life!" "You can count on me!" "Till death do us part." Yet words can be autumn leaves in November's wind. That's why we can become a bit squeamish when someone says, "You have my word!"

Someone we trusted, someone we respected, someone we looked up to, broke their word. Now what? Flight is a normal reaction. Escape presents itself as a fast and easy solution. No one wants to hurt. But the temptation is to escape into addictions. Alcohol, spending too much money, working all hours of the day and night—the list is endless. Addictions only multiply our sorrows. They are short-term gain that leads to long-term pain.

God breaks into our darkness with His Word. And what a Word it is! In Genesis 1:3, God says, "Let there be light. And there was light." Your words can't do that. Neither can mine. But God's Word can. God's Word does. Consider more verses that extol the power of God's Word.

- "Not one word of all the good promises that the LORD made to the house of Israel has failed." (Joshua 21:45)
- "Your word is a lamp to my feet and a light to my path." (Psalm 119:105)
- "The grass withers, the flower fades, but the word of our God will stand forever." (Isaiah 40:8)

God's Word is the most powerful force in the universe. By His Word, God called Abraham from Ur in the land of the Chaldeans, spoke to Moses from a burning bush, gave manna and quail in the wilderness, thundered from Sinai, and spoke to Elijah in a still, small voice. God's Word even made dry bones come to life, standing on their feet, a vast army. That's in Ezekiel.

God said it. That settles it. Faith believes it. We have His Word.

God isn't the strong, silent type. God isn't a mystery or an enigma. God speaks. Over 1,900 times in the Old Testament, authors say God spoke. "Man does not live by bread alone, but man lives by every word that comes from the mouth of the LORD" (Deuteronomy 8:3). Many of these life-giving words came through the prophet Jeremiah. In fact, Jeremiah is the longest book in the Bible, word for word.

As a prophet—God's spokesman—Jeremiah was much like Moses (cf. Deuteronomy 18:15, 18). Jeremiah does for his generation what Moses did for his: confront and comfort people with the power of God's true and abiding Word. The expression "Thus says the LORD" appears 155 times in Jeremiah—more often than the rest of the Old Testament books combined.

The expression "declares the LORD" or "oracle of the LORD" appears 167 times in Jeremiah, accounting for over 60 percent of all occurrences in the Old Testament. The word "word" comes over 90 times in Jeremiah—by far the greatest usage of the term in any book in the Bible.

Jeremiah is obsessed with God's Word! In his book, God's Word calls, judges, overthrows, critiques, promises, creates, warns, empowers, kills, and makes alive. The divine Word wields absolute and ultimate authority, towering over every other promise of power, hope, or rescue. Jeremiah is so enthralled with this Word that he consumes it as though it were food, fire, or wine.

- "Then the LORD put out His hand and touched my mouth. And the LORD said to me, 'Behold, I have put My words in your mouth.'" (Jeremiah 1:9)
- "Behold, I am making My words in your mouth a fire." (Jeremiah 5:14)
- "Your words were found, and I ate them, and Your words became to me a joy and the delight of my heart." (Jeremiah 15:16)
- "Concerning the prophets: My heart is broken within me; all my bones shake; I am like a drunken man, like a man overcome by wine, because of the LORD and because of His holy words." (Jeremiah 23:9)
- "Is not My word like fire, declares the LORD, and like a hammer that breaks the rock in pieces?" (Jeremiah 23:29)

Jeremiah lives to read, mark, learn, and inwardly digest God's Word— then speak it and live it out. God's Word gives hope in the midst of loss; tenacity to live courageously; and a voice that dares still to sing in life's most crushing sorrows.

GOD'S WRITTEN WORD

Sometimes we feel like we're on our last leg, our last dime, our last breath. This anguish can lead to resentment. "She said!" "They did!" "He forgot!" Instead of finding someone to blame for our pain, Jeremiah invites us to turn to God's Word—His written Word.

God's written Word authorized Judah's undoing (Jeremiah 25:13). It also endorses its future—especially in Jeremiah 26–52. These chapters highlight the authority of God's recorded Word. In chapter 26, officials come to Jeremiah's defense by citing one of Micah's oracles (Jeremiah 26:16–19). Their appeal to written prophecy saves the day—and Jeremiah's life. At the end of the book, the prophet writes on a scroll the judgments that will come upon Babylon (Jeremiah 51:59–64). This symbolic action bears seeds of hope for captive Judahites. In between chapters 26 and 51, Jeremiah sends letters to exiles in Babylon to defeat despair (Jeremiah 29). At the Lord's command, Jeremiah also prepares a written scroll that takes dead aim at heartache and hopelessness (Jeremiah 30–33). God further instructs Jeremiah to preserve written documentation of a business transaction between his cousin Hanamel and himself (Jeremiah 32:6–44). The written materials that Baruch places in an earthenware jar serve as a testimony that the Lord would one day restore His people (Jeremiah 32:13–14).

A dramatic example displaying the power of God's written Word comes in the confrontation between King Jehoiakim and Jeremiah (Jeremiah 36). The prophet dictates God's Word to Baruch, who reads it before Jehoiakim. In turn, the king destroys the document, only to have Jeremiah create another one, which contains "all the words of the scroll that Jehoiakim king of Judah had burned in the fire. And many similar words were added to them" (Jeremiah 36:32). The chapter affirms that the prophet's seemingly innocuous scroll triumphs over the king. The written Word is victorious!

Another text where the prophet highlights God's written Word comes in Jeremiah 31:33. God says, "I will put My law within them, and I will write it on their hearts." The internalization of divine instruction empowers us to trust God when everything looks dim and dead. It also enables us to break out of guilt.

The cornerstone of this internal Word is divine forgiveness. The Lord resolves to "forgive iniquity, and . . . remember their sin no more" (Jeremiah

(Jeremiah 31:34). Even if Judah's trip over the waterfall is certain, God will pick up His people from the rocks below and mend the boat—even though there wouldn't be much left to work with. God's Word disarms enemies, undermines tyranny, mobilizes the faithful, and generates confidence in those suffering from trauma and loss.

God's recorded Word restores beyond our imagination. His judgments shatter our denial. His absolution overrides our despair. Jeremiah maintains that in lieu of fallen social and political supports—the temple and its liturgical systems, the king and his nation, the land and covenant assurances—the Word, and ultimately the God who utters it, forms the foundation for a new life.

It doesn't matter how many times we've been through God's Word. What matters is how many times God's Word has been through us. That's why Jeremiah inwardly digests/takes to heart God's Word. He calls it his "joy and . . . delight" (Jeremiah 15:16). "Joy" and "delight"—or, in the ESV translation, the voices of "mirth" and "gladness"—come together four more times in the book, and on each occasion they are paired with "the voice of the bridegroom and the voice of the bride" (Jeremiah 7:34; 16:9; 25:10; 33:11). By means of these word associations, Jeremiah evokes the connection between meditating on God's Word and the exuberance and excitement experienced by a "bride and bridegroom."

Yet when we have a huge hole in our heart from a significant loss, we doubt the power of the Word. We wonder, isn't there something tastier, more appetizing, with a bit more pizzazz? Here it is. For breakfast: half a grapefruit; one piece of whole-wheat toast, no butter; eight ounces of skim milk; coffee, black. For lunch: four ounces of lean broiled chicken breast, skin removed; one cup of steamed zucchini; herb tea, no sugar; one Oreo cookie. For a snack: the rest of the package of Oreo cookies, one quart of chocolate almond ice cream, and one jar of hot fudge. For dinner: two loaves of garlic bread, heavy on the butter; one large sausage-and-pepperoni pizza, extra cheese; a large milkshake with whipped cream. For desert: three Milky Way candy bars and an entire frozen cheesecake!

Oh, we try, don't we? We try to stay on a spiritual diet of God's Word that promises to bring vim and vigor, peace and power. Then we slip: One Oreo cookie. One crumb of coveting, one piece of pornography, one slice of slander, one sip of sarcasm, and then the rest of the package of Oreo cookies! Satan thrusts this junk food before us. With a sly grin, he watches it all disappear. Filled with his miserable morsels, our desire to regularly study, memorize, learn, defend, trust, believe, love, and live out God's Word becomes a chore, a bore, a snore, until we say, "No more!"

I invite you to reject Satan's diet. Instead, press into God's Word. Press *hard* into God's Word. When fear appears, say, "But God said . . ." When doubts arise, say, "But God said . . ." When guilt overwhelms, say, "But God said . . ." Search the Bible like a miner digging for gold. Once you find a nugget, grasp it. Trust it. Hold on to it. Never let it go.

Use God's Word to counter your negative feelings.

Please don't misunderstand me. Feelings are good. Feelings are fine. Feelings are God's gift. Where would we be without feelings? But feelings are not facts. Just because we feel like a failure doesn't mean we're a failure. Just because we feel hopeless doesn't mean we're hopeless. When we feel shame, guilt, and emptiness; when the prince of darkness points his accusing finger at us, mocking our feeble discipleship, our failed relationships, and our fatal attractions; we have God's Word.

God's Word directs history—Jeremiah's history and ours as well. Josiah (626–609 BC), Jehoahaz (609 BC), Jehoiakim (609–598 BC), and Zedekiah (598–587 BC) didn't have the last word in Jeremiah's life. God did. God always has the last Word. His name is Jesus.

THE WORD MADE FLESH

God gives us one more Word—Jesus, the Word made flesh. Jesus is God's Word with skin and bones and fingers and a spleen and toes. Jesus has a heart. Jesus has a heart for you. Jesus shed His blood for you.

John drives this point home when he writes about Jesus on trial before Pontius Pilate. Pilate has Jesus' flesh ripped, torn, dressed in purple, and crowned with thorns. Then he brings Jesus out before the crowd and says, "Behold the man!" (John 19:5). The Latin is, famously, *Ecce homo.* "Behold the man!" Here is the man. Flesh. Flesh and blood. Flesh and blood and a beaten body. That's God we're talking about. God in the flesh. The Word—the Word that was with God in the beginning and was God.

Why did He do it? "So that by the grace of God He might taste death for everyone" (Hebrews 2:9). Jesus tasted the Roman elixir called crucifixion. It included the soldiers' spit, their cheap wine, sweat running down His cheeks, and finally His own blood. Our Savior not only tasted death, He swallowed it, chewed it up, and spit it out. "Death is swallowed up in victory!" (1 Corinthians 15:54). Now the Spirit of the risen Christ creates in us a hunger and thirst for His Word. "Like newborn infants, long for the pure spiritual milk, that by it you may grow up into salvation" (1 Peter 2:2). God's Word—not the word of people—empowers us to overcome disappointments and disasters.

GOD'S WORD OF JUDGMENT AND HOPE

I remember two Chicago Cub infielders in the late 1980s. Mark Grace played first base and Vance Law was at third. Law and Grace. They went together on the baseball field. They also go together in Jeremiah's book. God says to the prophet, "See, I have set you this day over nations and over kingdoms, to pluck up and to break down, to destroy and to overthrow, to build and to plant" (Jeremiah 1:10). God's Word has two parts: it dismantles and it creates. It shatters the old and forms the new. These six verbs reappear (in varying degrees) in Jeremiah 12:14–17; 15:7; 18:7–9; 24:6; 31:4–5, 28, 38, 40; 32:41; 42:10; 45:4; 49:38. While Jeremiah is the subject of the verbs in Jeremiah 1:10, God is the subject in every subsequent use. The prophetic Word brings about God's plan—His plan to restore our lives.

It isn't only God's plan for Judah. It's His plan for nations and kingdoms. It's God's plan for us. We need both parts of His Word. Law without Gospel is legalism. Gospel without Law promotes license.

Law dominates Jeremiah's book—pluck up, break down, destroy, and overthrow. But the Gospel has the concluding word. Building and planting point to the future—a future that includes security (building) and satisfaction (planting). "Where sin increased, grace abounded all the more" (Romans 5:20).

GOD'S VISUAL WORD

God gives us His written Word—He even writes it on our hearts. God gives us the incarnate Word—Jesus Christ, our Lord. God also gives us His visual Word through two of Jeremiah's visions. We might call them "show-and-tell" lectures. God shows the prophet an almond tree (Jeremiah 1:11–12), a boiling pot (Jeremiah 1:13–16), and a fortified city, iron pillar, and bronze walls (Jeremiah 1:17–19). The divine Word will blossom forth and pour out judgment. Through it all Jeremiah will stand firm.

Depending upon where you live, there are always signs of spring. They may be robins or cherry blossoms. Bumblebees, frogs and tadpoles, wild garlic, bluebells, and daffodils also signal warmer weather. Almond blossoms announced spring in Jeremiah's hometown of Anathoth.

"The Word of the LORD came to me, saying, 'Jeremiah, what do you see?' And I said, 'I see an almond [*shaqed*] branch.' Then the LORD said to me, 'You have seen well, for I am watching over [*shoqed*] My word to perform it'" (Jeremiah 1:11–12). Before an almond tree has leaves, it puts forth white and snowy blossoms, announcing that spring is right around the corner.

The blossoms are the "show." Here is the "tell." Just as springtime blossoms herald the coming of almonds (the Hebrew word for "almond" is *shaqed*), so God watches (the Hebrew word for "watch" is *shoqed*) over His Word so it blossoms forth in beauty. Do you see the pun? *Shaqed, shoqed*—almond, watch. The almond tree is worth watching. It announces new life.

God's Word is worth watching too. Just as almond blossoms promise springtime and summer, the divine Word promises new spiritual life. There are many such promises in Jeremiah, but they all point to *the* promise. This one also uses the world of agriculture. "Behold, the days are coming, declares the LORD, when I will raise up for David a righteous Shoot, and He shall reign as king and deal wisely, and shall execute justice and righteousness in the land" (Jeremiah 23:5, author's translation). A shoot implies three ideas:

- New growth from what has been cut and trimmed.
- Continuity between the new and the old.
- A small and humble new beginning.

The Babylonians cut and trimmed the house of David. The final straw was when the empire blinded and deported Zedekiah, the last Judean king. Jesus—from the house and lineage of David and, hence, Zedekiah—is the shoot Jeremiah promises. Like a shoot, Christ's beginnings are small and humble—a cradle, then a cross. On the third day, Christ bursts forth from the tomb—like an almond tree in the spring—with resurrection power and beauty.

God's Word accomplished the divine plan. Life swallowed up death! It still does. Even when it appears as though God's promises are dormant and dead in the long winters of life, they are alive—just like an almond tree. The day is coming when everything God promised will burst into flower, creating an everlasting springtime in paradise, the new Jerusalem. That's the Gospel.

As we move from an almond tree to ordinary cookware, God lays down the Law. "[Jeremiah said,] 'I see a boiling pot, facing away from the north.' Then the LORD said to me, 'Out of the north disaster shall be let loose upon all the inhabitants of the land'" (Jeremiah 1:13–14). The expression "boiling pot" more literally means that it is being blown upon. This is an important point. The fire is being stoked. Someone is fanning the flame. The heat is on. The Lord is blowing upon the pot. He's stirring up a kingdom from the north that will wreak havoc on His people. The boiling pot, however, will have limits. Evil is not everywhere. Evil is not all powerful. Evil is contained. Evil is in a container. Evil is under God's control.

The pot does more than announce that trouble is brewing. Note that it's a tipped pot. Its boiling water will spill to the south. Judah and Jerusalem are directly in the path of its flow. The scalding water will wash the land. That's the "show." Here's the "tell."

The Babylonian juggernaut is on its way. Nothing can stop it. Yet the disaster coming from the north isn't vindictive. It's instructive. It's not an end in itself. It's purposeful. It's penultimate. What's ultimate? A renewed relationship with God. That's what washing does. It cleanses and restores.

Here is a broader look at this "foe from the north":

- It comes from a distant land (Jeremiah 4:16; 5:15; 6:22).
- It's an established and enduring nation (Jeremiah 5:15) whose men are mighty (5:16), showing no mercy (6:23).
- It will attack suddenly (Jeremiah 4:20; 6:26) with cavalry on swift horses (4:13, 29) and with chariots (4:13).
- Its warriors are armed with bows and spears (Jeremiah 4:29; 6:23) and use battle formations (6:23).
- Its soldiers have the audacity to attack a fortified city at high noon (Jeremiah 6:4).

At the end of the prophet's vision of the tipped, boiling pot, God says, "Every one shall set his throne at the entrance of the gates of Jerusalem" (Jeremiah 1:15). Fast-forward to chapter 39. Jeremiah reports, "All the officials of the king of Babylon came and sat in the middle gate" (Jeremiah 39:3). The Lord watches over His Word to accomplish that for which He sends it. He is the God of the almond tree.

Jeremiah Overcomes

God has one more visual presentation. This one is the most personal. He shows Jeremiah that he will be tough as nails. "I make you this day a fortified city, an iron pillar, and bronze walls, against the whole land, against the kings of Judah, its officials, its priests, and the people of the land. They will fight against you, but they shall not prevail against you, for I am with you, declares the LORD, to deliver you" (Jeremiah 1:18–19). Four times in these two verses the Lord employs the word "against." Almost everyone and his or her sister will be against Jeremiah! He will suffer because of rejection, betrayal, war, ridicule, humiliation, imprisonment, displacement, and loss. No wonder that, throughout his book, Jeremiah expresses bitterness, rage, sadness, melancholy, bewilderment, anger, and disillusionment. But still! He will be a fortified city, an iron pillar, bronze walls—triple protection.

The city of Jerusalem may crack and crumble. But not Jeremiah. He will be like a city that enemies cannot conquer. That's not bad for someone who started out saying, "I'm too inexperienced and too young."

In a forty-year ministry, through the most confusing and chaotic decades of Israel's history, Jeremiah was invincible. Inwardly, he was in great agony many times, but he never swerved from his course. There was enormous pressure on him to change, to compromise, to quit, and to cave in. He never did. Who is the Foreman behind this "city" called Jeremiah? The Lord of hosts is His name.

God fights for Jeremiah. God fights for us. God fights for our health and for our family. He fights for our salvation and for our restoration. Are the odds against us? Is the coach against us? Is the boss against us? Is our health against us? Are our emotions against us? Difficult, for sure. Nevertheless, God fights for us. God fights for people with a tortured childhood, an aging body, an absentee dad. God fights for you with the lost job. You with the bad back, the bad credit score, the bad grade, and the bad break.

Do you recall Sir Ernest Shackleton's great journey in 1914? Ice eventually crushed his ship and stranded his men. The crew drifted for over a year. Finally, Shackleton led a crew of five through the Drake Passage and miraculously reached South Georgia Island—650 nautical miles from his helpless ship. He made it. Shackleton made it across the Antarctic! Jeremiah made it too. He overcame untold sorrows. So shall we. We have God's Word.

3

OVERCOMING THROUGH CONFESSION AND ABSOLUTION

*"I said, 'I will confess my transgressions to the LORD,'
and You forgave the iniquity of my sin."*

(Psalm 32:5)

Sorrows are often followed by distorted thinking. Thinking that includes over-the-top feelings of guilt, shame, self-contempt, humiliation, and self-loathing. "Why didn't I see this coming?" "How could I have been so naïve?" "No one else has ever made such a stupid mistake!" "When will I ever learn?" We send a daily note to ourselves: "You're worthless. You're hopeless. It's time to give up." Sadness and sorrow often bring with them a wicked witch. We call it shame.

Shame runs deeper than embarrassment. We become embarrassed by what we do. We feel shame because of who we are—divorced, old, single, unemployed, forgotten. Jeremiah knows the feeling. He mentions shame throughout his book (e.g., Jeremiah 2:26, 36; 3:3; 6:15; 7:19; 8:12; 10:14).

We may liken shame to a movie rated IO. IO stands for "If Only." "If only I had been smarter!" "If only I had asked for help!" "If only I had listened!" "If only I wasn't so slow to figure things out!" "If only assistance would have come earlier!" "If only I had been more patient!" "If only my skin had been free from cancer, my life free from debt, and my body free from aging!" IO. If only.

What sucked you into shame? A divorce? A shortsighted decision with long-term ramifications? Maybe your shame isn't the result of a moment but of a season in life. You failed as a parent. You blew it in your career. You squandered your youth or your money—or both. The result? Now you're drowning in shame.

There are several options.

Numb it. Numb your shame with a drink during happy hour. Numb it through binge shopping; binge video gaming; binge eating; binge drinking; binge TV watching. "If I feel nothing, then nothing really happened. If I can turn off my feelings, then it won't feel like knives are carving up my stomach." We anesthetize ourselves so we can carry on as if everything is "just fine."

Deny it. Pretend the experience never happened. Concoct a plan to cover it up. One lie, though, leads to another lie, then to another. Before long we have to adjust the second lie to align with the first, then the third lie to align with the second. "Oh what a tangled web we weave."

Bury it. Bury your shame beneath a mountain of work and a calendar of appointments. The busier we are, the less time we have to spend with that one person we have come to dislike the most—ourselves.

Punish it. Cut ourselves. Flog ourselves. If not with whips, then with rules. Create a long list of things to do. Pray more. Study more. Show up earlier and stay up later.

Redirect it. Lash out at the kids. Lash out at your spouse, your co-workers, your cat, your dog, the driver in the next lane, the man in the yellow submarine—whoever!

Offset it. Build the perfect family. Create the perfect career. Score perfect grades. Then be completely intolerant of mistakes made by yourself or by other people.

Try as we might, our shame remains, turning us into miserable, angry, stressed-out people. Shame sucks the very life out of our bones.

Israel's Failed Marriage

Jeremiah offers a two-step program to overcome shame. Perhaps you've heard about it before. Confession and absolution. In chapters 2 and 3 of his book, Jeremiah invites us to lay our shame down and watch God take it away. To assist us, the prophet compares God's relationship with Israel to a marriage—a marriage that begins wonderfully but is soon shaken by infidelity and separation. Divorce is imminent.

There's a time to rehearse all this hurt. We do it through confession.

Just after the wedding, Israel displayed great affection for the Lord. "Go and proclaim in the hearing of Jerusalem, Thus says the LORD, 'I remember the devotion [*hesed*] of your youth, your love as a bride, how you followed Me in the wilderness, in a land not sown'" (Jeremiah 2:2). The Hebrew word for "devotion" is *hesed*. *Hesed* means a deep, abiding, compassionate, and unfailing love. It denotes unshakable loyalty, unbroken promises, unceasing affection. Consider Ruth, who showers Naomi with *hesed*. "For where you go I will go, and where you lodge I will lodge. Your people will be my people, and your God my God. Where you die I will die" (Ruth 1:16–17). Israel's marriage with God began with *hesed*.

As God pages through His wedding album, He remembers Israel's *hesed*. The memories crush His heart. Why, they had once been newlyweds, deeply in love!

That was then. This is now. What went wrong? Israel left God. Abandoned Him for other lovers. Packed her bags and slammed the door. Why would a bride abandon the perfect husband?

- "They did not say, 'Where is the LORD who brought us up from the land of Egypt, who led us in the wilderness, in a land of deserts and pits, in a land of drought and deep darkness, in a land that none passes through, where no man dwells?'" (Jeremiah 2:6)
- "The priests did not say, 'Where is the LORD?'" (Jeremiah 2:8)

There's the problem! "They did not say." Israelites forgot their creed—the recital of God's great acts of salvation that included the Promised

Land. "Land" is the dominant word in Jeremiah 2:6–7: the land of Egypt, the wilderness, a land of deserts and pits, and a godforsaken land that no one passes through or lives in. The Promised Land, flowing with milk and honey, became a defiled land—an abomination. Israel failed to remember their creed and, in turn, lost their land. The marriage turned sour because Israel forgot. "They did not say."

They Forgot

On September 1, 1923, the strongest earthquake ever recorded devastated Yokohama, Japan. It killed 200,000 people and left 2.5 million homeless. Within days, food, clothing, medicine, and supplies began to arrive from the United States. Over the next six months, more than 150 ships arrived from America with material to rebuild the destroyed city. Hirohito, the Japanese emperor, sent a handwritten note to President Calvin Coolidge. It ended with these words: "The people of Japan thank you. The people of Japan will never forget."

Ha! Eighteen years later, on December 7, 1941, Japan attacked United States installations at Pearl Harbor, killing 2,403 Americans. The Japanese forgot—in spades.

The heart of the confession in Jeremiah is the sin of forgetting God's generosity. "Those who handle God's Word did not know Me; the shepherds transgressed against Me; the prophets prophesied by Baal and went after things that do not profit" (Jeremiah 2:8, author's translation). An outbreak of spiritual amnesia spread through Judah and Jerusalem. Worship had become a dead ritual instead of a living relationship, thanks in large part to failed leadership. The priests, kings, and false prophets led a movement that erased people's memory.

That's why the prophet's love poem, dripping with nostalgia in Jeremiah 2:1–3, ends so abruptly. Soon after the wedding, the bride—Israel— went after other gods. Idols are worthless, so those who worshiped them became worthless (Jeremiah 2:5). Other English versions of the Bible translate the Hebrew word for "worthless" as "vapor," "vanity," "wind," or "breath." "Worthless" signifies what is fleeting, futile, and frustrating. It's thin air, zero, zilch, nada, goose eggs. That's life apart from the God who made us and loves us—a big fat nothing.

What could have been between God and Israel—a long and abundant marriage—never was. It's a story of lost love. The flame went out because the bride pursued other lovers—other gods. "My people have committed two evils: they have forsaken Me, the fountain of living waters, and hewed out cisterns for themselves, broken cisterns that can hold no water" (Jeremiah 2:13). If abandoning fresh water in a dry climate isn't crazy enough, building a cracked cistern that leaks fresh water demonstrates the height of folly. Idolatry always leaves us dying from thirst.

God suffers as a scorned husband while Israel pursues pseudo-lovers. This shapes the rest of Jeremiah 2. God feels like a jilted lover. He states His case with the logic of a lawyer and with the longing of a broken heart.

- "Has a nation changed its gods, even though they are no gods?" (Jeremiah 2:11)
- "Have you not brought this upon yourself by forsaking the LORD your God, when He led you in the way?" (Jeremiah 2:17)
- "And now what do you gain by going to Egypt to drink the waters of the Nile? Or what do you gain by going to Assyria to drink the waters of the Euphrates?" (Jeremiah 2:18)
- "Where are your gods that you made for yourself?" (Jeremiah 2:28)
- "Have I been a wilderness to Israel, or a land of thick darkness?" (Jeremiah 2:31)

God has legitimate grounds for ending the marriage. Each of His questions is full of longings for intimacy, deep hurt, inexpressible anguish, remorse, and intense suffering. God isn't above the fray. He's entwined and deeply engaged. He asks questions. He suffers. He weeps. God makes a list of His hurts. The list is long. Israel became like a stubborn animal, a wild vine, a restless camel, a thief caught in the act, and even a nymphomaniac (Jeremiah 2:20–28).

God is finally beside Himself. "Yet My people have forgotten Me days without number" (Jeremiah 2:32). This is the last straw. Israel has been unfaithful and doesn't even care. Indifference is the greatest insult of all. Forgetting implies callous apathy, total detachment. People didn't care that they didn't care! Will the bride ever remember her Husband's love?

- "They have forgotten the LORD their God." (Jeremiah 3:21)
- "You have forgotten Me and trusted in lies." (Jeremiah 13:25)
- "My people have forgotten Me." (Jeremiah 18:15)

The evidence is overwhelming. God has an open-and-shut case. He's not, however, only the rejected Husband and the Prosecuting Attorney. God is the Holy Judge. He prepares to render His verdict. Could this be the end of the marriage?

The End

One of the most explosive growth areas in the travel industry is in the area of exotic vacations. We don't have to settle anymore for a KOA Campground in Kalamazoo, a Motel 6 in Memphis, or a Best Western in Boston. The travel industry has opened countless new opportunities for some real chills, spills, and thrills. We can ride a zip line across the Amazon River, heli-ski in the Alps, or hunt for tigers in Siberia. We can race cars, skydive, bungee jump, and hang glide. You name it, there's a company that will help you do it.

My travel company of choice is Jonathan Lessing's Bike Tours of Fort Collins, Colorado. Several years ago, my son Jonathan took me on a two-day, 150-mile bike trip in the Rocky Mountains. Talk about chills, spills, and thrills! Several times, I thought I was going to die. That it was the end. *No kidding!*

The disaster that was the destruction of Jerusalem in 587 BC looked like the end, yet many Israelites still weren't ready to face the music. Why was Jerusalem a pile of rubble? Why all the horror and violence? "What did we do to deserve this?" God's people weren't ready to admit their sin and shame. Jeremiah prompts them to confess:

- "You said, 'I will not serve.'" (Jeremiah 2:20)
- "How can you say, 'I am not unclean, I have not gone after the Baals'?" (Jeremiah 2:23)
- "You said, 'It is hopeless.'" (Jeremiah 2:25)
- "[You] say to a tree, 'You are my father,' and to a stone, 'You gave me birth.'" (Jeremiah 2:27)

People were living in the land of pretense, claiming to be innocent (Jeremiah 2:23, 25). They tried to hide, deny, and cover up the huge debacle. No wonder the Lord ushered His estranged wife Israel to divorce court (Jeremiah 3:1). The marriage was over. Done. Finished.

Or was it?

Remorse

Have you ever been in a discussion when a person says something and you think to yourself, "If you only knew." They mention something about their childhood and suddenly our childhood nightmares return and we say to ourselves, "If you only knew." They mention something about their job, their marriage, their utter loneliness—and we think, "If you only knew." Our back tenses up, a polite smile masks our face, but all the while we say to ourselves, "If you only knew what I said, what I did, what I thought, you'd never talk to me again."

Yes, I'm still talking about shame.

You may not have a tattoo to mark your past, but we all carry shame, remorse, and guilt. What is it for you? A battle with the bottle? A meltdown at work? Maybe you haven't talked to your mother in a year. Perhaps you've fought with your spouse for so long that you don't know how to begin again.

Still, for others, relationships have gone south, jobs have been lost, and those who were once friends are now enemies. In the midst of it all, we get that sinking feeling, that fear in the pit of our stomach, wondering how we will survive. Memories haunt us. People have hurt us. Parents have disappointed us. Sin still clings to us. Satan still harasses us.

"If you only knew!"

God knows. God knew all about Israel's past—that's what Jeremiah 2 is all about. God knows all about our past as well. Pulsating with *hesed*, God longs for reconciliation and reunion. He even gives us words for our confession: "We have sinned against the LORD our God, we and our fathers, from our youth even to this day, and we have not obeyed the voice of the LORD our God" (Jeremiah 3:25). In fact, in Jeremiah 3–4, God makes four appeals for His people to confess their brokenness and return to Him. They appear in Jeremiah 3:11–13; 3:14–20; 3:21–25; and 4:1–4.

Confession isn't being melancholy, depressed, or introverted. Confession isn't groveling in self-pity. Confession isn't sentimental sorrow. Sentimental sorrow is feeling good about feeling bad. That's not the kind of confession God invites. God invites us to be honest—with Him, ourselves, and others. Honesty is the only way to be saved from shame.

God hopes His bride will return to His loving embrace. The word "return" or "turn" appears seventeen times in Jeremiah 3:1–4:4. Like the father in the parable of the prodigal son, God stands with open arms, anxious for His wayward people to come home. Yes, there is confession. But all the more, there is divine absolution that removes all shame.

Reunited

Jeremiah realizes that marital strife is a powerful way to describe deep-seated sorrows. A tense home life and broken family is an image that most people can relate to. Our identity changes. The economic fear is real. Familiar people, places, and routines could be lost. We all know that divorce undoes everything.

The divorce proceedings in Jeremiah 3:1–5 employ Deuteronomy 24:1–4 as their background. If a man divorces his wife and she becomes the wife of another man, the road is blocked for her to return to her first husband. To do so would defile the land. Jeremiah implies that both the Northern and the Southern Kingdoms are forever cut off from returning to the Lord. The covenant relationship is over, and that's that.

I'm tempted to enter the courtroom drama and tell God, "Forget about

Your wayward wife. You deserve better than that. There are plenty of other fish in the sea." But God won't listen to me. God won't let go. He hopes against hope. He keeps the light on and the door open.

Miracle of miracles, God says, "Return, O faithless children, declares the LORD; for I am your master [Husband]; I will take you, one from a city and two from a family, and I will bring you to Zion" (Jeremiah 3:14). This is a breathtaking statement! The marriage isn't over! Mercy triumphs over judgment! What kind of husband is this? It's one who abounds in *hesed*—loving devotion. He loves His wife and He still loves His children. David speaks for all of us when he tells God, "Your steadfast love [*hesed*] is better than life" (Psalm 63:3).

A Divine Metaphor

A metaphor compares two dissimilar things while bypassing the word *like*. Metaphors help us see what we've not seen before. They help us connect the dots. Jeremiah employs two metaphors in chapter 3: that of a father and that of a husband. Both give shape to God's absolution—His unrelenting *hesed*. Here they are, side by side.

"'I said, How I would set you among My sons, and give you a pleasant land, a heritage most beautiful of all nations. And I thought you would call Me, My Father, and would not turn from following Me. Surely, as a treacherous wife leaves her husband, so have you been treacherous to Me, O house of Israel, declares the LORD'" (Jeremiah 3:19–20). Why does God mix metaphors? What is He? A Father or a Husband? Israel rejected Him as both a parent and a spouse—the two relationships where we feel the most intimate connections and the most searing pain.

Just as the wife stands for the nation of Judah, so the children represent the next generation—Judean exiles in Babylon. God promises to bring them back to Zion. "Return, O faithless children, declares the LORD; for I am your master; I will take you, one from a city and two from a family, and I will bring you to Zion" (Jeremiah 3:14).

Home! What a most glorious absolution! God will give them shepherds after His own heart (Jeremiah 3:15). Jerusalem will be rebuilt so that "all nations shall gather to it" (Jeremiah 3:17). Judah and Israel will reunite and the land will be "most beautiful of all nations" (Jeremiah 3:19).

We make confession. We trust God's absolution. We return to the arms of our loving God. He is a tender Husband, reaching out to His bride. He is a compassionate Father, who yearns for His children. He heals our pain. He fixes what is broken. He wipes out our past—lock, stock, and barrel. Our God abounds in *hesed*.

Restoration

During World War II, the battle for North Africa boiled down to a drink of water—one drink of water.

As the Germans and the British fought in North Africa, both sides were hard-pressed for water. The Brits laid pipes from a nearby oasis. Their custom was to test the pipes by filling them with sea water—*salt* water. Nazi patrols happened upon the pipes while they were being tested. The Germans, desperate for water, thought they had struck gold. They tapped the pipe and began to gulp down water—*salt* water.

Soon, as you might expect, the Germans began to suffer agonizing pain. Hours later, British forces were shocked to see German soldiers approaching with their hands raised, their mouths parched, crying out for drinkable water. It was the turning point in the battle for North Africa.

There's another drink that can make history. It's when we drink from living water. God's absolution is like drinking from living water (cf. Jeremiah 2:13). "Living water," though, implies that there is "dead water." Dead water is the same negative tapes we play in our mind, day after day. Dead water is talking about the same regret, day after day. Dead water is staying buried in shame, day after day. If we don't stop drinking dead water, it will kill us!

John's Gospel furthers Jeremiah's idea of living water. It's one of John's major themes:

- "Unless one is born of water and the Spirit, he cannot enter the kingdom of God." (John 3:5)
- "The water that I will give him will become in him a spring of water welling up to eternal life." (John 4:14)
- "Whoever believes in Me, as the Scripture has said, 'Out of his heart will flow rivers of living water.'" (John 7:38)

Yet, in one ironic twist for the ages, Jesus, the source of living water, is reduced to just a drop, until He completely dries up. "I thirst" (John 19:28). Jesus gasps for water—just one sip of water. The most horrific part of Roman crucifixion wasn't the whipping, the nails, the nakedness, or the ridicule. The most horrific part of Roman crucifixion was that it created an unbelievable thirst for water.

Look! "At once there came out blood and water" (John 19:34). Water flooding from the One whose body is blistered and burned. A gushing river of water surging from the One who hangs dead upon a cross. From the cross comes water—the living water of Christ's absolution for you.

Shame leaves us spiritually dehydrated, dry, and feeling dead. Miles and miles we go. When offered living water, all too often we say no. Instead, we gulp down salt water. Jeremiah learned. "O LORD, the hope of Israel, all who forsake You shall be put to shame; those who turn away from You shall be written in the earth, for they have forsaken the LORD, the fountain of living water" (Jeremiah 17:13).

All that can change. Come to Jesus. Come to His cross. Marvel at the water gushing out of the Savior's side—forgiving your sin, defeating your death, and quenching all of your thirst. God doesn't wait until we get it all together. He doesn't wait until we fight our demons and conquer our past. "God shows His love for us in that while we were still sinners, Christ died for us" (Romans 5:8). It's not too late. It's not even close to over.

Comebacks don't depend on how much we love Jesus. They depend on how much Jesus loves us. Comebacks don't depend on what we do for Jesus. They depend on what Jesus does for us. Comebacks don't depend on us giving our life for Jesus. They depend on Jesus giving His life for us.

Our story isn't over with Jesus in it. Isn't that great? *Our story is never over when Jesus is in it.*

We don't have to work our shame away, explain our shame away, eat our shame away, cry our shame away, or bury our shame away. Jesus doesn't say, "Try harder. You haven't done enough." At our darkest point—when we feel the ugliest—Jesus says, "I love you!" He welcomes and heals people who are full of shame. Ugly shame. Haunting shame.

We aren't worthless. We aren't damaged goods. We are clean. We are whole. The Savior's liberating love sets us free from condemnation; free from the pain of our past; free from worry about our future. No one can take this freedom from us. No law can stop it. No power on earth or hell can destroy it. "Behold, we come to You, for You are the LORD our God" (Jeremiah 3:22).

4

OVERCOMING THROUGH HOPE

*"Set your hope fully on the grace that
will be brought to you at the revelation of Jesus Christ."*

(1 Peter 1:13)

Sometimes people ask me how to pronounce my last name. "Is it *Lee-sing* or *Less-ing*?" I often tell them, "It's *Blessing* without the *B*." I might be wrong, though. Some years ago, when the sainted Dr. Oswald Hoffmann of Lutheran Hour lore preached at our church in Broken Arrow, Oklahoma, he called me "Pastor *Lee-sing*." I guess if Ozzie said it, it must be true.

Confusion over my last name has created some awkward moments. I was once speaking at a conference and a pastor came up to me and said, "Hey, Dr. *Lee-sing*, it's so nice to see you!" It would have been rude to correct him. "And besides," I thought to myself, "no harm, no foul." The problem was, however, that this pastor began introducing me to his friends. Momentum kept building with each introduction. Lee-sing. LEE-sing. *LEE-SING*. After three or four more "Lee-sings," I realized I couldn't do a thing. I had reached the point of no return.

So had Judah.

What brought on Judah's sad state of affairs? They chased worthless idols. They didn't know the Lord. They defiled the land. Made it an abomination. Prophesied by Baal. Refused to fear the Lord. Became degenerate, guilty, unclean, restless, lustful, hopeless, forgetful, sinful, and proud. This list is from Jeremiah 2. Space doesn't allow me to consider the next fifty chapters in the book! Judah had reached the point of no return.

We know the feeling. We're all dreamers. We all envision that we will succeed, that we will be loved, that we will be happy. Eventually, though, we hit a wall. We run aground. We crash and burn. We become dazed, confused, broken.

What do you do when it happens to you? when everything terminates? when the deal falls through? when the love of your life walks out? when the police officer comes to your door and says your child is in jail for selling cocaine? What do you do when your dreams fall apart and you know there is no putting them together? What do you do—what do I do—when we reach the point of no return?

The End of the World

Jeremiah says a catastrophe feels like the end of the world. "I looked on the earth, and behold, it was without form and void; and to the heavens, and they had no light" (Jeremiah 4:23). The approaching Babylonian war machine brought with it the end of everything.

Life looks that way sometimes. What we believed about family, prayer, commitment, and trust was betrayed. We were lied to or intentionally hurt. Whatever happened, it strikes us at our very core.

Sadness and sorrow are creation's undoing. Everything is thrown into reverse. The Babylonian invasion of Judah felt like creation's collapse. Light, mountains, hills, birds, and cities are "without form and void" (*tohu wabohu* in Hebrew). In Genesis 1:2, Moses uses the same two words to describe the world before God spoke order and created light. *Tohu wabohu* denotes a world lacking in order, color, and symmetry. Other English versions of the Bible translate this Hebrew expression this way:

- "A formless wasteland" (NAB)
- "Formless and empty" (NIV)
- "Formless void" (NASB)

Tohu wabohu announces that our world has been destroyed. What looked permanent and lasting has crumbled before our very eyes. We have moved from light to darkness, from beauty to ugliness, from bounty to a wasteland.

Jeremiah cries out, "My anguish, my anguish! I writhe in pain! Oh the walls of my heart! My heart is beating wildly; I cannot keep silent, for I hear the sound of the trumpet, the alarm of war" (Jeremiah 4:19). The word translated "anguish" in other contexts denotes the stomach, belly, or our inner organs. The prophet's use of the expression "writhe in pain" compares his experience to a woman giving birth. Jeremiah's heart is also "beating wildly." Put it all together, and the prophet's emotions are off the charts.

Like Jeremiah, when we experience the end of our world, our emotions become a jumbled mix of anger, terror, and grief. We're bombarded with so many intense feelings. One minute we're angry and vindictive. The next minute we feel like a wet noodle, ready to give up. It's difficult to focus on anything for any length of time, because everything changes so rapidly.

What should we do with these emotions? Sometimes we suppress them. We clam up. We don't tell a soul. We hardly admit these feelings to ourselves. Whatever happens, we can't admit them to God. Our best bet is to pray for it all to go away.

When we don't weep over an alcoholic dad or an unloving mother or over mistreatment or prejudice or bigotry, it's like burying toxic waste in our heart. It's only a matter of time before the poison comes to the surface and we end up doing things that bring more pain. That aching neck? That upset stomach? That migraine headache? A lot of that is because we stuff our sorrow inside.

God understands raw emotions. He cares about them. Whether we're up or down today—in the valley or simply doing another load of laundry—

we can turn to God. He understands our deep angst. He knows about our nightmare. Do you need some examples?

- "The LORD regretted that He had made man on the earth, and it grieved Him to His heart." (Genesis 6:6)
- "When [Jesus] drew near and saw the city, He wept over it." (Luke 19:41)
- "They rebelled and grieved His Holy Spirit." (Isaiah 63:10)

There you have it. In Genesis 6:6, God the Father grieves. In Luke 19:41, God the Son grieves. In Isaiah 63:10, God the Holy Spirit grieves. The triune God invites us to grieve, lament, and cry with Him.

God made us to be psychosomatic creatures. *Psycho* comes from the Greek word *psyche*, which means "soul." We have feelings and emotions. *Somatic* derives from the Greek word *soma*, which means "body." We have skin and bones and muscles and eyes and ears. *Psychosomatic*. My feelings and my body go together. Example A? When we repress pain, we feel it, especially in our stomach.

Jeremiah's stomach churns, turns, and burns. He's unsettled and anxious. His heart is in his throat. He's beside himself. Everything is reverting back to the dark and murky world of Genesis 1:2—*tohu wabohu*. Jeremiah sees light going out (the sun, moon, and stars). The mountains and hills—symbols of stability—collapse. People and birds become nonexistent. The entire world is unglued. God's "very good" (Genesis 1:31) is now "very bad." Death is on the move, spewing forth destruction like hot lava from a volcano.

Jeremiah further describes his feeling of despair with five words that depict public unrest and violence: "war," "crash" (two times), and "waste" (two times). "Crash follows hard on crash; the whole land is laid waste. Suddenly my tents are laid waste, my curtains in a moment" (Jeremiah 4:20).

We continue with Jeremiah 4:23–26. Each of these verses begins with "I looked" and the term "behold"—a word that denotes shock and surprise. The prophet's sequence moves from the universal ("earth" and "the heavens") to the local ("mountains" and "hills") to the lack of inhabitants ("no man" or "birds") to finally the specifics of Jeremiah's home ("fruitful land," "desert," "cities," and "ruins"). The catastrophe dismantles "all the hills," "all the birds of the air," and "all its cities." Nothing is spared.

Tohu wabohu.

Tohu wabohu—utter chaos. It includes hunger, violence, rape, poverty, divorce, abortion, unemployment, and death. What's left when even one of these visits us? How can we cope? Can we pick up the pieces and begin again? What can we retrieve and what must we let go?

Any attempt at recovering bygone days is bound to fail. We can't live in the past. To deny this only puts us in a land of make-believe. There are fifty ways to fight a fire, but closing your eyes isn't one of them. Denial doesn't work.

Blind optimism doesn't help either. There's a story about a man falling from a twelve-story building. When he reaches the sixth floor, someone asks him how he's doing. His response? "So far, so good!" That's not what I'm talking about—unrealistic hope that ignores the problem.

Pretending doesn't get us very far either. I know. When I'm hurt, my default reaction is to say, "I'm okay." When I don't get what I need, I respond with the words "I'm okay." When life's events crush me and threaten to destroy me, I tend to shrug my shoulders and say, "I'm okay."

It's tempting to "put on a face" and masquerade as a superspiritual Christian who rises above life's *tohu wabohu*. Though it grants short-term relief, in the end, anesthetizing ourselves only invites more pain. It's time to put on the brakes. It's time to say, "I'm not okay."

Good Friday

"My God, My God, why have You forsaken Me?" (Matthew 27:46). This is Christ's lament from the cross as He watches His world end. This can be our cry as well. God invites us to grieve when we're left alone, feeling as though the breakup and brokenness are more than we can manage.

God encourages us to mourn over workaholic parents, abusive friends, and emotionally distant spouses.

There's a wife left by her husband of thirty years for another woman half his age. There's a college student left by his fiancée for another guy who is going to be "way more successful." There are parents whose children have left home, and "empty nest" means a gaping hole in their hearts. There's a child stricken with a rare form of cancer, left alone, confined to her bed for what feels like forever. "Nobody loves me. Everybody hates me. I just want to die!"

If we don't acknowledge and grieve life's chaos, it becomes an insidious virus that destroys our body, mind, and soul. Trying to self-medicate with food, alcohol, shopping, studies, work, or the internet only gets us further trapped in patterns of self-sabotage.

There is a better way. Tell God how you feel. Jesus did. He was mocked by the crowds, betrayed by Judas, denied by Peter, forsaken by the ten, unjustly accused in a kangaroo court, sentenced to death by a weak-willed Roman governor, crowned with thorns, and scourged by musclemen just short of death. There, against the dark sky, is Jesus—condemned, crucified, and all alone. *Tohu wabohu.* Everything is without form and void.

Jesus mourns the darkness and teaches us to do the same. First, cry out, "My God, my God!" Go to the God who loves you and forgives you and shows you mercy because of Christ's cross, Christ's blood, and Christ's sacrifice. Don't look the other way. Don't swallow hard. Don't keep calm and carry on. Jesus mourned, and so we mourn.

Were our Savior's cries His last words? Was this the end of the story? How could it be? "The end" are never God's last words. Three days later, Jesus becomes the Living One. He died, and behold, He is alive forevermore.

The end is never the end. I'll write that again. *The end is never the end.* There's death but there's resurrection. There's the darkness of the night but there's the dawn of a new day. There's Golgotha but there's Galilee. Galilee! That's where the disciples saw their risen Lord!

That credit card bill is not the end. That diagnosis is not the end. That impossible situation is not the end. That depression stalking and mocking you is not the end. Christ always brings a new beginning—always. The end is never a full end. Consider these verses from Jeremiah:

- "For thus says the LORD, 'The whole land shall be a desolation; yet I will not make a full end.'" (Jeremiah 4:27)
- "Go up through her vine rows and destroy, but make not a full end." (Jeremiah 5:10)
- "But even in those days, declares the LORD, I will not make a full end of you." (Jeremiah 5:18)
- "For I am with you to save you, declares the LORD; I will make a full end of all the nations among whom I scattered you, but of you I will not make a full end." (Jeremiah 30:11)
- "Fear not, O Jacob My servant, declares the LORD, for I am with you. I will make a full end of all the nations to which I have driven you, but of you I will not make a full end." (Jeremiah 46:28)

Jeremiah 52 describes the time from Zedekiah's reign (597–587 BC) through Jerusalem's destruction and deportation to Babylon. The chapter concludes with an event that takes place in 560 BC when the Babylonian king Evil-merodach gives the Davidic king Jehoiachin of Judah a place of honor at the table.

The end of Judah is not the end of the Davidic monarchy. The nation of Judah lies in ruins. God's promise to the house of David marches on. As the Creator who de-creates, He also will re-create. "'Ah, Lord GOD! It is You who have made the heavens and the earth by Your great power and by Your outstretched arm! Nothing is too hard for You'" (Jeremiah 32:17).

First Class

In November 2010, I was on my way to attend a meeting in Atlanta, Georgia. Then my flight was canceled. I waited five hours for the next one and the airline rewarded me with an upgrade to first class. Then, lo and behold, several other professors going to the same conference showed up. They were surprised to hear I was now on their flight. Surprise turned to shock when I told them I was now in first class. I tried to explain things, and I even felt a bit guilty. Do you think I settled for coach to sit with them? Not on your life!

Because of God's tenacious love, we've been upgraded, from *tohu wabohu* to courage and confidence, faith and freedom. That's flying first class. Why settle for coach?

We may be looking at the end of a relationship or a job or a dream, but it's not the end of God's mercy or His plan for our lives. We may need to walk through a long, dark hallway—but it's a hallway. Hallways always lead to another room—a room where healing and hope are born anew.

5

OVERCOMING THROUGH WORSHIP

"I was glad when they said to me,
'Let us go to the house of the LORD!'"

(Psalm 122:1)

We know that suffering is part of life. That's why after one setback, we may feel down but still resilient. We tell ourselves that everything will be okay. Then, while we're still reeling from that setback, another one comes, then another. We aren't prepared for multiple sorrows when pain compounds exponentially. So we begin to sleepwalk through our days, aching with brokenness. Life becomes one deep sigh after another for months, years, sometimes for decades.

It can all feel like a prison sentence with no release date. We sit in the dark confines of sadness. The cold and gray surroundings create a greater fear: that we are stuck in sorrow forever. Agony doesn't come with a built-in bright side or a steady set of positives that outweigh the negatives. Help must break in from the outside. No matter how smart or strong we are, we need someone to lift us up from the pit. We need Jesus.

Seeking healing apart from Jesus is like holding cotton candy in the rain. We're left with a sticky mess of despair. But still. When it feels like our heart has stopped beating, we are tempted to turn away from Christ, to run as far away from God as we can. "God, if that's the way life is, then no thanks, God!" We're appalled, we're angry, we're shocked, we're heartbroken. So we run. We run from God. This is understandable. But it doesn't help. It doesn't help at all. We have to figure out how to worship again.

Waking Up to Worship

As you might imagine, over the years I've had some interesting feedback on my sermons. A man once told me, "Pastor Lessing, your sermons remind me of the mercies of God; they endure forever." Another time, a woman said, "Pastor Lessing, your sermon reminded me of the peace of God. It passed all human understanding."

The most humbling feedback came when I was the pastor at Trinity Lutheran Church in Broken Arrow, Oklahoma. One day, I overheard two older women. The first said, "I feel so bad. My doctor put me on a new medication that makes me drowsy. Last Sunday, I fell asleep during Pastor Lessing's sermon." The other woman replied, "Don't feel bad. I fell asleep too, and I'm not on any medication!"

From time to time, we all need to wake up to worship. That's why God gives us Jeremiah 7. The pain of Babylon had lulled God's people into spiritual sleep.

The Right Place and Right Words

Midway through the tenth century BC, Solomon built a temple in Jerusalem and dedicated it to God's glory (1 Kings 8). It became a vehicle for divine forgiveness and grace. By Jeremiah's day, however, the temple had become a form of escape. It consisted of three interrelated parts: (1) the temple is God's permanent residence; (2) the monarchy is God's permanent plan; (3) therefore, Jerusalem and the temple will endure forever.

Yet a catastrophe had just happened. Josiah, one of Judah's most godly kings, had been killed on the battlefield. Pharaoh Necho II mowed him down at the Battle of Megiddo in 609 BC. "All Judah and Jerusalem mourned for Josiah. Jeremiah also uttered a lament for Josiah" (2 Chronicles 35:24–25). It was a time of national mourning. People flocked to the temple. Jeremiah warns them, though, about having only the right place and right words.

There are times when we drag ourselves to church, thinking, "Get to the right place and say the right words and everything will be all right." We might even think, "I can think anything. Say anything. Do anything. Believe anything. Wish for anything. And all will be well! I attend the right place and say the right words."

Going to church—the right place—and saying the right words is a lot easier than having a relationship with Jesus. Showing up at church once a week and saying a hearty "Amen!" is a lot easier than engaging in a life of daily prayer and Scripture study. Jeremiah says as much: "Do not trust in these deceptive words: 'This is the temple of the LORD, the temple of the LORD, the temple of the LORD.' . . . Do not oppress the sojourner, the fatherless, or the widow, or shed innocent blood in this place, and . . . do not go after other gods" (Jeremiah 7:4, 6).

Jeremiah exposes the folly of ignoring God's concern for people on the margins, then attending church as if everything is just fine. It's easy to have the right place and say the right words. "This is the temple of the LORD, the temple of the LORD, the temple of the LORD." Such a shallow spirituality is like a house of cards, certain to fall at the slightest problem. Worship is not just about places and words; it includes life and love, mercy and faith. It includes our heart.

Places are important—immensely important. Sanctuaries and buildings are places where we gather to receive God's Gospel gifts and be motivated for fresh action. Yet standing in a sanctuary singing a hymn doesn't make us holy any more than standing in the backyard and barking at the moon makes us a dog.

And words are important—immensely important. Words express what we believe about the Bible, the Trinity, the Sacraments—the doctrines of the Church. What we say expresses what we believe. But mindlessly repeating holy words no more creates a relationship with Jesus than saying "I love you" twenty times a day makes us skilled as lovers.

The right place and the right words in and of themselves won't heal our broken hearts. The right place and the right words create the opportunity for wholeness and new life—but only an opportunity.

Jeremiah, speaking for God, continues, "Has this house, which is called by My name, become a den of robbers in your eyes? Behold, I Myself have seen it, declares the LORD" (Jeremiah 7:11). A robber's den is a secure place to hide between excursions into the countryside to pillage unprotected people. After the raids, robbers go back to the cave for safety. This describes the people in Jeremiah's day to a tee. They thought they could live one way outside the temple and a different way once they were worshiping in the temple.

Where did they get that idea? Judahites believed God had made irrevocable promises to Jerusalem's temple and Judah's monarchy. Both were immune from the enemy; therefore, so were the people. The prophet's response? External religion has become a narcotic to deaden the pain of reality. Jeremiah is against false notions about the temple, notions that make it a rabbit's foot or four-leaf clover.

Judeans were breaking the Ten Commandments (Jeremiah lists almost all of them in chapter 7) and then going to the temple to worship, thinking that using the right words would protect them. God says, "You spend all week doing what you want, taking advantage of others, then you come to the right place, say the right words, and pretend everything is just right." Paul warns us about this: "[They have] the appearance of godliness, but [deny] its power" (2 Timothy 3:5).

The Right Heart

As a child I loved the book *The Little Engine That Could*. The story's signature line is "I think I can." An engine pulling a long train over a steep mountain breaks down. After failing to draft a number of larger replacement engines, a much smaller engine agrees to give it a try, saying, "I think I can." While repeating these words, the little blue engine overcomes the mountain pass and does the impossible—he pulls the long train into the station.

Such determination might work for the little engine that could, but what about us when we can't? when our loss is too great, our pain too deep, our memories too fresh, and our mountain too high? Then what? Attend church to worship God and receive His gifts. God isn't for the little engine that could. God is for the train wreck that can't. In worship, we approach God with humility and lowliness. We are train wrecks that can't. That's why Jeremiah invites us to take a field trip to Shiloh.

Through the prophet, God says, "Go now to My place that was in Shiloh, where I made My name dwell at first, and see what I did to it because of the evil of My people Israel" (Jeremiah 7:12). Shiloh is about twenty miles north of Jerusalem. It's one of the most famous places in the Old Testament. When Joshua entered the Promised Land, Israelites assembled at Shiloh, set up the tabernacle, and parceled out the land among the twelve tribes. After that, God appeared to the child Samuel at Shiloh and called him into service.

Shiloh was the right place. At Shiloh people spoke the right words. But when the right place no longer launched a walk with God, when the right words no longer expressed love and faith, the Philistines destroyed Shiloh, in 1050 BC (1 Samuel 4). They even carted off the ark of the covenant. There was nothing left. In Jeremiah 7:12–15, the prophet reaches his stunning and devastating conclusion: Jerusalem will fair no better than Shiloh. The "it won't happen here" crowd needed to look north twenty miles.

If it happened at Shiloh, it will happen at Jerusalem—and any other place where people gather to worship God with a fake faith. It's not enough to be in the right place. It's not enough to say the right words. Shiloh is any place where God once lived but is no longer there. Through God's example of Shiloh, He calls us to approach Him with humble hearts.

Jeremiah's temple sermon isn't against the temple, per se. The prophet's demands aren't put forth as an alternative to the temple. The Means and the Grace go together. The temple (the Means) is where God delivers forgiveness of sin (the Grace). The Means of Grace empower a life that follows the Ten Commandments—albeit imperfectly. Jeremiah invites us to make a clean break from heartless worship by asking God to create in us a new heart.

For You

We gather in worship to hear God's Word, call upon Him in prayer and praise, and receive the gifts of Word and Sacrament. Through these Means of Grace, God says, "I have loved you with an everlasting love" (Jeremiah 31:3). The "you" in Jeremiah's Hebrew is singular, not plural. It's "you," not "you all." Singular "you" denotes a focus that is individual and intimate, particular and personal. God's care is cosmic and universal, to be sure. Yet here God employs the singular "you."

That's the power of worship. We hear promises like "Your sins are forgiven"; "Christ died and rose for you"; "I have called you by name." You! You! God loves you! There is a name for this. Mercy.

Mercy sent Jesus to a manger. Mercy sent Jesus to teach. Mercy sent Jesus to heal broken hearts. Mercy will send Jesus on the Last Day to sit on the throne of glory. There was another throne before the throne of glory. Did you know that?

It was the cross. The Romans nailed a placard above Christ's head that read, "*Iesous Nazarenus Rex Ideorum*." That's Latin for "Jesus of Nazareth, King of the Jews." Do you see what the soldiers did? They turned the cross into a mock throne for what they took to be a mock king and a mock messiah who led a mock movement. That's why they gave Him a mock crown made of thorns. For Rome? The cross is a throne of mockery. For us? The cross is the throne of mercy.

Mercy! Overflowing mercy. Unlimited mercy. Marvelous and miraculous mercy. God's mercy means we have forgiveness for every sin, direction at every turn, and hope for every deep sigh of despair. God delivers mercy through His means of mercy—the Gospel and the Sacraments of Baptism and Holy Communion. It's all "for you."

And So We Sing

Three times in his book, Jeremiah announces that hardships silence our singing (Jeremiah 7:34; 16:9; 25:10). Now the song is back. When we're in the right place with the right words coupled with the right heart, divine love overrides all sighing and silence. Stunned muteness gives way to merriment and joy (Jeremiah 33:11).

J. S. Bach helps us sing.

People have called Johann Sebastian Bach "the classic Lutheran layman," "a sign of God," "the Preacher," "the Teacher," "the Theologian," "the first great German voice since Luther," and "the Fifth Evangelist." Bach not only gives us words and melodies and choruses. He also gives us a theology of worship. It stems from 1 Chronicles 25—a list of 288 Levitical musicians.

I know. It's best to avoid lists, shun lists, never look at biblical lists. That is, unless you want to worship from the heart. In Bach's three-volume Calov Bible of 1733—which are the only books of any sort from Bach's library that have survived to this day—with red ink the master musician wrote in the margins of 1 Chronicles 25: "This chapter is the true foundation of all God-pleasing church music." Bach also underlined Calov's comments on verse 1: "The musicians are to express the Word of God in spiritual songs and psalms, sing them in the temple, and at the same time play with instruments." He noted that 1 Chronicles 25 is "the true foundation of all God-pleasing church music" because it states that hymnody's role is to proclaim God's Word.

What does God's Word say in our hymns and our liturgy? We were dead; now we're alive in Christ. We were sinking in sand; now we're standing on the Rock. We lived like victims; but now we live in victory—Christ's victory. God brought us out of bondage to sin, and now we're living in His wonderful promises. That's our song and we're sticking to it!

In the Absolution, the pastor doesn't say, "God has forgiven you." Though that's true, that's not what he says. The pastor says, "God forgives you." *Present tense!* Martin Luther doesn't teach us to say, "I was baptized." Though that's true, that's not what Luther emphasized. He said, "I am baptized!" *Present tense!* When we receive the Holy Supper, the pastor doesn't say, "Take, eat, this was Christ's body." Not at all. He says, "Take, eat, this is Christ's true body and Christ's true blood." *Present tense!* And when we celebrate Easter, we don't say, "Christ has risen." Though that's true, that's not what we say. We shout out, "Christ is risen!"

Here's my point.

In worship, Christ meets us in the here and now, giving us courage to face the day, spine to face tomorrow, and hope to face the week to come. No wonder Jeremiah says, "Sing to the LORD; praise the LORD! For He has delivered the life of the needy from the hand of evildoers" (Jeremiah 20:13).

I understand if you don't have a song to sing just yet. Go ahead and hang your head. Shake your fist. Cry out loud. Stomp your feet. It's tough. It's heartbreaking. It's sometimes beyond words. But trust me. The worst parts of life are the gateways to the best parts of life. Your crazy train will stop someday and you'll get off, singing songs of thanksgiving. That's because suffering is redemptive. Consider the man of John 9 who was born blind. Jesus says it happened so that the works of God might be displayed. We trust God who allows pain. We trust God who uses pain for good. Let's attend worship this weekend with this prayer: "Create in me a clean heart, O God, and renew a right spirit within me."

6

OVERCOMING THROUGH EXPRESSING GRIEF

"Weeping may tarry for the night,
but joy comes with the morning."

(Psalm 30:5)

Maybe you heard about this incident that appeared on a company accident form. "When I got to the building, I saw that the earthquake had knocked off some bricks around the top, so I set up a beam with a pulley at the top of the building and hoisted up two barrels full of bricks. After I fixed the damaged area, there were leftover bricks. I went to the bottom and began releasing the line. Unfortunately, the barrel of bricks was heavier than I was and, before I knew it, the barrel started coming down, jerking me up. I decided to hang on since, in a matter of seconds, I was too far off the ground to jump. When I hit the beam at the top, the barrel of bricks hit the ground, spilling the bricks. I was now heavier than the barrel. I started down at high speed. When I hit the ground, I landed on the bricks. I let go of my grip on the rope, and the barrel came down, hitting me in the head."

When life hits us hard, we land on bricks. Just then, a barrel hits us on the head. We're hurt so deeply we wonder if we can ever love or trust again.

It's tempting to cut everyone out of life. We no longer have the energy it takes to invest in relationships. Depression and anxiety overwhelm us. Sadness and fear become our constant companions. We can't let go of our anger toward people who destroyed us. It's the end of life as we know it.

Then, some hope. We begin a new job or a new relationship. Yet even these turn out to be false starts. The disappointment fuels more sadness and grief. "What's the use of trying anymore?" We made ourselves vulnerable, and vulnerability led to more suffering. We vow never to share our heart again. Loneliness and isolation are the new normal.

The Weeping Prophet

Michelangelo's painting of Jeremiah on the ceiling of the Sistine Chapel depicts the prophet as downcast and deep in thought. His face is dark. His eyes are closed. His shoulders are slumped. His left hand covers his mouth as if to say that he's done talking and he has given in to despair.

The prophet fills his book with grief. Jeremiah weeps. God weeps. Israel weeps. At one point Jeremiah writes, "For the wound of the daughter of my people is my heart wounded; I mourn, and dismay has taken hold on me" (Jeremiah 8:21). "I mourn" in this verse literally means "I am dark" or "black." Jeremiah is referring to the color of mourning clothes. Jeremiah goes through a box of Kleenex once a day. It's not surprising that people call Jeremiah "the weeping prophet." Additionally, the noun *jeremiad* denotes a lament or a list of woes

Expressing our pain is the first step toward healing our pain. Emotional angst is like a warning light on the dashboard of a car. I know all about red warning lights in cars. In the fall of 1979, I was on a trip from Nebraska to Texas, and I ignored the bright red flashing light—the oil light—on my dashboard. I failed to put oil in my Denver Bronco–orange 1974 Volkswagen Bug. You can imagine what happened. The engine exploded. I called my dad. My dad exploded—not from the lack of oil in *his* car. My dad exploded from the lack of a brain in *his* son! My dad asked me why I failed to put oil in the engine. For once in my life, I was speechless.

The warning light was trying to help me. So are my tears.

The Daughter of My People

What brought tears to Jeremiah's eyes? God's people were spiritually clueless. "Even the stork in the heavens knows her times, and the turtledove, swallow, and crane keep the time of their coming, but My people know not the rules of the LORD" (Jeremiah 8:7). Without any mechanical aids, birds navigate across great distances. In one test, a number of Manx shearwaters, which nest off the coast of Wales, were tagged and released. One was turned loose in Boston, some 3,200 miles from home. In just twelve days, the bird returned to its nest, having traveled 250 miles a day. Birds not only know when to migrate; they know when to care for their young, ward off intruders, and forage for food.

Birds find their way home. Judeans appear forever lost. "How can you say, 'We are wise, and the teaching of the LORD is with us'? But behold, the lying pen of the scribes has made it into a lie" (Jeremiah 8:8, author's translation). The prophet calls out Judah's scribes—the Bible experts. What's Jeremiah's point? Possessing the Scriptures isn't the same as practicing the Scriptures. We can possess the Bible. We can even profess the Bible. None of this is the same as practicing the Bible.

On top of all this, God's people lived in denial. Jeremiah warns that fields will be ruined (Jeremiah 8:13, 16), cities will be destroyed (Jeremiah 8:16), and God's people will cry out (Jeremiah 8:19). When the enemy arrives, it will be like drinking poison (Jeremiah 8:14), experiencing an earthquake (Jeremiah 8:16), or being attacked by venomous snakes (Jeremiah 8:17). Little wonder, then, that the people's heart will be deeply wounded (Jeremiah 8:21).

What did Judeans do? They embraced false prophets, charlatans who were full of hot air, saying, "Peace, peace," when there was no peace. Here is what Jeremiah calls them:

- Empty wind (Jeremiah 5:13)
- Deceitful physicians (Jeremiah 6:14; 8:11)
- Dispensers of chaff (Jeremiah 23:28)

- Ruthless and selfish (Jeremiah 23:1–4)
- Agents of ungodliness (Jeremiah 23:15)

These pseudoprophets were masters at denial. We succumb to denial to protect ourselves. Denial is a defense mechanism that shelters us from painful facts. We insist that the evidence isn't true despite overwhelming and irrefutable documentation. "Who, me? Sick? I'm not sick!" Consumerism is closely related to denial. We try to buy our way to wellness. A new car, house, wardrobe, motorcycle, or piece of expensive jewelry will surely make us feel better. We're right. It will. But not for long.

God Weeps

While Israelites live in denial, Jeremiah weeps. So does God. The Lord doesn't view our pain with detached objectivity. He isn't aloof. God has great passion and emotion. Throughout the Bible, He experiences sorrow, grief, pain, anguish, heartache, and regret. This isn't, however, like a car mechanic fixing an engine from the outside, or like a welfare administrator signing vouchers for food stamps. God enters deeply into our suffering and feels our pain.

In some cases, the pain of God and the pain of Jeremiah are indistinguishable. Both feel grief and have wounded hearts. Both mourn and are full of dismay. Both shed tears. God is wrenched apart as He burns with loving desire for His people. So is Jeremiah. The following verses describe how *both* the Lord and His prophet respond to the horrendous experience of exile.

- "My joy is gone; grief is upon me; my heart is sick within me." (Jeremiah 8:18)
- "Oh that my head were waters, and my eyes a fountain of tears, that I might weep day and night for the slain of the daughter of my people!" (Jeremiah 9:1)
- "I will take up weeping and wailing for the mountains, and a lamentation for the pastures of the wilderness." (Jeremiah 9:10)

In spite of Judah's stubbornness and lack of faith, God and Jeremiah together exhibit a passionate yearning for them. God and His prophet care deeply. This is no syrupy and sentimental sorrow. It's a fierce love that leads to broken hearts.

To be sure, God is holy, sovereign, and utterly removed from us. Yet, at the same time, God is immanent, personal, and relational. Because of Jesus, most of us recognize this intimate side of God in the New Testament. A closer reading of the above verses in Jeremiah, however, indicates that God also suffers in the Old Testament. God didn't become incarnate until Mary's conception by the Holy Spirit. Yet Christ's incarnation wasn't something completely new. It culminated God's long-standing relationship with the world as being both transcendent and immanent, sovereign and saving, mighty and merciful. God is traumatized in both the Old and New Testaments. How could it be otherwise? "Jesus Christ is the same yesterday and today and forever" (Hebrews 13:8).

A Time to Weep

Marie Antoinette, the last queen of France, once said, "Nothing tastes." She meant that nothing seemed worthwhile, nothing gave joy. Albert Camus, a twentieth-century French philosopher, once wrote, "Life is a bad joke." There is no rhyme or reason to life. We're born. We live. We die. That's it. *Life is a bad joke.*

This is how we feel when the rug has been pulled out from beneath our feet. Everything becomes void of meaning. The initial shock is numbing. Given time, though, the pain seeps into our heart and begins to erode our emotional life.

Take, for instance, the death of a loved one. We don't lose that person all at once. We lose them in pieces—the mail stops coming, we no longer share stories about our day, their scent gradually fades from our home. Then, just when we think we're doing better, something is said and the feelings of loss overwhelm us—again. *Nothing tastes!*

It's tempting to treat loss like a car alarm. Car alarms go off so frequently, often for no reason at all, that we ignore them. We become numb to the sirens, buzzers, whistles, and beepers. We can't let that happen to our heart.

I wish I could tell you that we overcome pain by going around it, tunneling underneath it, or taking a big jump over it. That's not what Jeremiah does. Jeremiah goes through it. So does God. So does David. He prays, "Even though I walk through the valley of the shadow of death" (Psalm 23:4). The death of a spouse, a dream, a job, our health—it's a "time to weep," a "time to mourn" (Ecclesiastes 3:4).

God and Jeremiah summon the grief brigade to help us. "Call for the mourning women to come; send for the skillful women to come; let them make haste and raise a wailing over us, that our eyes may run down with tears and our eyelids flow with water" (Jeremiah 9:17–18). Dirge-singing women are commanded to weep, but also to pass on their lamentation skills to their daughters (Jeremiah 9:20). Modeled by God and Jeremiah and amplified by women and their daughters, exiles are invited to shed tears. It's the only way forward.

It probably strikes you as odd that Jeremiah mentions women who got paid to mourn. Yet the more you think about it, the process makes sense. Expressing the despair brings buried feelings into the light of day. Most of Israel's professional mourners were women, but men could also sing laments (e.g., 2 Samuel 1:11; 3:33; 2 Chronicles 35:25). Mourning rites include the following:

- Tearing your clothes (Genesis 37:34; 2 Samuel 1:11–12)
- Wearing sackcloth, a course fabric of camel or goat hair, probably next to the skin (2 Samuel 3:31)
- Tearing or shaving off hair (Micah 1:16)
- Throwing dust on your head (Ezekiel 27:30)
- Sitting on the ground (Lamentations 2:10)
- Rolling in dust or ashes (Ezekiel 27:30)
- Fasting (2 Samuel 1:11–12)

There's a cost to grieving. It takes large amounts of time and energy. There's a higher cost to remaining emotionally blunted and paralyzed. That's why God commands people to mourn. He mandates it. "O daughter of my people, put on sackcloth, and roll in ashes; make mourning as for an only son, most bitter lamentation" (Jeremiah 6:26). This verse announces that there is much to mourn. To lose an only son means the family line has ended. There will be no male heir to pass on the family name. That's the legal toll. The emotional toll is impossible to explain. Losing an only son, losing *any* child, is perhaps life's greatest loss. The shock and devastation are beyond description.

God wants us to lament over what we have lost. Tears bring us back to life. Painful life, to be sure. But life. Tears tell us that our feelings are coming back—that *we* are coming back. Numbed shock and bottled-up emotions will not have the final say. Weeping leads to restoration.

While visceral cries are part of Israel's relationship with God, we often neglect them in the Church. Prayers of lament have largely dropped out of lectionaries and liturgies—with the exception of Psalm 22 on Good Friday. We are inclined to hurry past loss and grief, rushing quickly to resolution. "Everything will be all right." "Time heals all wounds." "The sun will come up tomorrow." The goal is to have a church where "seldom is heard a discouraging word." Jeremiah teaches us about grieving. So does Jesus.

Jesus Wept

One of the most well-known verses in the Bible is John 11:35, "Jesus wept." We need some context. Lazarus is sick. Lazarus is very sick. "The sisters sent to Him, saying, 'Lord, he whom You love is ill'" (John 11:3). Lazarus has two sisters, Mary and Martha, who send word to Jesus, asking Him to drop everything and come. *There's no time to waste.*

Lazarus gets worse. His sisters keep looking for Jesus as their brother drifts in and out of consciousness. Mary and Martha cry out, "Hold on, Lazarus! Hold on! Jesus is coming soon!" But the knock on the door never comes. The visit never happens. Jesus doesn't show up. Not to comfort.

Not to heal. Not to pray. Not even to attend the funeral after Lazarus dies.

"Now Jesus loved Martha and her sister and Lazarus. So, when He heard that Lazarus was ill, He stayed two days longer in the place where He was" (John 11:5–6). Jesus loved Mary, Martha, and Lazarus, so what does Jesus do? He lingers. He takes His time. He doesn't rush to see Lazarus. If you love someone and they're dying, you drop everything and go see them, pronto! Right? Jesus doesn't.

John tells us why. "When Jesus came, He found that Lazarus had already been in the tomb four days" (John 11:17). Many Jews in Christ's day believed that after death, a person's soul hovered over the dead body for three days. On the fourth day, however, the soul departed. That's when death became irreversible. That's when Jesus shows up—on the fourth day.

Jesus doesn't want to do a difficult miracle. Jesus wants to do an impossible miracle—something that demonstrates beyond any doubt that He is God. That's why Jesus waits until the fourth day. He wants to demonstrate absolute power over death.

Lazarus has been in the tomb for four days. The funeral? Over. The body? Buried. The grave? Sealed. Martha is hurt. Martha is deeply hurt. Her words have been echoed a billion times. "Lord, if You had been here, my brother would not have died" (John 11:21). Lord, where were You?

You've been there, at the hospital, watching your husband die; or at the cemetery, kissing the casket of the one you love so much. Your heart is crushed. *Lord, where were You?*

It's in this context that Jesus wept. Christ's love isn't cold and calculating. It's not distant and aloof. Christ's love is emotional—Christ's love for you is deeply emotional. "Jesus wept." It's one of the most treasured verses in the Bible.

Here is an emotional bond that refuses to let Lazarus remain in the tomb. Christ isn't only powerful enough to defeat death. Christ is also compassionate enough to do it. Psychology can deal with depression. Pep talks can deal with a losing team. Plane trips to Florida can deal with the winter blues. Only Jesus can deal with our ultimate enemy—death. And He does it with tears in His eyes.

Jesus promises solidarity with all who mourn. Far from relating with the icy indifference of a judge, Jesus expresses deep grief. When you suffer, He suffers. Your pain is His pain. Jesus tells Paul, who was ravaging the Church and killing Christians, "Saul, Saul, why are you persecuting *Me*?" (Acts 9:4, emphasis added). We follow a Savior with scars, who took on flesh, who took the full weight of human sin and lived to tell about it.

This has enormous ramifications for how we interpret suffering. If we think of God as remote and removed from our pain and agony, then we'll fashion ourselves in like manner. We will become self-reliant and aloof. Our goal will become avoiding all commitments that bring pain and suffering.

It's much more liberating to feel and grieve our losses. They are serious. They are weighty and difficult. They are real. They will never stop being a part of our lives. Nevertheless, we are not the primary carrier of those losses. Jesus is. And Jesus is coming again. On the Last Day, Jesus will return and our bodies will rise out of the grave. We will be more alive than ever before. Our eyes will see God in His glorious splendor. We will rejoice over the new creation in all its majesty and perfection. Colors will burst forth in plants and animals with a rainbow of beauty. There is more.

We will reach out and hold the hand of that person we so dearly loved—taken from us by death. What a grand reunion. And our taste buds? You think chocolates on Valentine's Day are delicious now? Just wait until Jesus gives us redeemed bodies. Our tongues will explode with tastes and flavors like never before. And the sounds we will hear! Songs of praise, music, birds, laughter—all the happiest sounds, amplified in ways that will fill our hearts with joy.

"Blessed are you who weep now, for you shall laugh" (Luke 6:21).

7

OVERCOMING THROUGH RENOUNCING IDOLATRY

"You turned to God from idols to serve the living and true God."

(1 Thessalonians 1:9)

Let me take you to a St. Louis success story, the Build-A-Bear Workshop. In 1997, Maxine Clark opened the first Build-A-Bear at the Saint Louis Galleria shopping mall. Today there are more than four hundred workshops worldwide. If you have never been to Build-A-Bear with five squealing seven-year-old girls, all who are on a sugar high from birthday cake and Mountain Dew Code Red, let me tell you the rules. First, you choose from over thirty models of bears. Next, you take your bear and stuff it, stitch it, fluff it, dress it, accessorize it, and name it. The result is that you have your "beary own bear." To prove it, an employee gives you a customized birth certificate. This is your creation. Ta-da!

We don't build bears. We build gods. We conceive them in our mind. We build them with our hands. We choose what they look like. We personalize them with our preferences. They are just what we want. They like what we like, share our opinions, and vote the same way we do. These gods increase our standard of living and happiness. They give us what we want and stay out of our way the rest of the time.

When going through emotional upheaval, we find ourselves between two lives. Our old life is gone. Our new life has yet to appear. We often become desperate for love and acceptance—looking in all the wrong places. It's tempting to follow false gods and pseudo-saviors when our heart has such huge holes. Money, sex, influence, property, and power are of little help when our world is falling apart. Idols offer everything. Idols deliver nothing.

A Build-a-God Workshop

Jeremiah recognizes this reality. That's why he takes us on a tour of a build-a-god workshop. Jeremiah 10:1–16 is like a duet. There are two singers. The first voice announces that fake gods always fail us. The second voice revels in the God who made heaven and earth. Here's an outline:

- Verse 1: Introduction
- Verses 2–5: The failure of foreign gods
- Verses 6–7: The Lord is King
- Verses 8–9: The failure of foreign gods
- Verse 10: The Lord is the everlasting King
- Verse 11: The failure of foreign gods
- Verses 12–13: The Lord is the Creator
- Verses 14–15: The failure of foreign gods
- Verse 16: Conclusion

Jeremiah makes foreboding declarations throughout this section. Foreign gods "cannot speak; they have to be carried, for they cannot walk. . . . They cannot do evil, neither is it in them to do good" (Jeremiah 10:5). Those who trust in them are "both stupid and foolish" (Jeremiah 10:8) because their "images are false, and there is no breath in them" (Jeremiah 10:14). "They are worthless, a work of delusion" (Jeremiah 10:15). Jeremiah 10:3, 8, and 15 call idols a vapor, stupid, foolish, and worthless. It doesn't matter how attractive these gods look; they aren't real. Paul, for his part, says that we self-destruct when we worship "the creature rather than the Creator" (Romans 1:25).

Jeremiah goes so far as to say that phony gods are "scarecrows" (Jeremiah 10:5). Do you remember the Scarecrow in *The Wizard of Oz*? He was a few bales short of a haystack. His song? "If I only had a brain." Jeremiah takes this further. Idols are not only brainless. They are powerless, lifeless, and graceless. Is there another option?

You bet there is! The Lord is great and His name is great (Jeremiah 10:6). He is the "King of the nations" (Jeremiah 10:7). There is none like Him (Jeremiah 10:6, 7, 16). The prophet continues:

- "The LORD is the true God; He is the living God and the everlasting King." (Jeremiah 10:10)
- "It is He who made the earth by His power, who established the world by His wisdom, and by His understanding stretched out the heavens." (Jeremiah 10:12)
- "When He utters His voice, there is a tumult of waters in the heavens, and He makes the mist rise from the ends of the earth. He makes lightning for the rain, and He brings forth the wind from His storehouses." (Jeremiah 10:13)
- "He is the one who formed all things." (Jeremiah 10:16)

There's no one like the Lord (Jeremiah 10:6, 7, 16). He "made," "established," and "stretched out" (Jeremiah 10:12). He "utters His voice," "makes," and "brings forth" (Jeremiah 10:13). He "formed all things" (Jeremiah 10:16).

All of these verbs take us to Genesis 1–2, where God displays His majestic creational power. It's hardly surprising that Jeremiah calls the God of Abraham, Isaac, and Jacob "the true God," "the living God," and "the everlasting King" (Jeremiah 10:10), as well as "the portion of Jacob" and "the LORD of hosts" (Jeremiah 10:16). Creation language also appears in, for instance, Jeremiah 10:12–13; 27:5; 32:17; 33:2; 51:15–19. The Lord continues to uphold creation (Jeremiah 31:35–36; 33:20, 25). There is no god like our God!

Our Ever-Present God

God not only made the heavens and the earth. He is present throughout creation. "Am I a God at hand, declares the LORD, and not a God far away? Can a man hide himself in secret places so that I cannot see him? declares the LORD. Do I not fill heaven and earth? declares the LORD" (Jeremiah 23:23–24).

Footballs fans, remember the 1996 season? A player for the Dallas Cowboys did something that hadn't been done since the early days of football. He started on both offense and defense. On offense, he played wide receiver. On defense, he played left cornerback. During one game, he tackled a running back behind the line of scrimmage. When Dallas got the ball, he caught a touchdown pass from quarterback Troy Aikman. John Madden, announcing the game, said, "He's all over the field. He's everywhere!" Who was John Madden referring to? Deion Sanders. Neon Deion Sanders was everywhere!

Now, Deion Sanders wasn't everywhere *literally*. If you left your seat to buy some pretzels and a hamburger, Deion wasn't working the concession stand. If you left the stadium early, Deion wasn't playing the trombone. Deion Sanders wasn't everywhere *literally*. God is.

When Jeremiah writes that God is everywhere, it's not just hype. It's not just hyperbole. God is everywhere. There is no place where God is not. God is here. God is there. God is everywhere! God isn't limited by space. God isn't limited by place. This is so hard to wrap our minds around because we're limited creatures. How many times have we wanted to be in two places at the same time but couldn't be? This is no problem with God.

That God is everywhere doesn't mean that God is everything. "God is everything" is pantheism. Pantheism blends the Creator with His creation. God is not everything, but God is everywhere.

When I'm lonely, God is my companion. "Turn to me and be gracious to me, for I am lonely" (Psalm 25:16). There are all kinds of lonely people. There are lonely people on business trips. There are lonely people in schools, jobs, cities, and churches. There are lonely people who live alone.

There are lonely people whose children have grown up and left home. What do we do when we experience moments of uncontrollable loneliness?

I'm sure you recall Jacob. Reflecting on his life, he says, "Then let us arise and go up to Bethel, so that I may make there an altar to the God who answers me in the day of my distress and has been with me wherever I have gone" (Genesis 35:3). As a young man, Jacob ran away from home because his brother Esau had vowed to kill him. Jacob ended up working for Laban for seven years so he could marry Laban's daughter Rachel. Laban, however, tricked Jacob into marrying Leah. After their one-week honeymoon, Jacob married Rachel and then worked for Laban another seven years, only to see Rachel die while giving birth to their second son, Benjamin. Years later, Jacob would think that his favorite son, Joseph, was dead. Through all of this, Jacob can still say, God "has been with me wherever I have gone."

There's a survival saying that goes like this: "One is none and two is one." The idea is simple. If we only have one flashlight and the switch malfunctions, we have nothing. We're in the dark. If, however, we have two flashlights and a malfunction occurs, we still have light. When I'm lonely, God is my companion. I'm never alone. I'm never just one.

When I'm discouraged, God is my comforter. "The LORD is near to the brokenhearted and saves the crushed in spirit" (Psalm 34:18). If you're discouraged there is one thing I can say with great confidence: God is near you. Is your heart breaking? God is near you. Is your life falling apart? God is near you. God isn't some impersonal force. God isn't some far-off, distant power. God is personal. God is near you when you're brokenhearted and crushed in spirit.

God is present because He abandoned Jesus. Let me write that one more time so it sinks in. God is present with us in our darkness because on Good Friday, He abandoned Jesus in His darkness. The chief priests, Annas and Caiaphas, paid Judas thirty pieces of silver to betray Christ. They sent temple soldiers to arrest Him in Gethsemane. They brought His case before Pilate, then stirred up the crowd to demand that Jesus be killed. They placed a crown of thorns on His head. They spit on Him and railed against Him, and finally, with three nails, Roman soldiers crucified Christ. Christ cried out, "My God, My God, why have You forsaken Me?" (Mark 15:34). The Father forsakes His Son on Good Friday so that we may know beyond any doubt that God will never forsake us. You can bank on that today. You can bank on that tomorrow. You can bank on that forever. We need no other god! His name is Emmanuel—*God with us!*

Welcome to Babylon

One day when I was eight years old, I was riding my bike when a red-headed boy in the back of a pickup truck threw a rock at my head. The rock hit me just above my left eye, and I fell off my bike. "My bike!" I screamed. "My bike is ruined!" I went to the closest house and began telling the woman who answered the door, "My bike! My bike is ruined!" She screamed and then pointed to my red shirt. My red shirt that used to be white. Only then did I realize I had a much bigger problem than a broken bike. I was bleeding profusely from a hole in my head.

Our biggest problem isn't a broken bike, or lack of money, or a bad job. Our biggest problem is idolatry. Jeremiah writes this about Babylon: "It is a land of images, and they are mad over idols" (Jeremiah 50:38). The name *Babylon (Bab-ilu)* means "gate of the gods." The city promised heaven on earth. As people entered Babylon through the Ishtar Gate and walked onto the great Processional Way, they would step on imported limestone slabs. Each one was inscribed with the phrase "To the honor of Marduk." Not Marmaduke; that's a dog in a comic strip. I'm talking about Marduk; that's a god in the Babylonian pantheon.

Judean exiles in Babylon were tempted to cave in and worship Marduk. After all, when in Babylon, live like the Babylonians. Many of Babylon's prisoners of war accepted the empire's indoctrination that claimed Marduk governed and directed history.

Judean exiles decided to accommodate to this Babylonian propaganda and conform to the religion of the day. The empire was not only a military superpower; it was also an advanced, sophisticated economic powerhouse.

"Why not give in and worship Marduk?" Jeremiah counters throughout chapter 10 of this book, saying in effect, "Hear, O Israel: The LORD our God, the LORD is one" (Deuteronomy 6:4).

Idolatry

The word *idolatry* often evokes pictures of primitive people worshiping gods like Marduk. We might additionally think about Paul in Athens, who took note that the city was filled with gods and goddesses (Acts 17:16). Idolatry, however, isn't just a problem in biblical times. Idolatry is a human problem for all times.

One of Sir Arthur Conan Doyle's first books about Sherlock Holmes helps us discover the idol in our heart. The story involves Holmes trying to determine where a woman has hidden a valuable object in her home. In order to find the treasure, the sleuth cunningly stages the threat of fire outside the house. Thinking that her home is in trouble, the woman's panicked eyes instinctively dart in the direction of her prized possession, giving away its location. That's pretty clever, Sherlock! If a fire began to engulf your home, what would you rush in to save? A car? A TV? A boatload of cash?

Idols dominate our culture. Altars include office towers, spas, stadiums, studios, tanning salons, classrooms, and vacation destinations. Idolatrous shrines appear anywhere people offer sacrifices to achieve ultimate happiness. In antiquity, false gods were bloodthirsty and impossible to appease. They still are. Counterfeit gods are slave masters that we can never satisfy. They always demand more.

Often, when demoralized by hardship, we become even more susceptible to idolatry. It begins with "when and then" thinking. "When I get more friends, then I'll be satisfied." "When I get a better job, then I'll be satisfied." "When I fall in love, then I'll be satisfied." "When I have more success, more good looks, and more health, then I'll be satisfied."

What do you need to be satisfied? A bigger home? A slimmer body? A wrinkle-free face? Successful children? Loving parents? A padded savings account? It's okay to want these things. It's emotional suicide when we become obsessed with and possessed by these things. When they become our idols—what we look to for ultimate satisfaction—we will sink deeper and deeper into loneliness and frustration.

John Calvin, a sixteenth-century reformer of the Church, once stated that the human heart is a perpetual idol factory. It mass-produces counterfeit gods. Often these idols aren't evil in and of themselves. They are God-given gifts that we substitute for the real God. They are things or people of value, but we ascribe to them ultimate value. Idolatry takes *good* things—our job, money, and health—and turns them into *ultimate* things. It takes *valuable* things and makes them into *supreme* things.

Often the object of our worship becomes another person—a spouse, friend, or child. Our affection for them turns into adoration. It's easy to deify people until they become the center of our existence. Once they occupy the innermost part of our heart, we tell ourselves that we can't live without them. Then we break God's Commandments, rationalize indiscretions, destroy relationships, and do significant harm to ourselves, just to get what we want. Counterfeit gods always torment us and, if left unchecked, they will most certainly destroy us. Why?

The Bible teaches that we become what we worship, either for ruin or restoration. The psalmist puts it this way: "Their idols are silver and gold, made by the hands of men. They have mouths, but cannot speak; eyes, but they cannot see. They have ears, but cannot hear; noses, but they cannot smell. They have hands, but do not feel; feet, but do not walk; and they do not make a sound in their throat. Those who make them become like them" (Psalm 115:4–8, author's translation; cf. Psalm 135:15–18). Paying homage to anyone or anything other than the Creator dehumanizes us and takes away our ability to spiritually see, hear, smell, feel, walk, and talk. We become like the gods we worship.

It's much like the Walt Disney 1940 movie *Pinocchio*. In one part, Pinocchio is taken away—along with a bunch of other young troublemakers—to Pleasure Island, where they all smoke cigars, play pool, and get drunk.

Before long, they all turn into donkeys. They lived like donkeys so they became like donkeys.

The golden calf episode in Exodus 32 is a stellar example of people becoming what they worship. Aaron shouts out orders for Israelites to bring him golden earrings. He then creates a tool and makes a golden calf. "They said, 'These are your gods, O Israel, who brought you up out of the land of Egypt!'" (Exodus 32:4). Do you see the connection between the calf and the people? Calves are stubborn and prone to running away. So are the Israelites. "They have turned aside quickly" (Exodus 32:8). They are "a stiff-necked people" (Exodus 32:9).

Why do idols have such power? Why do they so easily seduce us in our sorrow? Demonic powers accompany idols (e.g., Leviticus 17:7; Deuteronomy 32:17; Psalm 106:37). Paul asserts that the worship of idols is worship "[offered] to demons" (1 Corinthians 10:20). Satan is the spiritual reality behind our addictions, compulsions, and obsessions.

Idolatry leads to the breakdown of every human relationship. Once our relationship with the Creator is ruptured, we're unable to have satisfying relationships with the people He made. Without fellowship with the one true God, we are at odds with everything and everyone else in creation.

Paul commands us to "flee from idolatry" (1 Corinthians 10:14; cf. 1 John 5:21). It's incompatible with new life in Christ (1 Corinthians 5:10–11; 6:9; 10:7). Becoming a believer is to turn aside from idols and serve the living God (1 Thessalonians 1:9; 1 Corinthians 12:2). Ongoing fellowship within the Church is based on a constant vigilance toward the shunning of idols (Acts 15:20).

The summons is clear. Turn to the true God, the one revealed at Sinai and at the cross. This is the only God who heals us. This is the only God who completely forgives us.

Stand Firm

Judean exiles in Babylon included Hannaniah, Mishael, and Azariah. Maybe you know them by their VeggieTales names—Shack, Rack, and Benny. Some affectionately call them "Your Shack, My Shack, and a Bungalow." In Daniel 3, they're called by their Babylonian names, Shadrach, Meshach, and Abednego. With a Babylonian name, I'll act like a Babylonian.

Not Shadrach, Meshach, and Abednego.

The three Hebrews stand on the plain of Dura in Babylon. King Nebuchadnezzar has made a golden statue that is 12 feet wide and 125 feet high, and he has issued this decree: "When you hear the sound of the horn, pipe, lyre, trigon, harp, bagpipe, and every kind of music, you are to fall down and worship the golden image that King Nebuchadnezzar has set up" (Daniel 3:5). Violators will be thrown into the fire.

Shadrach, Meshach, and Abednego are ready to take the heat. They would rather burn in Babylon than turn away from the living God. "Our God whom we serve is able to deliver us from the burning fiery furnace, and He will deliver us out of your hand" (Daniel 3:17). Let me accent these words: "God is able." God is able to deliver us from the clutches of idolatry. God is able to free us from its false claims. God "is able to do far more abundantly than all that we ask or think" (Ephesians 3:20).

When the heat is on and we're tempted to worship fake gods, it's natural to think that Christ doesn't care, that He isn't close, that Christ doesn't have any compassion. Nebuchadnezzar said, "I see four men unbound, walking in the midst of the fire, and they are not hurt; and the appearance of the fourth is like a son of the gods" (Daniel 3:25). Nebuchadnezzar is wrong. It's not a son of the gods. It's the Son of God. It's Jesus. It's Jesus in the furnace. There's always a fourth Man in the furnace.

One afternoon on a hill called Golgotha, Christ entered the furnace again. The heat was cranked way up. The Palestinian sun was out. The temperature was up. Sweat was rolling down His bleeding and butchered body. It was as hot as hell, literally, because Jesus Christ was taking the heat for your sin and mine. Three days later, Jesus came out of the fire alive to make us this promise: "When you walk through the fire, you will not be burned; the flames will not set you ablaze. For I am the LORD your God, the Holy One of Israel, your Savior" (Isaiah 43:2–3).

Shadrach, Meshach, and Abednego came out from the fire—alive. They're unshakable. They're also unbakeable! The Bible says they didn't get burned, that their clothes weren't singed. I can't walk into a bowling alley without coming out smelling like smoke. But not these three. They don't even smell like smoke!

The next time you feel weak and are tempted to turn away from the one true God, stand with Shadrach, Meshach, and Abednego. Turn in your tools, stop building substitutes, throw away your idols, and never, ever again do business at a build-a-god workshop.

8

OVERCOMING THROUGH LAMENTS

"You will be sorrowful, but your sorrow will turn into joy."

(John 16:20)

There are parts of the United States that people call "flyover country" because they don't see these areas as being very exciting. You have to fly over them to get to more exotic places, like New York or LA. Without stepping on too many toes, I suggest that Iowa, Nebraska, and Kansas are the top three flyover states.

Have you noticed there are portions of the Bible that are "flyover" books? Perhaps one of yours is Leviticus with all of its rites, rituals, and regulations. Maybe it's the Book of Numbers with all of its, well, numbers! The Book of 1 Chronicles is right up there on my list of "flyovers." It begins with nine chapters of genealogies. Another biblical flyover might include the Old Testament laments. Life can be depressing enough. Why should I subject myself to screams in the night and cries full of despair?

Laments begin early in the Old Testament. When Moses is a state slave living in Egypt, he asks God, "Why have You mistreated this people?" (Exodus 5:22). When Joshua hears that Ammonites defeated the

Israelites, he asks God, "Why have You brought this people over the Jordan?" (Joshua 7:7). When Gideon is surrounded by fierce and ferocious foes, he asks God, "Why has all of this happened to us?" (Judges 6:13).

When Saul and Jonathan die on Mount Gilboa, David grieves over this deep and irreversible loss (2 Samuel 1:23–27). When his son Absalom is struck down in war, David again laments (2 Samuel 18:33). Even after Joab reprimands him, the king keeps crying (2 Samuel 19:4). Then there is Job, with his strident complaints (e.g., Job 14:20; 30:18–25). Sixty-five of 150 psalms are psalms of lament. There is even an entire book in the Old Testament called Lamentations.

Heart-wrenching questions permeate Israel's protests. Why did this happen? Why did God allow it? Why is life so unfair? Who is responsible? Is there any order in the world? Is the Lord really the Creator and Redeemer? Will He really come through?

Old Testament laments exhibit a candor about life's desperate moments and a profound honesty regarding disappointment. They express fury over the deep fissures of life and frequently blame God for everything gone wrong. The principal complaint, though, is divine absence—often called "the dark night of the soul." God claims to have power over injustice, but it doesn't seem that way. Present realities appear to negate divine promises.

What is our response to these primal cries? "Fly over!" After all, we're AmeriCANs, not AmeriCAN'Ts. We can make our way through anything. "Keep your chin up!" "Big boys don't cry." "Play with pain." "When the going gets tough, the tough get going!" "Tough times don't last but tough people do." This isn't what Jeremiah says.

Jeremiah's Laments

Protest. Mourn. Wail. Complain. Scream. Cry. Weep. Melt down. Rage. Jeremiah doesn't dance around issues. "Why is my pain unceasing, my wound incurable, refusing to be healed?" (Jeremiah 15:18). Jeremiah doesn't lament in the sense of giving up and resigning. He laments as someone who has been wronged and expects God to vindicate him. Jeremiah's cries demand divine action.

The prophet's laments appear in Jeremiah 11:18–12:6; 15:10–21; 17:14–18; 18:18–23; 20:7–18. These are some of the Bible's most transparent, vulnerable, and raw prayers. For instance, in chapter 15, Jeremiah complains that he is "a man of strife and contention to the whole land" and "all of them curse me" (Jeremiah 15:10). Although the prophet has been faithful, he suffers unceasing pain; his wound is incurable (Jeremiah 15:18). He faces ridicule, rejection, scorn, and reproach. His fellow citizens hold a vendetta against him because he faithfully speaks God's Word.

Jeremiah rages at God and accuses God of betraying him. "I was like a gentle lamb led to the slaughter" (Jeremiah 11:19). The prophet was playing quarterback and got blindsided—not by the opposition, but by his own teammates from his hometown of Anathoth. They tackled, sacked, crushed, and took Jeremiah off the field on a stretcher. He was then beyond himself. God, he said, makes "the way of the guilty prosper" by planting them and enabling them to "grow and bring forth fruit" (Jeremiah 12:1–2). The prophet blames God for acting like a stream that dries up, "a deceitful brook, waters that fail" (Jeremiah 15:18).

People scheme against Jeremiah, so he feels like a tree about to be destroyed (Jeremiah 11:19). Even his own family betrays him (Jeremiah 11:21–23; 12:6). He is persecuted (Jeremiah 15:15; 17:18); there are plots to kill him (Jeremiah 18:23); he is "a laughingstock," shamed, and ridiculed all day long, denounced by scorners (Jeremiah 20:7–10).

Despite attacks on his life (Jeremiah 11:18, 21–23; 12:6; 20:10), his isolation from others (Jeremiah 15:17), and his sense of abandonment by his community and, above all, by God (Jeremiah 12:1; 15:18; 20:7), laments keep Jeremiah engaged with his faith. The prophet keeps wrestling with God in the midst of his unspeakable pain.

Why?

I once heard a story about a freshman in college who was taking a philosophy course. He had studied and studied—and studied some more. Then came the final test. It had one question: "Why?" The freshman thought for a while, wrote one word down, and walked out. His one-word answer: "Because!"

Jeremiah's laments often begin with this tortured question: "Why?"

- "Why is the land ruined and laid waste like a wilderness, so that no one passes through?" (Jeremiah 9:12)
- "Why does the way of the wicked prosper? Why do all who are treacherous thrive?" (Jeremiah 12:1)
- "Why should You be like a man confused, like a mighty warrior who cannot save?" (Jeremiah 14:9)
- "Why have You struck us down so that there is no healing for us?" (Jeremiah 14:19)
- "Why is my pain unceasing, my wound incurable, refusing to be healed?" (Jeremiah 15:18)
- "Why did I come out from the womb to see toil and sorrow, and spend my days in shame?" (Jeremiah 20:18)
- "Why has the LORD dealt thus with this great city?" (Jeremiah 22:8)

Why was our baby stillborn? Why did a mother of three young children die of breast cancer? Why did a teenager die by suicide? Why? We long for broken things to be fixed, empty things to be filled, hurt feelings to heal, and tragic events to end. We plead with God to change things, but we keep waking up to unchanged circumstances. Why?

Theodicy

Jeremiah's protests have a name. They are called theodicy. *Theodicy* is a compound of two Greek words, *theos* and *dika*—"God" and "justice." God, where is the justice? Where is Your power when I'm in over my head? Theodicy presents us with this unanswerable riddle:

- God may be powerful and good if there is no evil.

- God may be good and there can be evil if God is not powerful.
- God may be powerful and there can be evil if God is not good.

Of these three elements—goodness, power, and evil—skeptics say that any two together can be affirmed, but in no logical way can all three hold together. How should we respond?

First, we acknowledge God's goodness. The Bible defines God's goodness in two ways. One has to do with His character; the other, with His actions. Psalm 119:68 captures both when it says, "You *are* good and [You] *do* what is good" (emphasis added). The first half of this verse describes God's character. God isn't an angry judge. God isn't a mean ogre. God is good. The second half of the verse describes God's actions. God doesn't do evil. He isn't malicious or sinister. God redeems. God restores. God does good.

God hears our cries of lament and says, "I don't condemn you. I don't belittle you. I don't scorn you or shame you." He says, "You haven't earned it and you don't deserve it, but I love to pour out extravagant goodness in your life." God is good. God does what is good—all for us.

I heard about a woman in Michigan who found a skunk in her cellar. She called police, who told her to open her cellar door, make a trail of breadcrumbs to her backyard, then wait for the skunk to follow the crumbs. The next day the woman called the police and said, "Guess what? Instead of one skunk in my cellar, I now have two skunks in my cellar!"

Sometimes life stinks. God is still good and God still does good. We say this when we see Jesus embracing lepers and washing feet. We trust God's goodness when we hear Jesus describing a shepherd who leaves ninety-nine to find one lost sheep, or a heartbroken father who never stops yearning for the return of his lost son. We believe in God's goodness when we read about a clamoring crowd surrounding Jesus and He stops to give His full attention to someone others ignore.

God's ultimate goodness is revealed in Jesus nailed to a cross. Jesus allows His body to be beaten, stripped, whipped, and pinned to wood to forgive every sin of every person who ever lived. Jesus sees Mary and John at the cross to comfort Him and instead He comforts them. Jesus promises paradise to a dying thief. With His final breath, Jesus prays for forgiveness—for the very people who crucified Him. What does the cross tell us? God is good—very good.

Second, in the face of doubters, God's Word itself attests that God is powerful. "Who has measured the waters in the hollow of His hand and marked off the heavens with a span, enclosed the dust of the earth in a measure and weighed the mountains in scales and the hills in a balance?" (Isaiah 40:12). There are 430 quintillion gallons of water on our planet. God has measured them all in the hollow of His hand. The universe is over 30 billion light years from one end to another. God measures it all with a span of His hand. The mass of earth is roughly 13,170,000,000,000,000,000,000,000 pounds. God places it all in scales on a balance. That's power.

On November 16, 1532, in what would later be called Peru, South America, Spanish conquistador Francisco Pizarro and his 168 Spanish soldiers defeated between 5,000 and 7,000 armed Inca Indians. How did they do it? Pizarro had stuff that the Incas didn't have—guns, horses, and steel. Pizarro had the power.

God has more. The sun produces more energy in one second than has been used in the history of the world. The sun, at its current rate, will be able to burn for another 30 billion years. That's power!

Third, suffering is real. The Bible is realistic. Suffering isn't an illusion. Affliction is real. It disrupts God's good creation. Suffering didn't exist before the fall and will not be experienced by God's people after Christ returns (Genesis 1–2; Revelation 21–22).

There you have it. God is good. God is powerful. Evil is real. These three ideas constitute Jeremiah's worldview. If we deny or soften any one of them, his book loses its punch; there is no problem with which to wrestle. The thought of faithful people suffering and wicked people prospering poses no problem for polytheists, dualists, atheists, agnostics, naturalists, and fatalists. It does for monotheists. It does for Jeremiah.

What does Jeremiah say about theodicy? He says that theodicy is an irrelevant exercise—a chasing after the wind. We can't explain God's actions because (1) we're not Him, (2) we don't have access to the heavenly court, and (3) we can't see the whole picture.

Looking for an answer as to why we hurt so bad is like trying to manually inflate a beach ball the size of Alaska. It can be done, but we'll pass out in the process. After all, we don't need answers. We need Jesus. Jesus doesn't call us to understand. Jesus calls us to follow. It's time to let go of unsolvable questions and, instead, learn to lament.

Learning to Lament

Sorrow can transform our heart into stone. We turn off emotions. We build walls. What's the solution? Laments. Laments aren't signs of weakness. Laments are signs of strength. They melt the icebergs frozen on the inside. They bring us back from the dead.

Some people, however, are uncomfortable with grief. When we open our heart they change the subject, leave the room, turn on the TV—anything to avoid awkward displays of emotion. We live in a society that wrongly concludes it's best not to discuss loss and it's better for people to privately cry. However, we must find ways to express our sadness about what once was, is no longer, and will never be again.

The Book of Psalms is God's gift to all who mourn. Psalmists often acknowledge the raw experiences of life. They cry out to the Lord, "How long?" (e.g., Psalm 6:3; 13:1–3); "Where is God?" (e.g., Psalm 42:3; 44:24; 79:10); "Why?" (e.g., Psalm 10:1; 22:1; 43:2; 74:1); "Are you asleep?" (e.g., Psalm 44:23); "Wake up!" (e.g., Psalm 35:23; 59:4); "Listen!" (e.g., Psalm 17:1; 27:7; 30:10). Psalms reject a fake and pretentious faith and affirm that suffering is real.

These laments correct euphoric and celebratory notions of faith that romantically portray the Christian life as consisting of only sweetness and light. These biblical cries of anguish help us avoid a one-sided, happiness-only mind-set that fails to deal forthrightly with life's tragedies. We never get past sorrow, but we can overcome it by going through it. How? Complain. Appeal. Remind. Express. Seek.

- *Complain* to God. We need to be ourselves to succeed in any relationship. This means the curtain is pulled away, and the one hiding behind is exposed. "It's me, it's me, it's me, O Lord, standing in the need of prayer." *It's me!* Honest expressions of fear and anger open the way for hope and healing.

- *Appeal* to God's love. Appeal to His character. Trust His mercy and compassion in Jesus.

- *Remind* God of His promises. "God, You said that You are faithful." "God, You said that You would answer my prayers."

- *Express* trust in God's wisdom and the things you don't understand. Our Father in heaven knows best.

- *Seek* help from a professional. Your pastor, a Christian counselor, or another health care professional will be able to assist you.

We can be confident that a new day will dawn. "Weeping may tarry for the night, but joy comes with the morning" (Psalm 30:5). When did God save His people from their long night in Egypt? In the morning (Exodus 14:24, 27). When does Psalm 46 say God delivers? In the morning (v. 5). When did Jesus rise again? In the morning. When does God deliver us from the long nights of life? According to Lamentations 3:23, His mercies are new every morning. What is the last name the Bible gives Jesus? The Bright Morning Star (Revelation 22:16).

Feelings of raw pain are like a river flowing from our heart. This river needs a "bank" so our feelings take on depth and direction. Apart from Jeremiah's laments—and others like them—we are left with our culture's shallow prescriptions for healing. But biblical cries and protests give us words and expressions that allow our brokenness to come before God's healing throne of grace.

Go ahead. Weep. Acknowledge your pain. *Refuse to fly over your sorrow.* Also know this: joy will come because Christ's Good Friday lament turned into the Easter song of victory and resurrection.

Flying Blind

In 2008, Jim O'Neill was flying from Glasgow, Scotland, to Colchester, England, when his vision failed. Initially he thought the sun had blinded him, but soon O'Neill realized it was much worse. He had suffered a stroke.

O'Neill groped around, found the radio, and issued a Mayday alert. Paul Gerrard of the Royal Air Force quickly took off and, finding O'Neill, hovered within five hundred feet, guiding the blind pilot to the nearest runway. O'Neill would have to land the plane flying blind.

We've all been struck, perhaps not with a stroke, but with a rejection letter, a sudden expense, or a cancer-ridden body. Losing sight of the landing strip, we've issued our fair share of Mayday prayers. We know the feeling of flying blind.

There are times when I know why bad things happen. I run a red light. The cop pulls me over. He writes a ticket. I'm out $275. Why did that happen? Because my nickname is "Lead-Foot Lessing." Jeremiah's suffering, on the other hand, was undeserved. This doesn't mean Jeremiah was sinless. The prophet was, however, a godly man. He was a man of faith. Jeremiah was an innocent sufferer. He didn't earn or deserve any of his excruciating pain.

This points to Jesus. *It all points to Jesus.* Jesus, like Jeremiah, is an innocent, righteous sufferer—only Jesus is without sin in the fullest and most complete sense imaginable. God didn't test Jeremiah to the point of death. With Jesus, God allows His enemies to marshal every weapon of mass destruction. Jeremiah is reduced to tears and utter despair. Jesus is stripped naked and nailed to wood like a scarecrow.

When we cry out, "Where are You, God?" Jesus says, "I'm here, on the cross, suffering with you and suffering for you. I feel your pain, your hurt, and your loss. The day is coming, though, when I will wipe away every tear from your eyes. There will be no more death, no more mourning, no more crying, and no more pain. The old order of things will pass away." After the cross, there was an empty tomb where the Conqueror stands, with the palms of His living hands outstretched, offering us the gift of eternal life.

On that day in 2008, on his first try, Jim O'Neill hit the runway and bounced up again. Paul Gerrard continued speaking words of assurance and hope. Finally, on the eighth try (the eighth try!), the blinded pilot managed to make a near-perfect landing.

When we're flying blind, many voices clamor for our attention: voices like self-pity, fear, and indulgence. When we listen to these voices, we crash and burn. Let us listen instead to Jesus. "Take, eat, this is My body for you. Take, drink, this is My blood of the new testament for the forgiveness of all your sins." This voice guides us. His loving heart hears our laments. Jesus does it all so we land safely in His loving arms—forevermore.

9

OVERCOMING THROUGH GOD'S TESTS

"Beloved, do not be surprised at the fiery
trial when it comes upon you to test you."

(1 Peter 4:12)

Perhaps you remember a time you were watching TV or listening to the radio when, unexpectedly, an announcer broke in with these words: "This is a test of the Emergency Broadcast System." Then, for the next sixty seconds, you would hear a loud, piercing sound. After that, the announcer would say, "The broadcasters of your area, in voluntary cooperation with federal, state, and local authorities, have developed this system to keep you informed in the event of an emergency. This concludes this test of the Emergency Broadcast System."

No one likes a test, whether it's an emergency broadcasting test, a true-or-false test, a multiple-choice test, or a driver's license test. No one especially likes the hardest test of them all—a final test.

What test is God putting you through? I'm not talking about mild annoyances or setbacks, such as hitting all the red lights on your commute to work, the vending machine being sold out of your favorite candy bar, spilling your drink on your dress, stubbing your toe on the end of the bed, or enduring another meltdown from your three-year-old. Dig down past those things.

Dig all the way down to your biggest test—the test of your life. Unrelenting abuse. Someone you love dying way too soon. Alcoholism destroying your family. Your career blown apart by one lapse of judgment. The inability to have the child you so desperately want. We need to dig down because we've buried it deep inside our heart. It's the one thing that we don't know how to deal with, no matter how many sermons we hear or Bible classes we attend.

God Tests Jeremiah

Jeremiah tells us about his test. "Righteous are You, O Lord, when I complain to You; yet I would plead my case before You. Why does the way of the wicked prosper? Why do all who are treacherous thrive?" (Jeremiah 12:1). The prophet says God is righteous—that God makes promises and sticks by them. Why, then, must Jeremiah suffer while the wicked prosper? "The men of Anathoth" (Jeremiah 11:21, 23) are about to get away with murder. Their target? Jeremiah. Now that's a test!

The Lord asks His prophet, "If you have raced with men on foot, and they have wearied you, how will you compete with horses? And if in a safe land you are so trusting, what will you do in the thicket of the Jordan? For even your brothers and the house of your father, even they have dealt treacherously with you; they are in full cry after you; do not believe them, though they speak friendly words to you" (Jeremiah 12:5–6). These verses sound a lot like God's answer to Job. Beginning in Job 38 and continuing to the end of Job 41, God takes Job on a tour of the universe, and along the way He asks Job seventy questions. The point of it all is that God has things under control. God doesn't deal with disillusionments according to our timetable but according to His. God summons Jeremiah, Job, and all believers to walk by faith, not by sight. *This is a test.*

Jeremiah's test isn't a short episode in an otherwise happy existence. It's the defining event of his life. God explains it this way: "She who bore seven has grown feeble; she has fainted away; her sun went down while it was yet day; she has been shamed and disgraced" (Jeremiah 15:9). Seven, when connected with maternal fertility, signals divine favor (Ruth 4:15; 1 Samuel 2:5). Now everything is turned on its head. Now seven announces ultimate shame and disgrace. That's why the sun has set for a long night. She—the nation of Judah—now sits in the dark. Jeremiah looks at this and wishes he had never been born (Jeremiah 15:10). God is "a deceitful brook" (Jeremiah 15:18). God promises so much and delivers so little.

A deceitful brook was a familiar sight for Jeremiah. Seasonal streams in Judah run with water only after a heavy rainfall. Thirsty people approach one of these wadis to quench their thirst. They see what looks like a streambed. As they get closer, they see the stream is depleted. Jeremiah likens this to God. Now you have Him, now you don't.

Do we share this disappointment with God? Do we ask Him about our unmet desires and longings? Jeremiah did. We looked at the prophet's laments in the last chapter. Here, I point out that God's tests bracket the prophet's protests and cries (Jeremiah 11:20; 20:12).

The word *test* in the Bible implies refining. "The bellows blow fiercely; the lead is consumed by the fire" (Jeremiah 6:29). Paul also speaks about God's plan to refine His people (e.g., Romans 5:4; Philippians 2:22; 1 Corinthians 16:3; 2 Corinthians 13:5). God wants to develop a mature faith in us, marked by depth and compassion. Our devastating disappointments are not—repeat, *not*—for nothing. They make us more like Jesus.

God Tests Our Heart

Chronic. Writers often link the word with pain, disease, and problems. *Chronic.* It feels like forever. There's no end in sight when we're forced to retire, forced to move, forced to cut off a relationship. What do we do? Where do we turn? Is there any hope?

Many say, "Follow your heart." Several years ago, if you were looking for a show in a big city, you could buy tickets for the "Disney on Ice: Follow Your Heart Tour." Today you can make an appointment at the Follow

Your Heart Counseling Center. There's a book with the subtitle *Finding the Courage to Follow Your Heart.* We may hear the advice "Go with your gut" or "Follow your feelings."

Is this bad advice? Eight times in his book, Jeremiah says that the heart of Judah's problem is a problem of the heart. "The heart is deceitful above all things and beyond cure" (Jeremiah 17:9, author's translation). Here, the word "deceitful" literally means "Jacob." Jacob was a liar, a trickster, and a major-league conniver. What does that look like? Let me count the ways! Jacob deceives Esau. Laban deceives Jacob. Not to be outdeceived, Jacob returns the favor and deceives Laban.

We have Jacob-like hearts—deceived and deceiving. We are blind to our own blindness. It's like that piece of lettuce caught in someone's teeth. They have no clue, so they keep smiling and talking. We can't pay attention to what they're saying because a piece of lettuce is lodged in their teeth. That's our heart. Most of the time we have no clue as to its capacity to deceive.

"The sin of Judah is written with a pen of iron; with a point of diamond it is engraved on the tablet of their heart" (Jeremiah 17:1). In the ancient Near East, people used iron pens and diamond points to make stone inscriptions. With this metaphor, Jeremiah accents the deep-seated and enduring sin in our heart. We should see red flags and hear loud sirens when someone says, "Just trust your heart."

Do you see why God tests our heart? All our Jacob-like deceptions need to be purged and forgiven. "O LORD of hosts, who tests the righteous, who sees the heart and the mind" (Jeremiah 20:12). *This is a test!* God hooks us up to a spiritual electrocardiogram (EKG).

That's because the Bible consistently and repeatedly says that *the heart of every problem is always the problem of the heart.* The Bible calls us to trust God—that's a response of the heart. The Bible calls us to hope in God's promises—that's a disposition of the heart. The Bible describes Christians as those who seek the Lord, which is the yearning of the heart. The Bible expects the godly to grieve over their sin, mourn the plight of the lost, and lament over sickness, disease, and death. All this is done with

the heart. The Bible invites us to give thanks to the Lord, rejoice with singing, and worship Him with gladness—none of which can be done without
the heart. And the Bible, above all things, calls us to love—both God and
our neighbor—from the heart. No wonder the Bible employs the word
heart more than 760 times.

We often employ the word *heart* to mean our emotions. We say, "She
broke my heart," meaning we're emotionally crushed. At other times, we
use the word *heart* to mean support: "I'm behind you with all my heart."
Still, at other times, we use the word *heart* to mean someone stopped living one way and started living a different way: "He had a change of heart."

In the Bible, however, the word *heart* doesn't only mean our emotions,
or only our support, or only taking a different way. Nor does *heart* mean
the large, muscular, pumping organ in our chest that keeps our blood
flowing. The Bible employs *heart* to mean our inner life. This includes our
emotions, thoughts, desires, and thinking.

"Create in me a clean heart, O God, and renew a right spirit within
me" (Psalm 51:10). David isn't praying for two things—a clean heart *and*
a right spirit. Our heart and spirit are the same thing. *Heart* sums up our
entire inner life—the intellectual, emotional, and spiritual part of who we
are. That's why God tests our heart. Our heart is who we are.

Ingredients in God's Tests

I hate to admit it. In fact, I'm not totally comfortable telling you about
it, but once my mother tried to kill me. She really did. No, I'm not talking
about when I was in high school and made, let's just say, some less than
stellar decisions. In those situations, she just screamed, "Reed! I'm going
to ring your neck!" When I was six years old, though, my mother actually
tried to kill me. Let me explain.

As a small child, I often marveled over my mom's great pancakes. One
morning when she was about to cook up her mouthwatering delicacies,
our dog Spotty ran away. Here was my chance! While she searched for
Spotty, I would search for the secret.

The first item I saw was a container of flour. Since this was the largest item around, I put a spoonful into my mouth. "Yuck!" I thought to myself. Then I reasoned, "It must be the eggs." The eggs tasted awful. Next I tried a container marked "Baking Powder." This had to be the secret to her pancakes. I put an extra-large spoonful of baking powder into my mouth. Talk about "gag me with a spoon"—literally.

Then it dawned on me. My mother was trying to kill me. Right? Wrong. My mother was taking individual ingredients, working them together, and creating amazing pancakes. The secret—*the secret*—is understanding how it all works together.

There are five ingredients to God's tests.

Shock when our world falls apart. We're never prepared for the day when we get a call and something tragic has happened; or we're at the doctor's office and he says the "c-word"—cancer. When bad stuff goes down, it's like jumping into an ice-cold lake. You know, the Polar Bear Plunge. We can prepare all we want, but when we jump, the shock to our system still astounds us.

We've heard about Murphy's Law: anything that can go wrong will go wrong. We drop a piece of jellied bread, and which side does it land on? The jelly side. Every time! Shell-shocked and dumbfounded, we look out the window and the sky gets darker by the minute. We think that things can't get worse, and guess what happens? Things get worse. "It never rains but it pours."

Silence when God doesn't show up. Jesus promises, "Ask, and it will be given to you; seek, and you will find; knock, and it will be opened to you" (Matthew 7:7). When something goes wrong, I believe Matthew 7:7. I ask, seek, and knock. Yet God doesn't reply to my email. God doesn't call or text back. God doesn't respond to my Facebook post.

Hernando Cortez wanted to lead an expedition into Mexico to capture its vast treasures. When he told the Spanish governor his strategy, the governor got so excited that he gave Cortez eleven ships and seven hundred men. In the spring of 1519, Cortez and company landed in Veracruz, Mexico. As soon as soldiers unloaded the ships, Cortez had all eleven ships burned. Why do that? If the fighting got too fierce, there would be no talk of sailing home. Like it or not, there was no way out.

God sometimes brings us to the point where all the ships are burned. There's no way out. It looks impossible. We panic. *This is a test!*

Struggle when we don't understand. *Why?* Why *this*? Why is this *happening*? Why is this happening *to me*? Why is this happening to me *right now*? Why did my husband walk out? Why did my wife die in that awful car accident? Why did I lose my job? Why didn't I get that promotion? Why was my son born with spina bifida?

Life can get dark—really dark. Tragedies beat us down and we get stuck in the darkness. Say what you want about Jeremiah, but at least he keeps struggling with God. He keeps holding on.

If we keep up the struggle we'll eventually advance from our adversity (advance, not gain complete victory), learn from our losses, profit from our pain, and be transformed by our troubles. Don't give up the struggle. Refuse to let the pain silence your prayers. Run from that four-letter word straight from the pit of hell: Q-U-I-T. Quit. Never, ever, ever quit!

Shaping by the Spirit when God turns evil into good. The Holy Spirit uses suffering to make us more like Christ. Too often, I think God's plan is to make me happy. Then the Book of Jeremiah breaks the news to me. God's plan is to make me holy, to make me more Christlike. That means every problem has a purpose. Other people may mean it for evil, but God uses it for good. Anybody can turn good into good. God specializes in turning evil into good. His tests aren't intended to destroy us. God's tests are intended to develop us.

Do you remember God telling Abraham to sacrifice his son Isaac? "After these things God tested Abraham" (Genesis 22:1). As the clock struck midnight, God provided a ram of sacrifice to take Isaac's place. Abraham passed the test and called the mountain, "The LORD will provide" (v. 14).

The same divine strategy appears in the Book of Judges. God says, "I will no longer drive out before them any of the nations that Joshua left when he died, in order to test Israel by them" (Judges 2:21–22). Israelite men and women called judges stood up—including Shamgar, Ehud,

Deborah, Jephthah, Samson, and my favorite, Giddy-Up, Get-Along Gideon. God's tests brought out their best. David goes further. He asks God, "Test my heart and my mind" (Psalm 26:2). Israel's second king longs to become more spiritually mature.

Sometimes a storm's fury looks like it might crush an eagle against a rocky cliff. But the eagle faces the storm and tilts its wings, and the whirlwind that might have crushed it begins to drive it upward until it rises above the storm. What's true of eagles can be true of us. The fierce storm that looks to destroy us is the same power by which we rise to new heights. God sends tests to bring us to a greater Christian character.

It was a massive storm on Good Friday when Christ died for your sins and mine. Arrested abruptly. Tried unjustly. Sentenced callously. Mocked repeatedly. Abandoned ruthlessly. Beaten brutally. Crucified barbarously. But risen triumphantly. God reversed the curse. Christ is alive, never to die again.

Turbulent times aren't random events serving no purpose. The resurrection of Jesus means they are wounds suffered in a cosmic battle where God is turning evil into good. That's what Paul teaches: "We know that for those who love God all things work together for good, for those who are called according to His purpose. For those whom He foreknew He also predestined to be conformed to the image of His Son" (Romans 8:28–29).

Paul doesn't say, "All things are good." All things are not good. They haunt us and hurt us and mess with our minds. Neither does Paul say, "We're pretty sure that . . ." or "Wouldn't it be nice if . . ." No. Paul is convinced. "We know." We know that the God of Jeremiah, the God and Father of our Lord Jesus Christ, takes bitter things and works them together to create lives of amazing beauty—"to be conformed to the image of His Son." God uses tests to save us from becoming self-absorbed, self-focused, self-centered, and self-reliant. We trust God's process. He will never forsake us. He will always remake us.

Service when we use our pain for God's glory. God wants to take our greatest pain and turn it into His glory. He wants to use our tests for a testimony. God wants to take the things we are most embarrassed about, the things we're most ashamed of, the things we most regret happening, and He wants to use them for good in the lives of others. Paul blesses God, who "comforts us in all our affliction, so that we may be able to comfort those who are in any affliction, with the comfort with which we ourselves are comforted by God" (2 Corinthians 1:4).

When I was a teenager, I remember my grandmother watching a soap opera called *Secret Storm*. We all have a secret storm—something we're so ashamed of that we don't tell a soul. But think about it. Who can better help the parents of a child with Down syndrome than parents who themselves have a child with Down syndrome? Who can better help someone going through a divorce than someone who's been divorced? Who could better help somebody struggling with an addiction than somebody who struggled with an addiction? The very thing we want don't want to talk about is the very thing God wants us to use to help other people.

That's the recipe. Shock. Silence. Struggle. Shaping. Service. It's a divine recipe in which God's tests are working for our good and the Father's glory.

A Good Pilot

A good pilot knows how to get people safely through the storm. I invite you to wrap your head and your heart around that idea. A good pilot knows how to get people home safely through the storm. What's true of a good pilot is all the more true of God. He knows how to get people safely through the storm. Isn't that the message of the Bible? God doing whatever it takes to get His people safely through life's unpredictable, ferocious, and sometimes hellish storms? For Abraham and Sarah, it was a storm called infertility. For Moses, it was a storm called slavery and then another one called forty years in the desert. For David, it was Goliath—Mr. Storm himself. For the disciples, it was the sudden storm on the Sea of Galilee. For Jeremiah, it was a Category 5 storm called Babylon.

We're all in some kind of storm. What's yours? Are you raising teenagers? Did you get cut from the team? Did you lose the love of your life?

Are finances tight? What about your health? Is old age getting the best of you? *This is a test!*

And this is the honest-to-God truth: our Pilot gets us through the storm because He entered into *the* storm. God the Son, Jesus, joined us in the storm—in the storm of life and in the storm of death. On Good Friday, God didn't fly above the storm, below it, or beside it. God was *in* it. "God was in Christ reconciling the world to Himself" (2 Corinthians 5:19, author's translation). God, in the storm. Listen. Can you hear Him? "Father, forgive them, for they know not what they do." "Today you will be with Me in paradise." "I thirst." "It is finished!"

Are you hurting? Jesus hurt. Are you bleeding? Jesus bled. Do you feel like you're gasping for air? Jesus gasped for air. Are you crying? Jesus cried. Is your heart broken? Jesus' heart was absolutely broken. You are not alone in your storm. You are never alone in your storm.

Jeremiah knows. God speaks to him in the storm. "And I will make you to this people a fortified wall of bronze; they will fight against you, but they shall not prevail over you, for I am with you to save you and deliver you" (Jeremiah 15:20). The prophet had heard these words in his youth (Jeremiah 1:18–19). Everything God promised then He promises now. God's promises hold in the storm. "What a friend we have in Jesus, All our sins and griefs to bear! What a privilege to carry Ev'rything to God in prayer!" (*LSB* 770:1).

To the father who holds a rose taken from his son's coffin, God speaks. To the couple with the barren womb and the fervent prayers, God speaks. To any person who has tried to see God through shattered glass, He speaks.

When it looks as though everything is going to be wiped off the map, should we freak out? have our nineteenth nervous breakdown? do something we'll regret for the rest of our life? No. Sit down. Buckle up. Take a deep breath. Relax. Then trust the Pilot to get you safely through the storm and take you all the way home. He will. Then we will sing with joy-filled hearts, "What a friend we have in Jesus."

10

OVERCOMING THROUGH LISTENING

"Samuel said, 'Speak, for Your servant is listening.'"

(1 Samuel 3:10, author's translation)

In September 1939, the British government distributed a poster that said, "Your Courage, Your Cheerfulness, Your Resolution, Will Bring Us Victory." Soon another poster was printed and distributed. "Freedom Is in Peril; Defend It with All Your Might."

During World War II, these two posters showed up all over England—on railroad platforms and in pubs, in stores and in restaurants. The government created a third poster in the series but it never saw the light of day. British officials held it in reserve for an extreme crisis, like a German invasion of Britain. More than 2.5 million copies of this third poster were printed, yet the public never saw it until 2001. That's when a bookstore owner in northeast England discovered one in a box of old books. What did that poster say? "Keep Calm and Carry On."

"Keep Calm and Carry On" became so popular that the bookstore began putting it on items like coffee mugs, postcards, and T-shirts. The rest, as they say, is history.

Management guru Jim Collins studied leadership in turbulent times. He looked at more than twenty thousand companies, sifting through data in search of an answer to this question: in an extreme crisis, why do some leaders make it while others don't? Collins concluded that successful leaders in a crisis aren't more creative, more visionary, more ambitious, or more risk-taking. What sets them apart? They're more self-controlled. They keep calm and carry on.

How about us? What do we say when things go south? "Life is too hard!" "This problem is too big!" "I've never been this low in my life." "I'm David against Goliath!" Consider these statistics:

- 60 percent of all illnesses and diseases are related to stress.
- 75 percent of all doctor visits are connected to stress.
- 13 percent of all Americans between the ages of 18 and 54 suffer from ongoing acute stress.
- 44 percent of all Americans lose sleep every night because of stress.
- If you're 65 years of age or older, your number-one health issue is stress.

Don't let stress tempt you to do something crazy. Don't let anxiety overwhelm you. Don't let fear intimidate you. Keep calm and carry on. The Bible has a word for that. "Listen." *Listen to God in His Word.*

A wedding anniversary card depicts a husband and wife in their golden years, sitting on a park bench. The wife snuggles up to her husband and says, "It's so nice to have you near." To which the husband responds, "Why yes, I'd like another beer!"

Sometimes it's hard to listen—especially to God, especially when today is chaotic and tomorrow looks more so. Instead of listening, our energy goes toward creating more stress for ourselves as well as for others. We become dumbfounded as to what to do next. Listening to God's voice seems impossible.

Keep Calm and Listen On

It was difficult for Judahites and residents in Jerusalem to listen. Babylon was breathing down their necks. Traumatized by the thought of exile, disease, hunger, and wholesale chaos, the people rejected God's Word. Take a look.

- "Their ears are uncircumcised, they cannot listen; behold, the word of the LORD is to them an object of scorn; they take no pleasure in it." (Jeremiah 6:10)
- "They did not listen or incline their ear." (Jeremiah 7:24, author's translation)
- "They did not listen to Me or incline their ear." (Jeremiah 7:26)
- "This is the nation that did not listen to the voice of the LORD their God." (Jeremiah 7:28, author's translation)
- "They did not listen or incline their ear." (Jeremiah 11:8, author's translation)
- "They did not listen to the voice of the LORD." (Jeremiah 43:7, author's translation)
- "They did not listen or incline their ear, to turn from their evil and make no offerings to other gods." (Jeremiah 44:5)

Since faith comes through listening (Romans 10:17), Judah's faith went down. People's stress went way up. In the face of despair, instead of turning *to* God, Judahites turned *away from* God. After all, God didn't instantly fix their problem. He didn't give them enough military muscle to defeat Babylon. And He wants them to listen to Him?

There are times when we also become disillusioned with the whole God thing. His words no longer hold our attention. What He says doesn't capture our hearts. We need something more than words.

Prophetic Sign-Acts

At almost every turn in his book, Jeremiah faces traumatized people who don't want to listen, who go to great lengths to silence him. If they can't silence him, some are prepared to kill him. What's a prophet to do? How about combining God's Word with a visual object? It worked for Moses. Do you recall his leprous hand and stick/snake? Those signs certainly got people's attention! Jeremiah 13:1–11 describes the prophet's first prophetic sign-act. Others include the following:

- Remaining single (Jeremiah 16:1–13)
- Visiting a potter's house (Jeremiah 18:1–12)
- Breaking a clay pot (Jeremiah 19:1–15)
- Wearing an iron yoke (Jeremiah 28:1–17)
- Buying a field (Jeremiah 32:6–44)
- Commanding that a scroll be thrown into the Euphrates River (Jeremiah 51:59–64)

Jeremiah isn't the only prophet who communicated with visual aids. Isaiah walked around barefoot and naked for three years (Isaiah 20). Hosea married a prostitute named Gomer (Hosea 1:2–3). Ezekiel, whose book contains the greatest number of prophetic sign-acts in the Bible, lay bound in ropes (Ezekiel 4:1–8), shaved his head and struck some of his hair with a sword (Ezekiel 5:1–2), and dug through a wall (Ezekiel 12:3–7). If all of this sounds strange, that's exactly the point. People could ignore a prophet's words, but it would be hard to forget their actions, which stayed in people's minds and reinforced the prophet's preaching point.

Jeremiah's Loincloth

When John Molloy wrote his book *Dress for Success* in 1975, I'm confident he didn't have me in mind. If it wasn't for the caring people in my life, I would still be wearing orange ties and pink shirts with the leisure suit my mother bought me in 1976. I would be the geek of the week and the head Hebrew nerd of the herd. "Dressing for success" isn't my spiritual gift. That's why I like Jeremiah.

The prophet's first sign-act commences with God telling Jeremiah to go shopping. "Thus says the LORD to me, 'Go and buy an *aezor*'" (Jeremiah 13:1, author's translation). The Hebrew word *aezor* may be translated "waistband" or "undergarment." But for my Hebrew money, a better translation would be "Fruit of the Loom" or "Hanes." That's right. An *aezor* denotes underwear, which in the Old Testament normally consisted of leather. The Lord, however, commands Jeremiah—who in this sign represents God's people—to sport *linen* underwear. According to Leviticus 16:4, only priests in Israel wore linen undergarments. Therefore, Jeremiah's clothing announced the truth of Exodus 19:6—namely, that all Israel was "a kingdom of priests." Not just Jeremiah but the entire nation was holy; they were all sacred, and they were all consecrated to the Lord.

What's more, a loincloth was an undergarment—a *personal* piece of clothing. Long ago, God bound Himself to Israel. The imagery of a loincloth suggests intimacy—that the Lord and Israel were inseparable. It was all very personal. "I will take you to be My people, and I will be your God" (Exodus 6:7).

The verb rendered "cling" in Jeremiah 13:11 further describes this close relationship. The word for "cling" first appears in Genesis 2:24, where Moses writes, "Therefore a man will leave his father and his mother and cling to his wife and the two will become one flesh" (author's translation). In Ruth 1:14, the verb describes Ruth's relentless and tenacious commitment to Naomi. Later Ruth says, "Where you go I will go, and where you lodge I will lodge. Your people shall be my people, and your God my God" (Ruth 1:16). The two—God and Israel—were one. His mission was their mission. His plan was their plan. Israel went where God went. They stayed where He stayed. He was their God and they were His people.

The undergarment symbolism continues. Israelites would wear their undergarments by day and wash them by night so they could wear them again the next day. God commands Jeremiah, however, "Do not dip it in water" (Jeremiah 13:1). The prophet wears his underwear without washing it for several days. Or was it several weeks? Or dare I ask, did Jeremiah leave it on, unwashed, for several months? The Bible doesn't say. His underwear smelled to holy high heaven. I'm sure the prophet took some heat. "Jeremiah, don't you have different underwear?" "Jeremiah, haven't you heard of prophetic etiquette?"

Then God directed the prophet to lose his lousy loincloth. Because a trip to the Euphrates River would have been a journey of over five hundred miles, many interpreters point out the similarities between "Parah" (Joshua 18:23), a local city in the territory of Benjamin, and *Perat*, the Hebrew word for "Euphrates" in Jeremiah 13:4. In all likelihood, God commands Jeremiah to go to the village of Parah, some five miles northeast of Jerusalem, and bury his underwear. "Good riddance!" Jeremiah must have said. "See you later, dirty underwear!" Many days later, God orders him to go and dig it up (Jeremiah 13:6). "Oh no!" the prophet must have gasped. "Now my underwear is good for nothing!"

That's God's point. Jeremiah then quotes God as saying, "This evil people, who refuse to hear My words, who stubbornly follow their own heart and have gone after other gods to serve them and worship them, shall be like this loincloth, which is good for nothing" (Jeremiah 13:10). Babylon eventually buried Judahites through conquest and exile because God's people had grown spiritually deaf. They refused to listen.

Jesus and Jeremiah

At one point in His ministry, Jesus led His disciples to a place north of the Sea of Galilee—Caesarea Philippi. There He asked them, "Who do people say I am?" They answered, "Some say John the Baptist, others say Elijah, and others Jeremiah or one of the prophets" (Matthew 16:14). Why did some link Jesus with Jeremiah?

Jesus, just like Jeremiah, didn't dress for success. He wore swaddling clothes as an infant. On another occasion, He girded Himself as a menial slave to wash feet. These events pale when compared with the day soldiers stripped Jesus naked and beat Him to a bloody pulp. Later that same day, our Savior put on the most shocking item ever—your sin and mine.

Paul puts it this way: "He who had no sin became sin for us" (2 Corinthians 5:21, author's translation). Peter states, "He Himself bore our sins in His body on the tree" (1 Peter 2:24). The Father placed upon Jesus every cruel word and every evil thought. Jesus bore every act of dishonesty and every white-collar crime. Jesus took on Himself every lustful look and every dishonest deal. Those who orchestrated the bloody mess did it because they believed Jesus was good for nothing. What do you do with that? Ask Jeremiah. You dig a hole and bury it.

God could never leave Israel buried in Babylon. God could never leave Jesus buried in the tomb. God will never leave you burdened and buried in your pain. By faith alone, God dresses you in Christ's robes of righteousness. "These are the ones coming out of the great tribulation. They have washed their robes and made them white in the blood of the Lamb" (Revelation 7:14). There is more. "For all of you who were baptized into Christ have clothed yourselves with Christ" (Galatians 3:27, author's translation).

God's Word

Because neat and tidy answers to pain are often elusive, we lose hope. We give up. Just there, in our weakest moment, God still invites us to listen to His Word. He also encourages us to internalize it. Jeremiah says, "Your words were found, and I ate them and Your words became to me a joy and the delight of my heart, for I am called by Your name, O LORD, God of hosts" (Jeremiah 15:16). Do you long for a more robust and intimate relationship with God? He encourages you to "read, mark, learn and inwardly digest" His Holy Word ("The Collect for the Word," *TLH*, p. 14). What does this Word do? It kindles faith, creates resolve, and dispels darkness until hope is born anew.

In Jeremiah 26, the prophet's enemies accuse him, but God's Word comes to his rescue. Government officials stand up for Jeremiah. They point out that the prophet is echoing Micah 3:12. In chapter 29, Jeremiah hears about hopeless exiles, so he sends them God's Word by means of a letter that promises them a future and a hope. In chapters 50 and 51, Babylon overwhelms Jeremiah with its raw evil, so God gives him a word on a scroll that announced the empire's demise. And in chapter 36, when King Jehoiakim slices, dices, and burns God's Word, the prophet rewrites his book. Call it *Jeremiah 2.0*!

In the prophet's lifetime, Judah lost everything: the temple, sacrifices, the monarchy, cities, and the land. However, just like Jeremiah, people still had God's Word to mobilize and energize them. No wonder Jeremiah calls this Word his joy and delight—the love of his life (Jeremiah 15:16).

God has spoken His final Word. It's a more vindicating Word than Micah 3:12. It's a more hopeful Word than Jeremiah's letter penned to exiles. It's a more victorious Word than the one spoken against Babylon. It's a more enduring Word than the scroll rewritten by Jeremiah. Coming down past the galaxies, past our solar system, past the moon and the stars, this Word became flesh. Jesus came in a body to carry our sin to the cross, bear our burdens on His shoulders, defeat sin and Satan—and then live to tell us about it.

God's Word doesn't offer quick solutions to complex problems. It does something better. It announces that Christ was crucified for our sin and raised again for our justification. Everything else pales into secondary importance compared with the promise of the free gift of eternal life through Christ Jesus our Lord (Romans 6:23).

With a Word like this, we can say goodbye to stress. We keep calm and listen on!

11

OVERCOMING THROUGH TRUST

*"Trust in the LORD with all your heart,
and do not lean on your own understanding."*

(Proverbs 3:5)

A few years ago, David Borgenicht and Joshua Piven wrote a book called *The Worst-Case Scenario Survival Handbook: Expert Advice for Extreme Situations.* One section is called "How to Survive If Your Parachute Fails to Open." Another section is titled "How to Fend Off a Shark." How good are your survival skills when your parachute doesn't open or when a shark attacks?

Better yet, how good are your survival skills when you're taking an afternoon stroll and you run into a lion that just escaped from the local zoo? I don't like cats, but I've got an honest respect for lions! What survival skills should we employ if we come face-to-face with a lion?

A. Run?

B. Play dead?

C. Make yourself appear bigger by opening your coat?

D. Sing the hymn "Stricken, Smitten, and Afflicted"?

According to *The Worst-Case Scenario Survival Handbook*, the answer is C: "Make yourself appear bigger by opening your coat." The moral of the story? Don't forget your coat!

Jeremiah is an ancient survival handbook. The prophet teaches how to trust God when we face lions, tigers, and bears. Add this to the list: loneliness.

All the Lonely People

Jeremiah 16:1–9 describes the prophet's personal life. God tells him that he should "not take a wife, nor shall you have sons or daughters in this place" (Jeremiah 16:2). It was rare for an Israelite man to stay single. So rare, in fact, that Hebrew doesn't have a word for "bachelor." Jeremiah's isolation continues. "You shall not go into the house of feasting to sit with them, to eat and drink" (Jeremiah 16:8). The prophet laments his God-ordained solitude. "I did not sit in the company of revelers, nor did I rejoice; I sat alone, because Your hand was upon me" (Jeremiah 15:17). People never saw Jeremiah at the corner bar laughing with friends. They never met his wife or children. Jeremiah had few friends. He lived alone.

This is what cataclysmic events in our lives often do. They separate us from people. We become detached from family and community rhythms. After a few months or years, we begin to feel as though we don't fit anywhere. Emotionally, we become a block of cement.

A Harvard political scientist named Robert Putnam published a book called *Bowling Alone: The Collapse and Revival of American Community*. He describes how American life is becoming more isolated. Putnam cites membership losses in civic organizations like the PTA, the League of Women Voters, the Lions, the Optimists, and the Kiwanis clubs. The number of people who bowl in leagues has also dropped dramatically; hence Putnam's title, *Bowling Alone*.

The results have been devastating. Americans are experiencing more depression, more suicides, and more chemical addictions than ever before. In fact, according to one study, our hyper-individualism is the reason we are eight times (*eight times!*) more depressed than people who live in the world's poorest countries, where close-knit relationships are valued and treasured.

Seven times in Genesis 1 God declared that everything was "good." God even says that it's "very good" (Genesis 1:31). Then God says, "It is not good." What? Say again? The world is still perfect. Sin hasn't entered the picture. What isn't good? "It is not good that the man should be alone" (Genesis 2:18). Something was lacking in Adam's life. That would be people.

We can't overcome life's sorrows if we face them alone. We need other people to help us adapt to our new circumstances. People convey God's Word and walk with us through our trauma. Friends and family members are God's gift to support us, give us insight, love us, and lead us back to health.

Two Plants

Jeremiah gives us a metaphor. It's about two plants. The first plant describes people who trust in themselves. They choose to go through life alone. The second plant are those who trust in God. Trust in God always brings with it a community of like-minded trusters. *People!*

"Thus says the LORD: 'Cursed is the man who trusts in man and makes flesh his strength, whose heart turns away from the LORD. He is like a shrub in the desert, and shall not see any good come. He shall dwell in the parched places of the wilderness, in an uninhabited salt land'" (Jeremiah 17:5–6). Most of us have been in a desert—in Arizona or California, or perhaps we've been to the Sahara Desert. There isn't bountiful, lush life with bright greens and water flowing.

None of us gets up in the morning and says, "Today I think I'll be like a shrub in the desert. I think I'll live in the parched places of the wilderness, in an uninhabited salt land." Instead, the decision to trust ourselves and turn away from the Lord happens incrementally. It often begins with a crisis in our family, with our health, or with our money. "If God really loved me, this wouldn't have happened." Then we stop praying. "If God really loved me, He would have answered my prayers." Then we stop worshiping. "If God really loved me, He would have provided a way out."

What's the problem in all of this? We interpret events through our grid and not God's; we make flesh our strength. "Flesh" is throwing ourselves into things like financial stockpiling and relational manipulation. The God thing isn't working, so why not try working the market or working the room? "If it's going to be, it's up to me!"

When we place trust in ourselves, before we know it, we're like a dwarf juniper in the desert, living in parched places of the wilderness. We become isolated from God and from people. Listening to our own counsel and insight creates a very small world.

Let me be blunt. I'm going to say this with love and respect. Most days, we're our own worst enemies. The biggest problem we have in our lives is us. We tell ourselves lies. We believe the lies. Then we turn around and convince ourselves that we're living in the truth. We become shrubs in a wasteland—parched and barren. Our roots can't go deep enough to be nourished by the living water of God's grace. Even when showers of blessings fall, they disappear into the sand. We blame others, our circumstances, or both. Then what? We isolate, insulate, and separate. There's a better way!

God tells Jeremiah, "Blessed is the man who trusts in the LORD, whose trust is the LORD. He is like a tree planted by water, that sends out its roots by the stream, and does not fear when heat comes, for its leaves remain green, and is not anxious in the year of drought, for it does not cease to bear fruit" (Jeremiah 17:7–8). Jeremiah found these ideas in Psalm 1. Note these connections:

- "Blessed is the man." (Jeremiah 17:7; Psalm 1:1)
- "He is like a tree planted." (Jeremiah 17:8; Psalm 1:3)
- "Its leaves remain green." (Jeremiah 17:8); "Its leaf does not wither." (Psalm 1:3)

- "It does not cease to bear fruit." (Jeremiah 17:8); it "yields its fruit in its season." (Psalm 1:3)

The Hebrew verb rendered "planted" in the ESV translation denotes "transplanted." This makes sense. In Holy Baptism, God moves us from parched places to water—living water that cleanses and refreshes. Baptismal water that gives life.

What's the primary difference between a dry shrub and a well-watered tree? Location! The location of our trust is the difference between night and day. The transplanted tree/person doesn't fear when heat comes. We don't get anxious in the year of drought. And we don't give in to one of the greatest obstacles to our healing—worry.

Worry sucks the life out of us.

Worry!

Worry goes by other names: "anxiety," "apprehension," "angst." Country cousins include "frazzled," "fretting," "in a stew," "on pins and needles," and, with Elvis Presley, "all shook up!" The German word *würgen* gets to the heart of what worry does; *würgen* means "strangle, choke, take by the throat."

Paul writes, "Don't worry about anything" (Philippians 4:6, author's translation). In the apostle's Greek, the word *worry* means "divide the mind." That's what worry does. It divides our mind, and then we only squeamishly believe that God has baptismally transplanted us by soul-refreshing waters.

Paul doesn't encourage us to live without worry while lounging on a beach in the South Pacific. Paul is in a Roman prison. Recall what led to his imprisonment. He was arrested in Jerusalem, almost murdered by forty men, caught up in political machinery for two years, shipwrecked on the Island of Malta, then placed under house arrest in Rome. It's after all this that Paul writes, "Don't worry about anything."

Worry can't change the past. I remember the *Back to the Future* series of movies. Marty McFly and Doc Emmett Brown get in the DeLorean that takes them back to the past. They live in the past and are able to change the past.

I've got bad news. Those movies? They aren't real. We can't go back. Worry can't change the past. I've got more bad news. Only God controls the future. Worry can't change the past. Worry can't change the future. Worry can only destroy today. Worry crushes our confidence, sabotages our sanity, strangles our spirits, throttles our thinking. And worry torpedoes our trust.

Worry works like this: I have to pass my test tomorrow. If I don't pass my test tomorrow, I'll go on academic probation. If I go on academic probation, I could get thrown out of school. If I get thrown out of school, I'll never find a job. If I don't find a job, I'll never be able to buy a house. If I can't buy a house, how can I ever get married? If I never get married, then I'll never know the joy of having children. Conclusion? If I don't pass my test tomorrow it will be the end of the world! Worry is like sitting in a rocking chair, going back and forth and expending a lot of energy to go nowhere.

You and I don't have to cave in to worry. Each of us is a transplanted tree! What kind of tree is Jeremiah talking about? An olive tree.

Olive trees are the most valuable trees in Israel. They produce fruit and oil and have long been an economic and dietary staple in the Mediterranean world—cultivated for the past six thousand years. Olive trees are beautiful (due to their numerous leaves) and durable (they can live for as long as a thousand years). An olive tree can theoretically survive for an unlimited length of time. When its trunk becomes broad and hollow, its roots produce young shoots that surround the trunk and replace collapsing parts. In the Bible, when God identifies people with olive trees, the connection implies abundance (Judges 9:9; Psalm 128:3) and closeness to God (Psalm 52:8).

Would you like to be more of an olive tree and less of a desert bush? It boils down to overcoming worry with trust—trust in God.

Trusting God

Horton Hatches the Egg is one of my favorite Dr. Seuss books. It's a story about Horton the elephant, whom Mayzie the bird tricks into sitting on her egg while she takes a permanent vacation in Palm Beach, Florida. Horton sits on the egg, repeatedly pledging his faithfulness "100 percent."

Already in the first chapter of the Bible, God makes a case for His faithfulness. The Hebrew phrase *wayyomer Elohim*, or "God said," appears nine times in Genesis 1. Without exception, what God said happens. God spoke and there was light and land and a sun and a moon and everything. In Genesis 1, God says, "I meant what I said and I said what I meant, I'm faithful for sure, 100 percent." God is completely faithful and worthy of all our trust.

When Abraham lied about Sarah, God didn't give up. When Moses asked, "Who am I to bring Israel out of Egypt?" God didn't give up. When the Israelites built a golden calf and worshiped it, God didn't give up. When Judah was exiled in 587 BC, God didn't give up. When soldiers spit in Christ's face, used a whip to rip open His back, and pounded nails to crush the nerves in His hands and feet, our Savior didn't give up. Come what may, God doesn't give up. *God will never give up on you.*

- "The Rock, His work is perfect, for all His ways are justice. A God of faithfulness [*emuna*]." (Deuteronomy 32:4)
- "The word of the LORD is right and true; He is faithful [*emuna*] in all He does." (Psalm 33:4, author's translation)
- "The LORD is faithful [*emuna*] in all His words and kind in all His works." (Psalm 145:13)
- "You have done wonderful things, plans formed of old, faithful [*emuna*] and sure." (Isaiah 25:1)

How did Hebrews respond to God's *emuna*—God's faithfulness? They said, "Amen." *Amen* is another Hebrew word, deriving from *emuna*. *Amen* means "Yes, Lord. I place my trust in You. It shall be so!"

Let's step back now and look at the big picture of Jeremiah 16–17. The section begins with Jeremiah's isolation and loneliness. It then moves to the prophet's reflections on Psalm 1, where he gives us two options: trust in self or trust in God. Chapter 17 ends with an oracle on the Sabbath. What do these motifs have in common? We need to rest when we're assaulted by loneliness, self-sufficiency, and worry.

God Gives Rest

I invite you to fill in the blanks.

- I'm ready to throw in the _____.
- I'm at the end of my _____.
- I'm just a bundle of _____.
- My life is falling _____.
- I'm at my wits' _____.
- I feel like resigning from the _____.

Sometimes we hear about collapsing ground that creates a depression called a sinkhole. Cars, sidewalks, lawn furniture, and sometimes entire houses fall into these holes. Sinkholes occur when underground water erodes the ground below so that the ground above—on the surface—loses its underlying support. Suddenly everything caves in.

Depression is a lot like a sinkhole. On the surface things look okay. "How are you?" "Fine!" But pain and loss erode our heart to the point that one day everything collapses. Suddenly—or so it would seem—life caves in and we fall into a deep, dark hole.

Looking up from our hole, we realize that we've spent the majority of our time and energy establishing life on the visible level—on the surface. We've replaced our losses with a lot of good and perhaps even excellent assets—academic degrees, work experiences, new relationships, money, and even physical strength and beauty. But if we neglect our heart—our inner life—it's only a matter of time until it all comes crashing down.

The results are in. People are caving in at the highest rate in our country's history. Sales for tranquilizers, sleep aids, and coping meds are at an all-time high. So is alcohol. Books on reducing depression become instant best sellers. I once saw a bumper sticker that read, "I'm planning to have a nervous breakdown. I've earned it and no one will keep me from it!"

Loneliness, Self-Sufficiency, and Worry

Loneliness, self-sufficiency, and worry placed Jeremiah in a hole. That's why he follows his oracle on shrubs and trees with a teaching about the Sabbath. *Sabbath* comes from the Hebrew verb for "cut off." There are times when we need to cut off from the internet, work, and routines. The prophet quotes the Lord as saying, "Keep the Sabbath day holy, as I commanded your fathers" (Jeremiah 17:22). God instituted the Sabbath (Genesis 2:3; Exodus 20:11). It's His gift to weary souls. The Book of Exodus expands on the idea.

The pharaoh in Exodus insists that Israelite state slaves must work all the time so that they keep pace with his building plans. When he no longer gives Israelites straw for their bricks, the work expectations become unbearable. "Why have you not done all your task of making bricks today and yesterday, as in the past?" (Exodus 5:14).

There is no Sabbath for anyone caught in this sick system. People had to keep reaching for more because Pharaoh wouldn't concede an inch: "You are idle, you are idle; that is why you say, 'Let us go and sacrifice to the LORD'" (Exodus 5:17). Pharaoh's foremen bark out these orders: "You shall by no means reduce your number of bricks, your daily task each day" (Exodus 5:19).

Life boils down to one word—productivity. Pharaoh cares for people only as they are instruments to produce wealth for those who wield all the power. He dehumanizes Israelites with his single pharaonic mandate: more bricks!

Seen in this context, the Sabbath is a countercultural idea. It offers wonder and celebration instead of the constant worry that comes from the rat race of production. The Sabbath is an intentional work stoppage. It's God's way to break our bondage to work, quotas, productivity, and busyness. God says, "Your highest values will not be professional and financial. If they rule your heart, you will end up destroying yourself as well as those you love."

Unlike the other six days, when it's easy to define people by means of their productivity, the Sabbath is an equal opportunity event that overrides all distinctions (Exodus 23:12; Deuteronomy 5:14). God mandates that Israel treat servants with kindness, remembering that they were once slaves in Egypt (e.g., Exodus 23:9; Leviticus 19:34; Deuteronomy 24:18–22). The Sabbath insists that our primary calling is not as workers but neighbors. Sabbath time, Sabbath practice, and Sabbath freedoms are neighborly because they are a departure from pharaonic brick quotas that produce fear and anxiety.

Rest is our protest against unreachable brick-making quotas. "Is not life more than food, and the body more than clothing?" (Matthew 6:25). Sabbath is a nonanxious alternative, an anti-pharaonic lifestyle in the midst of a society that believes in more technological inventions, economic expansion, and military mechanisms. The mantra is always "More!"

Sabbath is the way Israelites renounced autonomy and confessed their trust in the Lord. Sabbath is the way we surrender our lives to the God who created us and re-creates us in Christ. Sabbath turns us from shrubs to olive trees—lives that are beautiful and enduring. Lives intimately intertwined with others.

12

OVERCOMING THROUGH HUMILITY

"Humble yourselves . . . under the mighty hand of God."

(1 Peter 5:6)

Bohemian author Franz Kafka (1883–1924) once said the only reason to read a book is to have it hammer us in the head and break up the icy sea in our heart. *Jeremiah is such a book!* The prophet employs everything in his verbal arsenal to announce Babylon's impending assault against Jerusalem. He does whatever it takes to awaken people from their spiritual malaise and prepare them to overcome impending sorrow.

Jeremiah recognizes that anguish frequently triggers denial. Emotional upheavals shock our system. Chemicals in our body that normally flow harmoniously become unsettled by stress. To protect ourselves from raw emotions we shut down. Turn off. Cover up. Pain erodes our ability to use language. At times, it leaves us speechless—literally.

Here comes Jeremiah with his ice ax to break our frozen heart! When there are no words, Jeremiah helps us understand trauma with our eyes. His analogy of a potter and his clay takes us to God—His judgment and mercy, His wrath and love, His Law and Gospel. Jeremiah's goal? For us to sigh deeply. Weep softly. Groan inwardly. Hope expectantly. And come alive as we admit that we're clay. Clay is tough enough to be reshaped and fired. Clay is also soft enough to be pliable in the potter's hands.

A Potter's House

God tells Jeremiah, "Arise, and go down to the potter's house" (Jeremiah 18:2). Once at the house, the prophet spots a wheel (Jeremiah 18:3). Ancient potters used two stone disks in order to shape, form, and create with clay.

Before the invention of the pottery wheel in about 9000 BC, people lived a hand-to-mouth existence. Life consisted of daily survival as storage was limited to bulky stone bowls that served as containers. Try to imagine getting along with no functional containers—no pots or pans, no bowls or barrels, no cardboard boxes or brown bags. Life is reduced to what we can hold in our hands.

Then the revolution! Everything changed when people mastered pottery. They created bowls, jugs, plates, pots, and lamps by exerting pressure on the inside of a clay ball while using counterpressure from two stone disks. And the firing process in a kiln created a temperature high enough to make the clay durable. People began to store grain and carry water. Pottery became the most functional item on the planet.

Pottery also became one of the most beautiful items on the planet. Potters designed, shaped, and fired every pot and pan. It was their unique creation. Pottery was functional. Pottery was also beautiful.

We live in a different world. It seems the trend today is toward being either functional or beautiful, but rarely both. Grocery bags function well, but who really cares what color they are? Paintings and other pieces of artwork are beautiful, but most of them have no practical use. Ancient pottery, however, was distinctive. Vessels were both functional and fascinating, handy and handsome, practical and often quite pretty.

Jeremiah sees this miracle in the making. A potter is working at a wheel with a formless mass of clay. A little pressure here, more there, and a vessel begins to emerge out of shapeless mud. Then it dawns upon him.

Jeremiah sees the analogy. This is how God works in our lives. He is the potter. We are the clay. In spite of everything we've been through, we are still useful. We are still beautiful.

In chapter 1, Jeremiah finds out that he has been in the Potter's hands since before he was born. God tells him, "Before I formed [*yatsar*] you in the womb I knew you" (Jeremiah 1:5). The Hebrew word for "formed," *yatsar*, is the same word the prophet employs in Jeremiah 18:2, often translated "potter." Moses uses the word when he describes God creating Adam: "Then the LORD God formed [*yatsar*] Adam from the dirt" (Genesis 2:7, author's translation).

Adam didn't appear randomly. Neither did Jeremiah. Not one of us is here by chance. Fate has nothing to do with it. The Potter has formed us with skilled hands. Before we were born, God planned for us to be useful. Before we were born, God planned for us to be beautiful.

Past pain doesn't make us damaged goods. We aren't useless. We are new creations in Christ Jesus. This is all wonderful and beautiful and amazing; but we still have a problem. Jeremiah observes, "The vessel he was making of clay was spoiled in the potter's hand" (Jeremiah 18:4). Oh no! A spoiled vessel. A clay pot with impurities and blemishes because it resists the potter's shaping hands. Jeremiah calls that sin, rebellion, and iniquity.

What will the potter do? Kick the wheel and go home? Throw the clay at the dog? Purchase a different type of clay? Ditch the whole thing and give up? "He reworked it into another vessel, as it seemed good to the potter to do" (Jeremiah 18:4). God doesn't throw away what is cracked and chipped. *He works with the same clay.* God patiently sticks with it. God isn't afraid to keep getting His hands dirty.

On the cross, God gets dirty again. Only this time, it's not getting just His hands dirty. It's getting His feet, face, arms, legs—His entire body and soul—dirty and defiled for you.

Jesus is standing alone. Beaten and silent in front of a seething crowd. The sight of His skin flogged to shreds incites people to want more blood. The crown of thorns makes His head throb. Because of Good Friday, God never gives up on clay—that's us. God keeps working, keeps sculpting, keeps re-creating. He is making us more useful and more beautiful.

Suffering isn't pointless. It molds and shapes us, refines and renews us. There is meaning behind life's madness. Jeremiah writes, "Then the word of the LORD came to me: 'O house of Israel, can I not do with you as this potter has done? declares the LORD. Behold, like the clay in the potter's hand, so are you in My hand, O house of Israel'" (Jeremiah 18:5–6). The Potter can do whatever He wants with His clay. His hands hold all power, dominion, and authority. His hands bear Calvary's loving scars.

You Are the Potter, I Am the Clay

All isn't lost when a glass or dish breaks. We get glue and fasten pieces back together. What happens, though, when there aren't any pieces? when the shattering is so complete that everything looks like dust? What does God do with dust? He adds water and forms clay. Then He fires the clay to shine with added beauty and brightness. There's hope even when God doesn't have a lot to work with.

Please understand. God doesn't want our lives to turn to dust and ashes. God doesn't want sin. God doesn't want us to get cancer. Mass shootings aren't God's will. Pandemics aren't either. Please also understand this: God does His best work with dust.

Take Job, for instance. Job was the wealthiest man in Edom—worth $45 million by today's standards. Overnight, Job goes bankrupt. His ten children die. He gets a dreaded disease. His wife says, "Curse God and die" (Job 2:9). Then the Three Stooges show up—Curly, Moe, and Larry. Only the Bible calls them Bildad, Zophar, and Eliphaz. What does Job say? "When He has tried me, I shall come out as gold" (Job 23:10). God restored Job twofold (Job 42:10). The rest of Job's life was the best of Job's life.

Would you like another example? Jacob gives his son Joseph a coat of many colors. Do his brothers like it? They throw Joseph into a pit, then sell him to some Ishmaelites who are on their way to Egypt. The Ishmaelites sell Joseph to Potiphar. Potiphar's wife accuses Joseph of raping her. She said! He said! Joseph is seventeen. Joseph isn't vindicated until he is forty-one. What does Joseph say? "You meant evil against me, but God meant it for good" (Genesis 50:20).

The Potter wants us to look past pain and look to the purpose behind our pain. He is shaping us to become more mature, committed believers in Jesus. Useful and beautiful. That's God's goal.

Our pain has a purpose. So do our prayers. When all you've got is dust, it's tempting to think that God doesn't answer prayers. Have you ever prayed and felt like it was a waste of time? like your words were just bouncing off the ceiling? like prayer is just a bunch of mumbo jumbo?

If God wasn't the potter who has control of clay, then prayer would be a waste of time. Who wants to ask something of someone who can't help? Can you imagine God saying, "I'd really like to help, but I can't. Please know that it frustrates Me as much as it frustrates you!" Will that ever happen? Never!

Sometimes we say, "My children are out of control!" "My health is out of control!" "My finances are out of control!" Try this instead: "God is in control." When you're worried sick, say, "God is in control." When you feel hopeless, say, "God is in control." When you're standing by the casket wondering, "Why him? Why now? What now?" say, "God is in control." Say, "God is the potter, I am the clay." He takes dust and dirt and reshapes us into people who are useful and ever beautiful.

Beauty and the Beast

There was a time when he was a young, handsome prince living in his stately castle. That was before the curse. The enchantress, disguised as an old beggar woman, turned him into an ugly animal and changed all his servants into household items. Their names are now famous: Lumière, Cogsworth, Mrs. Potts, and my favorite, the little teacup named Chip. What did they call the prince? The Beast. Why? Because he was repugnant and repulsive, hideous and homely. The Beast hid in his castle, secluding himself from everyone and everything. All that changed one day when a sweet young lady named Belle came strolling along and into his life. Beauty loves the Beast and the Beast becomes beautiful.

Have you ever felt like the Beast? Rejected, alone, and living in the shadows? We run to our castle and hide so no one can see the ugly mess we make of our lives. It all looks like dust.

Following Jeremiah's tour of a potter's house, he describes our dust and ashes in graphic terms. In chapter 18, he uses words like "spoiled," "pluck up," "break down," "destroy," "evil," "disaster," "stubbornness," "false gods," "enemy," "calamity," "perish," "strike," "pit," "famine," "sword," "childless," "widowed," "death," "pestilence," "snares," "kill," "overthrown," and "anger." Jeremiah also includes the trifecta of "horrible," "horror," and "horrified." What a beastly chapter!

It's hard, though, to find a page in the Bible where the beast doesn't appear. Cain murders Abel. Saul hunts down David. Amnon rapes Tamar. Joab kills Absalom. One Herod kills babies and another Herod beheads John the Baptist. Pilate washes his hands of the whole mess. Even the sweet psalmist Asaph, who wrote twelve psalms, admits, "I was brutish and ignorant; I was like a beast toward you" (Psalm 73:22).

In 2011, I was riding my bike on a trail along the Mississippi River, just north of the St. Louis Arch. Cruising down a hill with the wind in my face, I was born to be wild! Suddenly my pedaling came to a screeching halt. A guy on a bike approached from the opposite direction. I hit my brakes to avoid a collision, lost control, and skidded on the gravel, scraping my right leg and arm and cracking two ribs. Then my helmet hit the ground. BAM!

What happened next contains both good news and bad news. The good news? I was still alive. The bad news? The guy on the other bike didn't care. He kept going!

So there I was, lying in the gravel, my head pounding, my right arm and leg bleeding, and let's just say I wasn't meditating upon the upward call of God in Christ Jesus. "How could he? That rude biker! Boy, if I catch up with him!" The brute beast reared his ugly head, again. I harbored my hurt as I pedaled my bent bike all the way home.

Why did I get so upset? Why was I so eager to have this impolite biker arrested and thrown in jail? Truth be told, this is just one of ten billion times I've reacted to life by behaving like a beast.

In a moment, in the twinkling of an eye, we lash out to maim and maul people with our deadly thoughts and explosive words. When we come to our senses, the temptation is to run to our castle and hide, obsess over how ugly we are, and get lost in all the dust. Don't do that. Please don't do that. Beauty loves the beast and the beast becomes forever beautiful.

How do I know?

The beast reared his ugly head another time. That time his goal was singular: make Jesus absolutely abhorrent. He was led like a lamb to the slaughter (Isaiah 53:7). The legionnaire's whip consisted of leather strips with lead balls on the ends. It beat His back beyond recognition. The crown of thorns left deep gashes on His head and caked His hair with blood. Crucifixion disfigured Christ's entire body as He twisted and turned, writhing in pain.

Golgotha was filled with rotting flesh and the stench of death. Corpses hung there for days, sometimes weeks, often consumed by birds and animals. This was where our savage human nature triumphed over the stunning beauty of the Father's only-begotten Son. The bloody mess shatters all analogies and all metaphors. Words collapse before the sheer atrocity of it all.

Here's what it means. Beauty loves the beast, and the beast becomes beautiful.

Here's what that means. The Potter knows what He's doing when we are in the furnace of suffering and pain. He's out to remake us forever beautiful.

13

OVERCOMING THROUGH GOD'S GRACE

"My grace is sufficient for you,
for My power is made perfect in weakness."

(2 Corinthians 12:9)

When I was in high school, once a year, for two solid weeks, I dedicated every ounce of my strength to one goal—making the basketball team. When I woke up, my first thought was basketball. At lunch, basketball. As three o'clock drew ever closer, I found myself less able to concentrate on school and more obsessed with basketball. I focused all my thoughts on one all-consuming goal—make the team, my high school basketball team.

Then the day came when the coach posted the list of who made it. The whole process left me understanding that to get anything in life, I would have to sacrifice, sweat, bleed, give it all—and then some. After all, "God helps those who help themselves." Right? I once saw a multimillion-dollar boat. Its name? *Deserved.* That's the American way. Work hard, make it big, then boast, "Deserved!"

Americans are pros at performance. The Lord is a pro at grace. God gives me what I need, not what I deserve. This is good news when life's losses trigger a crisis in faith. What does it mean that God doesn't answer my prayers the way I want? How do I keep going to church when I'm all alone? When I'm thrown a cruel curve, how can faith survive? In a word, *grace*.

High Noon

It's high noon at the OK Corral. Jeremiah is wearing a white hat. Who is the man in the black hat? Pashhur, a priest overseeing Jerusalem's temple. His job description is simple: come weal or woe, the status must remain quo. Pashhur's proverb? "This is the temple of the LORD, the temple of the LORD, the temple of the LORD" (Jeremiah 7:4). As chief of temple security, Pashhur polices the place and dispenses with all false prophets, placing a gag order on everyone critiquing the present arrangement of power.

In walks Jeremiah. He's not afraid to call the situation what it is.

The prophet's preaching was a threat to Pashhur's job. Take a look. "The priests did not say, 'Where is the LORD?' And those who handle Torah did not know me" (Jeremiah 2:8, author's translation). It's hardly surprising that people gave Jeremiah the name *Magor-misabib*. It means "terror on every side." The nickname summarizes the prophet's message in Jeremiah 6:25; 46:5; and 49:29. When people saw Jeremiah in the marketplace or walking in their neighborhood, they said, "Here comes good ol' fire-and-brimstone himself—Mr. Magor-misabib!"

Jeremiah comments on the Jerusalem temple. The priest Pashhur couldn't stomach the thought that God is against Solomon's temple, that Jerusalem will suffer irrevocable consequences for its unfaithfulness (Jeremiah 19:14–15). Jeremiah will mention the city of David almost two hundred more times from chapter 20 to the end of his book. Jerusalem is ground zero.

The stage is now set: Jeremiah versus Pashhur, prophet versus priest, the rebel versus the establishment. The Lord stands behind Jeremiah. The Judean monarchy stands behind Pashhur. The God of Israel commissions the prophet. The highest authorities in the land commission the priest. To say that the prophet and priest "crossed paths" is to understate the narrative in Jeremiah 20. According to a fundamental law of physics, the force of impact depends on speed and direction. Jeremiah and Pashhur are both moving fast, from opposite directions. One is bent on devotion; the other, on promotion. One is a servant; the other, a tyrant. One loves people; the other loves the establishment. One preaches and prays. The other maligns and manipulates.

What happens? It's a one-round knockout! As the guardian of the state and its sacred precincts, Pashhur strikes Jeremiah and puts him in stocks at the upper Benjamin Gate of the temple (Jeremiah 20:2). REJECTED!

Rejection

We've been there. We all know the pain of rejection. We slam-dunked the job interview, only to be informed that the company is going in a "different direction." We gave it all we had to reconcile, and the next week they ignore our texts and phone calls. We followed all the directions, but things still fell apart. We showed up for practice every day, giving it everything, but we lost every game. We spent time with our child, going out of our way to parent the best we know how. She still rebelled and now has vowed never to talk with us again. Being rejected damages our self-esteem, ignites anger, and erodes confidence.

"When it rains it pours." Sometimes multiple rejections come at the same time. A layoff, then a divorce. A breakup, a college rejection letter, then a D- in calculus. We can usually handle one rejection, but three or four at the same time? Being rejected activates the same area of our brain that responds to physical pain. Ouch!

It gets worse. We become our own prosecuting attorney, judge, and jury. The sentence? Life in prison with no parole. We tell ourselves, "I'm a failure." We feel disgusted with how things have turned out. It adds more pain.

One day, the devil put his tools up for sale, marking each with a sale price. The implements included hatred, envy, jealousy, deceit, lying, and pride. Set apart was a harmless-looking but well-worn tool—rejection.

Its price was astronomical, the highest of all. Why so pricey? The devil answered, "Because it's more useful than my other tools. I can crush a person's heart with rejection when I can't get near them with the other implements. Look how badly worn it is. That's because I use rejection on everyone." Rejection causes us to say things we shouldn't say, think things we shouldn't think, and do things we shouldn't do.

Pashhur arrested Jeremiah, beat him, and threw the petulant prophet in jail, locking him in stocks. Jeremiah writhed in pain. REJECTED!

God Gives Grace

"The next day . . . Pashhur released Jeremiah from the stocks" (Jeremiah 20:3). Why did the priest relent? What prompted him to free the prophet? Grace. God's grace. God always gives grace. Once released from the stocks, Jeremiah, with his back still throbbing and his wrists still contorted, delivered a scathing rebuke. The name *Pashhur* means "joy all around." His new name given by Jeremiah? "Terror all around." Pashhur becomes a sign for "all Judah" (Jeremiah 20:4). The Lord will make the priest a "terror" to himself and others when Babylon's king comes to plunder and pillage the land. Pashhur and his fellow priests will be exiled to Babylon, where they will eventually die (Jeremiah 20:6).

I would say that Jeremiah rebounded—and then some! His courage follows a long line of prophets who, by God's grace, challenged the status quo. Moses confronts Pharaoh with God's thunderous "Let My people go" (e.g., Exodus 5:1). Nathan courageously puts his career on the line when he rebukes David, "You are the man!" (2 Samuel 12:7). Elijah takes the heat from Ahab, who calls him the "troubler of Israel" (1 Kings 18:17). And Daniel's dream of the night subverts Nebuchadnezzar's illusion of the day (Daniel 4:1–27).

Israel's final prophet took the most courageous stand. Jesus also dared to turn His world of power politics upside down, making statements like "the last will be first" (Matthew 20:16; Mark 10:31; Luke 13:30), and "Whoever humbles himself like this child is the greatest in the kingdom of heaven" (Matthew 18:4). Jesus once had the audacity to make a whip and use it to cleanse His Father's house (John 2:15). Another time, He looked the religious leaders straight in the eye and said, "Woe to you, teachers of the law and Pharisees, you hypocrites! You clean the outside of the cup and dish, but inside they are full of greed and self-indulgence" (Matthew 23:25, author's translation).

Before Jesus stood before Pontius Pilate, He faced off with His Pash-hur—the high priest Caiaphas. The Savior said, "In the future you will see the Son of Man sitting at the right hand of the Mighty One and coming on the clouds of heaven" (Matthew 26:64, author's translation; cf. Mark 14:62).

Jesus didn't get crucified for giving to charity. He wasn't pinned to wood for helping people. Jesus was executed because He announced grace for all people. Jesus called for a new kingdom, and He was the new King. Societies don't execute conformists. They silence those who shake religious conventions to the core.

Jesus is a roaring Lion (Revelation 5:5). Jesus is also the bleeding Lamb (John 1:29, 36). His power is made perfect in weakness (2 Corinthians 12:9). Jesus allows soldiers to march Him through Jerusalem's streets while He shoulders His crossbar with blood dripping from His butchered back. Jesus allows these executioners to strip Him naked, shove Him to the ground, and nail Him to a cross with their tools of torture. Jesus takes the spit and the insults without calling His Father to immediately dispense twelve legions of angels (Matthew 26:53).

Jesus is the God of all grace!

Tell God How You Feel

Jeremiah 20 records the prophet's lowest point, the dark night of his soul. After his arrest and acquittal, Jeremiah blames God, rejects his calling, and curses the day he was born.

God invites us also to be honest with Him. God won't smirk, roll His eyes, furrow His brow, or look the other way. God doesn't get tired of us.

He invites us to draw near to His throne because it's a throne of grace (Hebrews 4:16).

Jeremiah's most intense lament isn't as a crisis of faith; it's a crisis of vocation (Jeremiah 20:7–18). The prophet prays, "O LORD, You have deceived me, and I was deceived; You are stronger than I, and You have prevailed. I have become a laughingstock all the day; everyone mocks me" (Jeremiah 20:7). Jeremiah says God tricked him into becoming a prophet.

Jeremiah was in a catch-22. He suffers if he speaks God's Word. He suffers if he doesn't speak God's Word. Yet hadn't God promised Jeremiah that he would become "a fortified city, an iron pillar, and bronze walls, against the whole land, against the kings of Judah, its officials, its priests, and the people of the land" (Jeremiah 1:18)? The prophet responds, "Empty words!"

Jeremiah had become a laughingstock. No one listened. No one paid attention. No one cared. God called Jeremiah into a situation that was more difficult than the prophet ever imagined. Now he's at the end of his rope. He cries out to God with great anger.

People ask me, "Is it wrong to be angry with God?" They're sometimes surprised by my answer: "If you feel anger toward God, you should tell Him. God is big enough to handle your anger. So tell Him about it. He wants you to pour out your entire heart to Him." Just like Jeremiah, our heart becomes filled with bitterness when we struggle to reconcile God's goodness with our intense suffering.

God invites us to express our complaint—even if it's a messy, inarticulate, tear-filled prayer. He wants us to go before Him as we are, not pretending to be someone we aren't. When we're honest with God, we will develop a deeper relationship with Him. With great grace, God says, "Call upon Me in the day of trouble; I will deliver you, and you shall glorify Me" (Psalm 50:15).

An Up-and-Down Ride

What an emotional roller coaster! Jeremiah moves from accusing God

(Jeremiah 20:7–8) to making one of the greatest statements of faith in the Bible: "If I say, 'I will not mention Him, or speak any more in His name,' there is in my heart as it were a burning fire shut up in my bones, and I am weary with holding it in, and I cannot" (Jeremiah 20:9). Jeremiah turns in his resignation and in the same breath tears it up. Jeremiah quits, then he doesn't quit.

Because of Pashhur's rejection, Jeremiah was ready to give up. But he couldn't. He wouldn't. The prophet was compelled to speak God's Word. It was like a fire in his bones that he couldn't extinguish. "Therefore thus says the LORD, the God of hosts: '. . . Behold, I am making My words in your mouth a fire'" (Jeremiah 5:14).

The Power of Praise

When we're rejected we tend to look inward—to our problems and frustrations. "What did I do wrong?" "How could I have avoided it?" "This? Again?" We need to look instead upward to God. He hasn't abandoned us. "The LORD is with me like a mighty warrior" (Jeremiah 20:11, author's translation). The prophet wasn't alone. Neither are we. Jeremiah would be victorious because the Lord is a mighty warrior. He fights for His people. He fights for us!

That's why we sing—even on our darkest days. "Sing to the LORD; praise the LORD! For He has delivered the life of the needy from the hand of evildoers" (Jeremiah 20:13). The prophet sings a song of salvation. It includes the Hebrew word *Hallelu*. It translates into English as "praise."

Praise takes our mind off rejection and focuses it on God. Praise acknowledges that God has the right to rule and reign how He sees fit. Praise confesses that God knows more about what we need than we do. Praise celebrates that God can do what He wants, when He wants, and how He wants. We don't see the finished product—but we still praise God for His plan.

Here's an example.

In 2 Chronicles 20, a Judean king named Jehoshaphat defeats

Ammonites, Edomites, and Moabites. "He appointed those who were to sing to the LORD and praise Him in holy attire, as they went before the army, and say, 'Give thanks to the LORD, for His steadfast love endures forever'" (2 Chronicles 20:21). What a sight! The church choir leading the charge against the enemies. Generals and lieutenants, sergeants and privates—along with their weapons and artillery—marching behind musicians thanking God for victory before the victory. Let me slow down. *Levitical singers are praising God for victory before the victory.*

Psalm 149:6 offers insight into this battle strategy: "The praises of God are in their mouths like a double-edged sword in their hands" (author's translation). When the praises of God are in our mouths, they—like double-edged swords—silence our memories of rebuffs and rejections. When biblical truth is set to music, it becomes memorable, teachable, and transformational. I encourage you to meditate on more of Jeremiah's praises:

- "Sing aloud with gladness for Jacob, and raise shouts for the chief of the nations; proclaim, give praise, and say, 'O LORD, save Your people, the remnant of Israel.'" (Jeremiah 31:7)
- "They shall come and sing aloud on the height of Zion, and they shall be radiant over the goodness of the LORD." (Jeremiah 31:12)
- "There shall be heard again the voice of mirth and the voice of gladness, the voice of the bridegroom and the voice of the bride, the voices of those who sing, as they bring thank offerings to the house of the LORD: 'Give thanks to the LORD of hosts, for the LORD is good, for His steadfast love endures forever!'" (Jeremiah 33:10–11)
- "Then the heavens and the earth, and all that is in them, shall sing for joy over Babylon, for the destroyers shall come against them out of the north, declares the LORD." (Jeremiah 51:48)

Jesus, like Jeremiah, knows the power of praise. "When they had sung a hymn, they went out to the Mount of Olives" (Matthew 26:30). Imagine that. Everything is about to go nuclear, so Jesus sings Psalms 113–118—

often called "the Egyptian Hallel." There's that Hebrew word for "praise" again. Psalms 113–118 praise God for His power that delivered Israel from Egypt. On Maundy Thursday, Jesus and His disciples sing verses like these:

- "He raises the poor from the dust and lifts the needy from the ash heap." (Psalm 113:7)
- "Our God is in the heavens; He does all that He pleases." (Psalm 115:3)
- "You [the Lord] have delivered my soul from death, my eyes from tears, my feet from stumbling." (Psalm 116:8)
- "The stone that the builders rejected has become the cornerstone. This is the LORD's doing; it is marvelous in our eyes. This is the day that the LORD has made; let us rejoice and be glad in it." (Psalm 118:22–24)

Christ is about to be betrayed by a kiss. Then, in staccato-like fashion, there will be deniers and slappers and beaters and spitters and whippers and mockers. There will also be nailers. So what does Jesus do? He sings. "I shall live, and recount the deeds of the LORD" (Psalm 118:17).

Jeremiah sings as well, but then he descends into despair and darkness. Jeremiah accuses God and then renews his commitment to God's Word. He confesses, worships, and extols. He denounces, doubts, and despairs. So which is it? You know. It's all of this. That's what rejection does. It puts us on a topsy-turvy path where one minute we're full of faith, and the next minute we want to die.

There is an odd (and deliberate) juxtaposition between Jeremiah 20:7–13 and 14–18. I would have placed the praise *after* the pout. "All's well that ends well." That's how I like things to work. That's not how faith works. Faith waxes and wanes from exuberant praise to bitter resentment—sometimes in the same hour. Sure, we're saints. We're also sinners. Jeremiah's last prayer in chapter 20 is hardly full of joy and confidence. It includes these laments:

- "Cursed be the day on which I was born!" (Jeremiah 20:14)

- "Cursed be the man who brought the news to my father, 'A son is born to you.'" (Jeremiah 20:15)
- "Why did I come out from the womb to see toil and sorrow, and spend my days in shame?" (Jeremiah 20:18)

Jeremiah's journey began before God formed him in the womb (Jeremiah 1:5). Now, in wanting death, he refers to the womb again. The prophet doesn't want to go on. He doesn't want life to end; he laments that it began. He wishes he had never been born. The prophet's prayer ends with the oft-asked question "Why?" The question lingers. God doesn't answer. The issue is left unresolved. Is there any hope? Yes! God gives more grace.

God's Grace

God delivers grace through Holy Baptism—a washing of regeneration and renewal in the Holy Spirit (Titus 3:5). Baptism delivers everything Jesus won for us by His perfect life, His sin-atoning blood, and His death-defeating resurrection. God's saving grace restores hope.

A lot of magazines and websites suggest that hope is restored when we become thinner, more muscular, more pimple-free, or more perfumed. Many movies and TV shows imply that hope is restored when we increase our popularity, our intelligence, our net worth—or all three.

Please read closely what I'm about to say. When we feel rejected, hope isn't restored by the number of pounds we lose, the kind of car we drive, or the type of clothes we wear. CEO, store clerk, carpenter, or field hand, it doesn't matter. Old or young, it doesn't matter. First string or cut from the basketball team—like me in high school, every year!—it doesn't matter. It's only God's saving grace that restores hope.

One of the biggest problems in our Christian life is that we begin with a relationship, then revert to rules. We reduce the joy of a relationship to routine and a dull regimen. How do we begin the Christian life? By grace. How do we continue the Christian life? By grace. God gives saving grace. God gives strengthening grace.

God also lavishly gives sufficient grace. "He said to me, 'My grace is sufficient for you'" (2 Corinthians 12:9). "He said" is a verbal form indicating present and ongoing action. Christ said and He continues to say! Christ says, "By grace you're saved. By grace you're strengthened. And My grace is always sufficient."

Rejection haunts us with two words: "What if?" *What if* I never recover? *What if* it happens again? "What if" twists us into emotional pretzels, makes our eyes twitch and our blood pressure rise, and causes our heads to ache.

God's sufficient grace empowers us to change "What if" to "Now that." *Now that* Jesus is risen from the dead . . . *Now that* Jesus is coming to make all things new . . . *Now that* Jesus has baptized me, absolved me, loves me, and communes me in His Holy Supper . . . *Now that* I have God's saving, strengthening, and sufficient grace, I will not allow rejection to have the final say. *Ever.*

14

OVERCOMING THROUGH THE GOOD SHEPHERD

"The good shepherd lays down His life for the sheep."

(John 10:11)

What creature are we most like? In the nineteenth century, Charles Darwin claimed people are most like monkeys. That was wrong then. That is wrong today. Many biologists now say people are most like rats. Pretty much whatever makes a rat sick makes us sick. Isn't that a happy thought? Other scientists believe people are a lot like bees because we're social creatures who live in highly structured societies. Still others compare us to dolphins because dolphins and people have a similar ratio of brain mass to body size.

Monkeys, rats, bees, and dolphins. According to the Bible, what creature are we most likened to? I bet you know. *Sheep.* Sheep are mentioned over five hundred times in the Bible, more than any other animal. Sheep need a shepherd, especially when they've been hurt—deeply.

When we get hurt, our memory takes on a life of its own. We try to forget it; our memory won't let us. We try to ignore it; our memory replays it. We try to get over it; our memory lingers and fixates on it. Our memory files the past away and recalls it when we least expect it. We think we have a memory. That's not right. Our memory has us. We wonder if the chaos and upheaval will ever loosen its grip on our heart. After all, we're just sheep.

Evil Shepherds

It was a common practice in the ancient Near East to call kings "shepherds." For example, Isaiah says the great Persian king Cyrus II (600–530 BC) is a shepherd (Isaiah 44:28). The Bible also calls King David a shepherd (2 Samuel 7:8). That's what God wants in a leader. Someone who is tough, but tender; mighty, but merciful. That's a shepherd. "Thus says the LORD: Do justice and righteousness, and deliver from the hand of the oppressor him who has been robbed. And do no wrong or violence to the resident alien, the fatherless, and the widow, nor shed innocent blood in this place" (Jeremiah 22:3). That's the ideal. Here's the real: "'Woe to the shepherds who destroy and scatter the sheep of My pasture!' declares the LORD" (Jeremiah 23:1). Judah's shepherds were fleecing the flock:

- "The shepherds transgressed." (Jeremiah 2:8)
- "The shepherds are stupid and do not inquire of the LORD." (Jeremiah 10:21)
- "Many shepherds have destroyed My vineyard." (Jeremiah 12:10)
- "My people have been lost sheep. Their shepherds have led them astray." (Jeremiah 50:6)

King David was the yardstick by which Judah's shepherd-kings were measured. For instance, King Ahaz "did not do what was right in the eyes of the LORD his God, as his father David had done" (2 Kings 16:2). Even the kings in the Joash-Amaziah-Azariah-Jotham succession—which gets a good report and whose kingships are generally likened to that of their father (e.g., 2 Kings 14:3; 15:3)—are measured against David's rule. Their failure to remove high places (where idols were worshiped) makes them inferior to him.

It was no different in Jeremiah's day. The kings, princes, and royal elite worshiped Canaanite gods on high places. They also deprived God's people of justice and righteousness. Jeremiah offers this critique: "They know no bounds in deeds of evil; they judge not with justice the cause of the fatherless, to make it prosper, and they do not defend the rights of the needy" (Jeremiah 5:28). Judah's shepherds were more like wolves. But not all of them.

Josiah, who ruled from 626 to 609 BC, did justice and righteousness (Jeremiah 22:15). "He judged the cause of the poor and needy; then it was well. Is not this to know Me? declares the LORD" (Jeremiah 22:16). Sadly, Judean kings who followed Josiah ignored people's cries. Jehoahaz (609 BC), Jehoiakim (609–598 BC), Jehoiachin (598 BC), and Zedekiah (598–587 BC) failed miserably.

Jeremiah singles out Jehoiakim, who restored his own palace during a national crisis (Jeremiah 22:13–17) and rejected God's Word (Jeremiah 36). Jehoiakim's death would leave him publicly disgraced. "With the burial of a donkey he shall be buried, dragged and dumped beyond the gates of Jerusalem" (Jeremiah 22:19).

Jehoiachin—like his father Jehoiakim—also falls under prophetic judgment. He and his sons would never again reign in Judah. Calling him Coniah, the prophet writes, "Is this man Coniah a despised, broken pot, a vessel no one cares for? Why are he and his children hurled and cast into a land that they do not know?" (Jeremiah 22:28).

What about Zedekiah, Judah's last king? "The king of Babylon made Mattaniah, Jehoiachin's uncle, king in his place, and changed his name to Zedekiah" (2 Kings 24:17). Zedekiah functioned as an imperial puppet. Yet he still vacillated—paying tribute to Babylon while also conspiring for Judean independence.

Judah's last four shepherd-kings cared nothing for the sheep. They were self-serving. Jeremiah observes, "Therefore thus says the LORD, the God of Israel, concerning the shepherds who care for My people: 'You have scattered My flock and have driven them away, and you have not attended to them. Behold, I will attend to you for your evil deeds, declares the LORD'" (Jeremiah 23:2).

Hurt by Authorities

There are times when authorities hurt us and do great damage. Called to extend justice and compassion, instead leaders use their position to bring us great harm. They act violently and irrationally. What was it for you? An employer? A parent? A teacher? A coach? A professor? For Howard Rutledge, it was a foreign government.

Howard Rutledge was an American fighter pilot during the Vietnam War who was shot down and captured by the North Vietnamese in 1965. They locked Rutledge in a prison in Hanoi, North Vietnam. What was the prison called? "The Hanoi Hilton."

Howard Rutledge was locked in a 6 × 6-foot cell. There were no books, no magazines, and no newspapers. The colors were drab gray and dirt brown. He fought to keep his sanity.

Sometimes life gets really dark when those in power choose to harm us and hurt us. After all, we're just sheep.

Sheep

Jesus asks a question: "What do you think? If a man has a hundred sheep, and one of them has gone astray [*planao*], does he not leave the ninety-nine on the mountains and go in search of the one that went astray [*planao*]?" (Matthew 18:12). The Greek of this verse expects that we say yes. Really? A shepherd leaves the ninety-nine to search for the one? Just one sheep? That's what Jesus says.

Two times in Matthew 18:12 the evangelist employs the Greek verb *planao*. It means "go astray, wander, meander." Ancient Greeks observed that most of the heavenly bodies stay in one place. They called them stars. However, some luminous objects wandered. They went astray. They meandered. The Greeks called those heavenly bodies planets—*planao*. Sheep are like planets. They wander around and get lost in the dark.

Sheep are dumb. Have you ever seen a group of trained sheep in a circus? I don't think so. There are three levels of stupidity. Dumb, dumber, and then there are sheep. If someone says that sheep are as dumb as a brick, they're actually insulting the brick.

Shepherds tell stories about one sheep falling off a cliff and the rest of the flock following over the precipice. In 2005, Turkish shepherds watched in horror as hundreds of sheep followed each other over a massive cliff. More than 400 sheep died, but their bodies cushioned the fall of the additional 1,100 sheep who followed them.

Sheep are dirty. Sheepskin is full of an oil called lanolin. Lanolin coats a sheep's wool so it stays warm in cold weather. Lanolin also makes sheep wool one of the most effective types of glue known to mankind! Every time sheep lie down, grass, dirt, cockleburs, dust—everything imaginable—sticks to their coat. Have you ever seen the southern end of a northbound herd? It's not a pretty sight!

Sheep are defenseless. Sheep can't see very far—less than fifteen yards. Sheep don't know what hit them until it hits them. They have no natural defenses—no claws, no horns, no fangs, not even a stink bag like a skunk. To make matters worse, sheep are top-heavy; their legs are thin and wobbly. Sheep are sitting ducks for ravenous wolves. There will never be an NFL team called the Las Vegas Lambs or the San Antonio Sheep. What would the cheerleaders say? "Fleece 'em! Fleece 'em! Bah, bah, bah!"?

Sheep are distracted. Sheep are distracted by nasal bot flies and warble flies. When tormented by these pests, it's impossible for sheep to lie down and rest. They get up on their feet, stamp their legs, and shake their heads. Sheep become so distracted that even a jackrabbit suddenly bounding from behind a bush can cause an entire flock to freak out and begin a stampede.

Dumb, dirty, defenseless, and distracted. That's us. "Prone to wander, Lord, I feel it; Prone to leave the God I love" (*LSB* 686:3). We wander like planets and get lost in the darkness. But remember what Jesus says: one sheep is worth everything. "And if he finds it, truly, I say to you, he rejoices over it more than over the ninety-nine that never went astray" (Matthew 18:13).

Through Jeremiah, God promises, "I will set shepherds over them who will care for them, and they shall fear no more, nor be dismayed, neither shall any be missing, declares the LORD" (Jeremiah 23:4). Jesus is the most amazing of these God-ordained shepherds.

The Good Shepherd

Like Jeremiah, the prophet Ezekiel was also greatly disappointed in Judah's last four kings—Jehoahaz, Jehoiakim, Jehoiachin, and Zedekiah. Through Ezekiel, God says, "Son of man, prophesy against the shepherds of Israel. . . . The weak you have not strengthened, the sick you have not healed, the injured you have not bound up, the strayed you have not brought back, the lost you have not sought, and with force and harshness you have ruled them" (Ezekiel 34:2, 4).

What will the Lord do? He will take matters into His own hands! God will become Israel's Shepherd. Here is my literal translation of God's announcement in Ezekiel 34:11–15: "Behold, I, I, I will seek. . . . I will search for My sheep. . . . I will search for My sheep. . . . I will rescue. I will bring them. . . . I will gather them. . . . I will bring them. . . . I will shepherd them. . . . I will shepherd them. I Myself will shepherd. . . . I Myself will cause them to lie down." Seventeen references to God in five verses! Sheep need this new shepherd!

His name is Jesus.

From the moment Jesus was born, His enemies—like ravenous wolves—set out to kill Him. They tried to butcher Him in Bethlehem, throw Him off a cliff in Nazareth, and stone Him to death in Jerusalem. Jesus could go forty days without food, then climb into the ring with Satan—the toughest opponent in the universe—and walk away a winner. There was no point in trying to drown Jesus. He walked away from that too—by walking on the water. There was only one thing that could finally kill Jesus. A cross.

A cross! Four times in John 10, Jesus says that He lays down His life for His sheep (John 10:11, 15, 17, 18). Christ's death stands at the center of the fourth Gospel. Let me run some numbers by you. John's Gospel has twenty-one chapters. Palm Sunday is in chapter 12 and Good Friday closes out chapter 19. That's 38 percent of the Gospel pointedly focused on events surrounding Christ laying down His life for the sheep—38 percent!

On Good Friday, there were no green pastures. Rather, spit and blood were caked on Christ's cheeks. There were no quiet waters. There was no water at all. Jesus cried out, "I thirst," as He passed through the valley of the shadow of death. There was no rod or staff for comfort. And the cup overflowed, all right. Jesus drank from the cup of the fury of the wrath of God Almighty. Surely goodness and mercy were twisted and perverted in the most inhumane way.

Like Ezekiel, Jeremiah predicted all of this. "Behold, the days are coming, declares the LORD, when I will raise up for David a righteous Shoot, and He shall reign as king and deal wisely, and shall execute justice and righteousness in the land. In His days Judah will be saved, and Israel will dwell securely. And this is the name by which He will be called: 'The LORD is our righteousness'" (Jeremiah 23:5–6, author's translation). Finally! A shepherd-king like David! Christ is our righteousness. We are covered in His blood.

Jeremiah calls Jesus "a righteous Shoot." "Shoot" also appears as a name for Jesus in Zechariah 3:8; 6:12. And, although Isaiah 11:1 and 53:2 don't employ the specific term "Shoot," they use plant imagery to describe Jesus.

Our Savior's shoot-like beginnings, His humble ministry, and His refusal to exercise divine power led the Jewish elites to conclude that Jesus was the wrong kind of shepherd-king. Jesus associated with the wrong kind of people, preached the wrong kind of sermons, called the wrong kind of followers, carried out the wrong kind of mission, and offered the wrong kind of redemption. It culminated on Good Friday. "And over His head they put the charge against Him, which read, 'This is Jesus, the King of the Jews'" (Matthew 27:37).

The Lord Our Righteousness

I took up jogging when I was in college. By the time I began seminary studies in St. Louis, Missouri, I considered myself a bolt of lightning and faster than a speeding bullet. I carefully screened my opponents, running only with people I was certain I could beat.

The St. Louis seminary had two races every year—the Faster Pastor and the Quicker Vicar. The Faster Pastor was five miles. The Quicker Vicar was a one-mile fun run. While thinking about which race I was best suited for, I met a student who was clearly over fifty—a classic couch potato. The guy told me, "Last year I ran in the Quicker Vicar. I came in tenth." I thought to myself, "If I came in tenth place in a one-mile fun run, I wouldn't tell a soul!"

The next day we went for a run. To make a long story short, the couch-potato guy beat me by at least a hundred yards. After our run I asked him, "You said last year you placed tenth in the Quicker Vicar one-mile fun run?" "Yes, I had a good day." I asked him, "What would have happened if you had run in the Faster Pastor Race?" "Faster Pastor? It would've been ugly. Slice and dice. Murder city!"

I sat there, stunned. How deceived can a guy get? I thought I was Faster Pastor material. But I'd lost to a guy twice my age and twice my weight. What was my problem? I had never objectified my skill level. I didn't have any benchmark to assess how fast I really was. The old, overweight guy was now my benchmark. What did my benchmark tell me? I had vastly overrated myself.

Running isn't the only area in life where we overrate ourselves. We overrate ourselves in the classroom, in the boardroom, in the workout room, and in the weight room. We overrate ourselves in cooking, singing, gardening, tennis, golf—you name it.

But nowhere does our problem of overrating ourselves happen more frequently than in our spiritual lives. Most of us vastly overrate how good we are in God's eyes. Most of us walk around believing that spiritually speaking, we're capable of competing in the Faster Pastor Race when we probably can't even finish the Quicker Vicar one-mile fun run. What do we call this? Moralism. Moralism is overrating ourselves in the spiritual realm.

Moralism is thinking I belong in the Faster Pastor Race. Moralism is thinking I will win the Faster Pastor Race. Moralism says, "I keep my nose clean and I'm right with The Man Upstairs." Moralism says, "Because I'm nice to people, because I pay taxes, and because I don't kick the dog, on Judgment Day I don't need to worry about standing before a holy and righteous God. Rapists, ax murderers, and drug dealers will get theirs on the Last Day. But me? I'll be just fine. Thank you very much!" Who among us hasn't thought, "I'm okay. *Really!*"

Jesus saved His harshest words for moralists. Who were they? The Pharisees and the scribes. Seven times in Matthew 23, Jesus employs the word "woe." That's how Jeremiah 23 begins. "Woe to the shepherds." "Woe" means people are spiritually dead. Jeremiah and Jesus reserved "woe"—their harshest word—for those who were leading sheep astray by thinking too highly of themselves.

After the dust of a heartbreak settles in, it's tempting to begin blaming. We get on our high horse and start pointing the accusing finger. "He said!" "She said!" "They forgot!" "How could they stoop so low!" Playing the blame game insures we lose—we lose the opportunity to learn from our loss. Jesus puts it this way: "Why do you see the speck that is in your brother's eye, but do not notice the log that is in your own eye?" (Matthew 7:3). Though tempting after a crushing disappointment, moralism gets us nowhere.

In a clear rebuff against Zedekiah—whose name means "Yahweh is righteous"—Jeremiah calls Jesus "Yahweh our righteousness" (Jeremiah 23:6, author's translation). Zedekiah had the name. Jesus gives the gift—the gift of righteousness. Jesus frees us from self-righteousness so we rest in His gift of declared righteousness. This is such a wonderful promise that the prophet says it again in Jeremiah 33:14–15. Good things are worth repeating! Note Jeremiah's additional promises of a Shepherd-King:

- "And it shall come to pass in that day, declares the LORD of hosts, that I will break his yoke from off your neck, and I will burst your bonds, and foreigners shall no more make a servant of him. But they shall serve the LORD their God and David their king, whom I will raise up for them." (Jeremiah 30:8–9)

- "Their prince shall be one of themselves; their ruler shall come out from their midst; I will make him draw near, and he shall approach Me, for who would dare of himself to approach Me? declares the LORD." (Jeremiah 30:21)

Jesus is this King-Ruler. He is the Christ, the King, the Son of David. Matthew hammers this point home by citing ten specific Old Testament promises with the words "so that what was spoken might be fulfilled." To make this even clearer, Matthew cites the Old Testament 67 times and alludes to it on more than 250 occasions. Everything promised, predicted, and prophesied in Israel's Scriptures points to Jesus.

People have given more adoration to Jesus, more attention to Jesus, more devotion to Jesus, and more opposition to Jesus than to any other person who has ever lived. People have analyzed, debated, scrutinized, and sifted through every recorded word Jesus ever said. After two thousand years, there is never one minute on earth that millions of people aren't searching the Scriptures to learn more about Jesus. Why? He still leaves the ninety-nine to find one—to find you.

Hope for the future isn't built on our righteousness. Moralism is a dead end. Our hope is built on nothing less, nothing more, and nothing else than Jesus' blood and righteousness. "I dare not trust the sweetest frame, But wholly lean on Jesus' name" (*TLH* 370:1)!

God's Presence with His Sheep

Jeremiah includes the promise in chapter 23 that Jesus, our Good Shepherd, is with us wherever we are. "Do I not fill heaven and earth? declares the LORD" (Jeremiah 23:24).

If we can't see Jesus when we suffer sadness, His promised presence prevails for us through Baptism. If we feel He is too far away when our heart is broken, He invites us to the Supper, saying, "Take, eat My body; take, drink My blood." When we say with Jeremiah, "I sat alone" (Jeremiah 15:17), Christ is our constant companion.

If you're discouraged, there's one thing I can say with complete confidence: Christ is close. Is your heart breaking? Christ is close. Is your life falling apart? Christ is close. Christ isn't an impersonal force. He isn't some far-off, distant power. Christ is a person. He is your Good Shepherd. He is near you when you're brokenhearted and crushed in spirit.

Here is the most accurate translation of Hebrews 13:5: Jesus says, "Never, never, never, never, never will I leave you or forsake you." Howard Rutledge believed that. He prayed for God's presence while imprisoned by the North Vietnamese in the Hanoi Hilton. One day, a glimmer of light dawned through the bottom of his prison door. That was all he needed. From that point, Rutledge knew that God would set him free. And He did!

There's another glimmer of light dawning. Can you see it? It's Easter light. It's Easter deliverance! Jesus is alive, for us. When we're wandering around like lost sheep, He leaves the ninety-nine and runs after us (Luke 15:3–7). When we're confused by the voices of demons and devils, He calls us by name and we know that voice (John 10:3). When we're caught in the web of moralism, He is the Lamb of God who takes away the sins of the world (John 1:29, 36). Jesus is our Good Shepherd, who gathers us in His arms until we're better, holds us until we can live with the hurt, and carries us close to His loving heart forever. Jesus is a Shepherd worth following all our days.

15

OVERCOMING THROUGH SEEING

"Open my eyes, that I may behold wondrous things from Your Torah."

(Psalm 119:18, author's translation)

By 1930, William Randolph Hearst owned more than thirty major American newspapers and had enough money to collect some of the most prized paintings in the world. One day Hearst decided there was one painting he had to have. He hired an agent who searched high and low for months, trying to find it. The agent traveled all over the world, with no success. Finally, he found the painting. Where? He found it in the warehouse of William Randolph Hearst!

You and I have the same problem. We have a much greater treasure—God's promises in His Word—but often we don't realize it. It gets lost in the clutter and chaos of our sorrow. We end up walking around, feeling utterly discouraged.

We need to open our eyes.

Paul writes, "I pray also that the eyes of your heart may be enlightened in order that you may know the hope to which He has called you, the riches of His glorious inheritance in the saints. And His incomparably great power for us who believe" (Ephesians 1:18–19, author's translation). God's power explodes darkness, demons, devils, and death. It's "incomparably great." Here's the problem: we can have the power but not see the power.

Prophets Are Visionaries

Visions are central to the ministry and message of Israel's prophets. The prophets regularly include them in their writings (e.g., Isaiah 6; Ezekiel 1:1; 8:1; 37:1; 40:1). Prophets are sometimes called "seers" (e.g., 1 Samuel 9:9), while several prophetic books begin with the term "vision" (Isaiah 1:1; Obadiah 1:1; Nahum 1:1). Sometimes prophetic visions occur in a series. For example, Jeremiah has two sequential visions (Jeremiah 1:11–13), Amos has five (Amos 7:1–9; 8:1–2; 9:1–4), and Zechariah has eight (Zechariah 1:7–6:15).

Generally speaking, pre-exilic prophets see visions anchored in earthly experiences. Amos describes locusts and a plumb line (Amos 7:1–3, 7–9), while Isaiah sees smoke and fire (Isaiah 6:4–6). Jeremiah looks at an almond tree and a boiling pot (Jeremiah 1:11–16). After the exile, visions aren't connected to mundane things and events. Ezekiel's inaugural vision is anything but ordinary (Ezekiel 1:1–28), and Daniel employs dramatic movement and action, along with complex symbolism (Daniel 7:1–15).

Prophetic visions describe what is real but unseen; what is spiritually true, though unapparent when we look at outward circumstances. Prophets expound upon things that by nature we do not know, we do not understand, and we could never imagine (1 Corinthians 2:9). Yet the Holy Spirit gives us insight to embrace these enduring truths (1 Corinthians 2:10).

Jeremiah's Upside-Down Vision

Upside down. That was my position as I went over a cliff on a mountain bike on July 6, 2008. I was biking with my son, Jonathan. We were in Devil's Den State Park in northwest Arkansas. What an embarrassing place for a pastor to die—Devil's Den!

Upside down. You know the feeling, on a roller coaster, connected to a bungee cord, or when you get unsettling news that flips you head over heels. Jeremiah knew the feeling. God's plan in his book is to capsize, invert, overturn, and upend everything: "to pluck up and to break down, to destroy and to overthrow" (Jeremiah 1:10). The prophet lived and preached in such a way that the monarchy, the temple, the covenant, God's election of Israel, and the gift of the Promised Land were all turned inside out and upside down.

At the heart of Jeremiah's upside-down ministry is his vision in chapter 24. Set in the years immediately following the second Babylonian deportation in 597 BC, Jeremiah goes to the temple and sees two baskets of figs. Good figs are in the first basket. They are plump and juicy, ripe to perfection, the best of the best. Bad figs are in the second basket. They are stinky and smelly, rotten to the core, the worst of the worst.

What does it mean?

"That's easy," you confidently claim. "The good figs are those who managed to avoid the exile. After 597 BC, life continued to function for them quite well. They were still able to move from party to party, from portfolio to portfolio. This group consisted of Zedekiah, the king of Judah, and his high-roller officials. These are Judah's best of the best!"

"And while I'm on a roll," you assert, "the bad figs are those who are part of the Babylonian deportation of 597 BC. This included King Jehoiachin and the prophet Ezekiel. They are stinky and smelly because they are landless, homeless, and futureless. Rotten to the core, these people should expect no mercy from God. These are Judah's worst of the worst!"

How did you arrive at this interpretation?

"Piece of cake," you say; "the land was promised to the patriarchs Abraham, Isaac, and Jacob. Look it up. It's in the Book of Genesis—in spades. Living in the land is a blessing and living outside the land is a curse. That's what Leviticus 26 and Deuteronomy 28 teach. The good figs are in the land. The rotten figs are outside the land. Case closed."

I suggest we buckle up and tighten our helmets because the Lord is about to turn us upside down. "Like these good figs, so I will regard as good the exiles from Judah, whom I have sent away from this place to the land of the Chaldeans" (Jeremiah 24:5). And those who remain in the land? "I will make them a horror to all the kingdoms of the earth, to be a reproach, a byword, a taunt, and a curse in all the places where I shall drive them" (Jeremiah 24:9).

You're aghast—completely beside yourself. "You mean to say that the first have become last and the last have become first? Who came up with that idea? God wouldn't treat the bigwigs, the movers and shakers, Zedekiah and all his officials like that. They are in the land, which means overflowing prosperity, right?" Allow me to point out this verse: "I will send sword, famine, and pestilence upon them, until they shall be utterly destroyed from the land that I gave to them and their fathers" (Jeremiah 24:10).

While it's difficult to see at first, the future belongs to the exiles, not those in the land. Need some examples? Haggai, Zechariah, Zerubbabel, Joshua the high priest, Ezra, and Nehemiah. They all traveled from Babylon to provide the necessary leadership to rebuild Judah and Jerusalem. It's true. "The last will be first" (Matthew 20:16).

Bad Eyesight

Have you ever seen that big *E* on the eye chart? I haven't. My vision is 20/400. That's why I wear contact lenses. When your vision is 20/400, there are no good-looking glasses!

Let's be honest. We all have fuzzy eyesight when it comes to GP. GP? God's Power. Sometimes we're spiritually farsighted. We can see things far away but not up close. "Oh sure," we say. "Someday God's power will explode death. I'll be with the Lord forever. Hallelujah!" But when asked about today, the up-close stuff—bills, budgets, bickering, and all the roadblocks—God's power is fuzzy. It seems like He's only got one firecracker.

Sometimes we're spiritually nearsighted. We can see things near but not far away. Today? Sure, God's got it covered. But the future looks so fuzzy. "God will take care of me now, but when I _____ (fill in the blank with "get older," "retire," "begin a new job," "have no children at home"), then life will get really rough. Poor God, all He has is one teeny, tiny little firecracker."

There's a remarkable story in 2 Kings 6. Elisha and his servants are surrounded by an invading army. A servant asks, "What shall we do?" He saw the circumstances and it looked disastrous. Then this. "'Do not be afraid, for those who are with us are more than those who are with them.' Then Elisha prayed and said, 'O Lord, please open his eyes that he may see.' So the Lord opened the eyes of the young man, and he saw, and behold, the mountain was full of horses and chariots of fire all around Elisha" (2 Kings 6:16–17).

Sometimes we feel surrounded, don't we? Surrounded by impossible circumstances and impossible people. We feel overwhelmed. O Lord, open our eyes that we may see!

Jeremiah's vision of figs gives us 20/20 vision to see GP—God's Power.

Interpreting the Vision

God pledges to regard the exiles as good (Jeremiah 24:5). The Hebrew verb rendered "regard" appears as a causative verb—God is the agent of the verb's action. God causes the exiles to be regarded as good. Those in Babylon are only good because God says they are good. The lowly are raised up. The downtrodden are exalted. Though displaced and shamed, the exiles are Judah's future.

The verb "regard" functions much like "counted" in Genesis 15:6: "[Abram] believed the Lord, and He counted it to him as righteousness." In grace, God regards/counts the bad as good, the unrighteous as righteous, the broken as whole. This decision accents God's mercy, not our merit; His grace, not our goodness. Salvation is God's doing, not ours. Take note of all the first-person references to God in Jeremiah 24:6–7: "I will set . . . I will bring . . . I will build . . . I will plant . . . I will give . . . I am the Lord . . . I will be their God." Against all expectations, God allies Himself with the community of exiles that have no land, no home, and no security.

God chooses exiles in Babylon instead of landed ones in Judah. He chooses the marginalized instead of the established. God is on the side of the powerless. Take, for instance, the matriarchs—Sarah (Genesis 11:30),

Rebekah (Genesis 25:21), and Rachel (Genesis 30:1). At one time, they were all barren. God also sides with state slaves (Exodus 11:7) and David instead of Saul (1 Samuel 16:1–3), and climactically, He vindicates His crucified Son by raising Him from the dead. The first will be last and the last will be first (Mark 10:31; Luke 13:30). The have-nots will become the haves. This world's definitions of power, worth, and value will not endure. Consider these verses:

- "The bows of the mighty are broken, but the feeble bind on strength. Those who were full have hired themselves out for bread, but those who were hungry have ceased to hunger. The barren has borne seven, but she who has many children is forlorn." (1 Samuel 2:4–5)

- "He has brought down the mighty from their thrones and exalted those of humble estate; He has filled the hungry with good things, and the rich He has sent away empty." (Luke 1:52–53)

- "God chose what is foolish in the world to shame the wise; God chose what is weak in the world to shame the strong; God chose what is low and despised in the world, even things that are not, to bring to nothing things that are." (1 Corinthians 1:27–28)

- "God opposes the proud but gives grace to the humble." (James 4:6)

Jesus, Mr. Inversion Himself, chooses fishermen instead of Pharisees, sinners instead of Sadducees, and whores instead of Herodians. Climactically Jesus chooses thorns for His crown instead of silver and gold, and spit and blood instead of sweetness and light. His choices lead to torment and torture, darkness and death. It led to the greatest inversion of all: "Why do you seek the living among the dead? He is not here, but has risen" (Luke 24:5–6). Jesus blew the rock open from the inside. He rolled away the stone. He surged out of the tomb and is still surging into the world to speak these grace-filled words to you: "I will set My eyes on them for good" (Jeremiah 24:6).

God Sets His Eyes on Us

"I Only Have Eyes for You." Harry Warren and Al Dubin composed this song in 1934. Numerous musicians have recorded it, including Peggy Lee, Frank Sinatra, and Art Garfunkel. *Rolling Stone* ranks the Flamingos' version of the song 157th on their list of the 500 Greatest Songs of All Time.

The Lord has His own version of this golden oldie. He only has eyes for exiles. Compare this with what Babylon said to Judean deportees: "You're slaves, prisoners, cogs in our vast and ever-growing political machine!"

Let me take you back to a favorite childhood memory. As a child, one of my rituals every summer was to go to Elitch Gardens in Denver, Colorado. The park had all kinds of rides and enough sticky cotton candy to amaze my little life. What fascinated me most, however, were all the fun house mirrors. Some mirrors would make me look tall and skinny. Others would make me look short and fat. Still others would make me look ugly and creepy. None of them reflected who I really was.

Neither do the mirrors that surround us. Just turn on the TV, surf the net, go to a mall, pick up a magazine. We see perfect people with perfect families and perfect marriages, each spouse with a perfect job. These images seduce us. Then what do we see? We don't measure up. You name it and we don't have it. Addicted to how others see us, we begin feeling tall and skinny, short and fat, ugly and creepy. Add to that our broken marriage, wayward teenager, and terminally ill mother, and these mirrors cause us to feel even more worthless.

When we feel worthless, we not only discount ourselves, we also begin discounting others. You name them, we discount them—spouse, child, colleague, parent, boss. When we feel like nothing, we treat other people like nothing. We sell each other off for cut-rate prices, slashing and burning reputations. Obsessed with what we don't have, we get stuck in the game of gossip, the silent stares, and the jungle of judgment.

Let me write this with the utmost clarity. How we stack up in the eyes of others doesn't reflect our value. Our true value comes from the Lord, who says, "I only have eyes for you." We're prized, priceless, preferred, and precious.

Value is derived from two things. The first is ownership. A car owned by Elvis Presley is worth a lot more than my Mazda Protégé that my three children dented, damaged, dinged, and almost destroyed! I think I sold it for $19.95.

God owns us. He created and claimed us, fashioned and formed us. We are His sons and His daughters through water and the Word. In Holy Baptism, God adopts us to be His children.

Value is also based on how much someone is willing to pay. What is God willing to pay for us? The blood of His Son, Jesus. Christ's sacrificial death on the cross.

I know what you're probably thinking. "Why trust God to place value on me? Just who is this God anyway?" He is the Maker of heaven and earth. Jeremiah presents a robust theology of creation:

- "It is He who made the earth by His power, who established the world by His wisdom, and by His understanding stretched out the heavens." (Jeremiah 10:12)
- "When He utters His voice, there is a tumult of waters in the heavens, and He makes the mist rise from the ends of the earth. He makes lightning for the rain, and He brings forth the wind from His storehouses." (Jeremiah 10:13)
- "He is the one who formed all things." (Jeremiah 10:16)
- "Do I not fill heaven and earth? declares the LORD." (Jeremiah 23:24)
- "Ah, Lord GOD! It is You who have made the heavens and the earth by Your great power and by Your outstretched arm! Nothing is too hard for You." (Jeremiah 32:17)
- "Thus says the LORD who made the earth, the LORD who formed it to establish it—the LORD is His name." (Jeremiah 33:2)

- "It is He who made the earth by His power, who established the world by His wisdom, and by His understanding stretched out the heavens." (Jeremiah 51:15)

This is the God who says, "I only have eyes for you." Who? You! You're what? Valuable, cherished, of infinite worth. Where? Not in the eyes of Babylon. There we are nameless numbers and state-owned statistics. Where are we valuable? Not in our eyes. When our eyes are wide open, we see our duplicity and dishonesty, our sin and our selfishness.

So where are we valuable? God says, "In My eyes!" In God's eyes, we are beloved, forgiven, washed, precious, cleansed, adopted, chosen, called, alive. HIS.

There is more. In the baptismal flood, God claimed you, and on a hill called Calvary, He paid for you with His Son, Jesus. God has more than just eyes for you. He has hands and feet for you, nailed to a cross. He has a head for you, crowned with thorns. He has a side for you, pierced by a spear.

There is still more. God has a heart for you. Jesus says, "As the Father has loved Me, so have I loved you" (John 15:9). God has ears for you too. Jesus says, "Ask, and it will be given to you; seek, and you will find; knock, and it will be opened to you" (Matthew 7:7). And God has body and blood for you. Jesus says, "Given and shed for you for the forgiveness of sins." Jeremiah's vision of figs testifies to this one indisputable fact. God loves these lyrics: "The moon may be high, But I can't see a thing in the sky. I only have eyes for you."

A New Heart

Jeremiah writes, "The heart is deceitful above all things, and desperately sick; who can understand it?" (Jeremiah 17:9). This is one of the most powerful statements regarding human depravity in the Bible. Apart from Jesus, our heart is spiritually dead. Our condition can't be cured. We can't make ourselves alive to God. We can't take stone-cold, lifeless hearts and make them beat with warmth toward God.

God knows. "Can the Ethiopian change his skin or the leopard his spots? Then also you can do good who are accustomed to do evil" (Jeremiah 13:23). The prophet refers to the concept of a stubborn heart eight times in his book (Jeremiah 3:17; 7:24; 9:14; 11:8; 13:10; 16:12; 18:12; 23:17). Thank God. He takes things into His own hands. Jeremiah's vision of figs includes this promise: "I will give them a heart to know that I am the LORD" (Jeremiah 24:7).

When the Bible talks about knowing God, it often uses the word *heart*. Whenever the Bible describes what it means to be a follower of the Lord, what's at the center? Our heart.

- "You shall love the LORD your God with all your heart and with all your soul and with all your might." (Deuteronomy 6:5)
- "Let the words of my mouth and the meditation of my heart be acceptable in Your sight, O LORD." (Psalm 19:14)
- "Trust in the LORD with all your heart." (Proverbs 3:5)
- "Princes persecute me without cause, but my heart stands in awe of Your words." (Psalm 119:161)
- "The aim of our charge is love that issues from a pure heart." (1 Timothy 1:5)
- "Have unity of mind, sympathy, brotherly love, a tender heart." (1 Peter 3:8)

God promises to give us a new heart. He doesn't repair hearts or fix hearts. Forget heart bypass surgery, a stent, a pacemaker, or a valve. If God does that, the old parts will still be there. We need heart transplant surgery.

In 1967, Dr. Christiaan Barnard performed the first heart transplant in South Africa. After the operation, the recipient lived for only eighteen days. The first American to receive a heart transplant was Everett Thomas in May 1968. He lived for nearly seven more months. Today the average patient survives fifteen years. When God gives us a new heart, how long will we live? That would be forever!

Death is our diagnosis. The Lord is our doctor. What is the missing element? A donor. We desperately need a willing donor. When a medical doctor performs a heart transplant, we know that the heart donor died. The donor gave life to another. Where will we get a living, beating heart? Who will it come from?

There's only ever been one Man who didn't suffer with the birth defect of a hard heart. There's only one Man whose heart is kind completely, tender totally, and loving abundantly. That would be Jesus. Only Jesus has a heart that is perfect toward the Father. Only Jesus can replace a broken heart with one that beats for Him and people. Only Jesus offers His heart—free of charge.

Let's say you see your doctor tomorrow and he says, "Here's the bad news: your heart is failing, it's riddled with disease, and you're going to die. Here's the good news: a perfect replacement has just come in. Would you agree to a transplant?" It would be strange to say, "I'll roll the dice and stick with the heart I've got." Why not say, "Doctor, where do I sign? Let's get it done!"

The Doctor is waiting to perform the operation—free of charge. The Donor's heart is available—free of charge. Do you agree with the diagnosis? Would you turn away an offer like that? Who doesn't want to stop feeling like a lifeless corpse? Who doesn't want to stop letting the Gospel ricochet off their heart like BBs off a cement driveway? Who doesn't want to stop being hooked to a spiritual EKG, registering no pulse? A new heart will give us new eyes to see Jesus. I'm signing up. How about you?

16

OVERCOMING THROUGH PERSISTENCE

"Let us run with endurance the race that is set before us."

(Hebrews 12:1)

In 1911, Roald Amundsen led a Norwegian team in a race to the South Pole. Robert Scott directed the contingent from England. Both teams had the same equipment and faced the same elements, yet Amundsen reached the South Pole thirty-four days ahead of Scott. Why the difference?

Amundsen listened to sound advice. Travel fifteen to twenty miles a day. Good weather? Fifteen to twenty miles a day. Bad weather? Fifteen to twenty miles a day. No more. No less. Always fifteen to twenty miles a day.

Scott, by contrast, ignored this counsel. He pushed his team to exhaustion in good weather and stopped in bad. Amundsen won the race without losing a man. Scott lost not only the race but also his life and the lives of most of his contingent. What's the point?

The tortoise always beats the hare.

Have you ever painted over a fence that was peeling and cracking? I have. I said to myself, "It will be so much faster and easier!" But the paint didn't last long. You know why. The old paint wasn't scraped off. Soon I was back where I started—with peeling and cracking! Let me reiterate. The tortoise always beats the hare.

Jeremiah took note. His challenge was about as complex as it gets: the country's demise and destruction.

Jehoiakim's Fourth Year

With Jeremiah 25, we come to the end of the book's first half. Note the links between the chapters 1 and 25: "word(s)" (Jeremiah 1:1, 2, 4, 9, 11, 12, 13; 25:1, 3, 8, 13, 30), "hand" (Jeremiah 1:9; 25:17), "send" (Jeremiah 1:7; 25:4, 16), and "north" (Jeremiah 1:13, 14, 15; 25:9, 26). Chapters 1 and 25 serve as bookends to bracket the first half of Jeremiah, and this makes chapter 25 pivotal.

Jeremiah 25 begins with these words: "The word that came to Jeremiah concerning all the people of Judah, in the fourth year of Jehoiakim the son of Josiah, king of Judah (that was the first year of Nebuchadnezzar king of Babylon), which Jeremiah the prophet spoke to all the people of Judah and all the inhabitants of Jerusalem" (Jeremiah 25:1–2).

The fourth year of Jehoiakim was a time of enormous significance. Hereafter, 605 BC would be indelibly marked upon Israel's memory. That was the year Nebuchadnezzar defeated the Egyptians and Assyrians at the Battle of Carchemish. Everything changed. Mention of this year reappears at other critical junctures in Jeremiah (Jeremiah 36:1; 45:1; 46:2).

We all have a "fourth year of Jehoiakim." We remember the year—and probably the month, day, and time. When she died. When he left. When we got the news. When our world ended.

What was it for you? Did the deal fall through? Did you get a pink slip? Did you run out of money? or patience? or health? or all three? What do we do when our dreams fall apart? and there's no putting them back together? What do you do—what do I do—when our world ends?

Jehoiakim's fourth year was Nebuchadnezzar's first year as king of Babylon. God was beginning His plan to uproot, tear down, destroy, and overthrow (Jeremiah 1:10). Judah would repeatedly be invaded and ravaged by

Babylonian hordes. The temple would be burned to the ground. It would be the end of everything.

The fourth year of Jehoiakim is zero hour. A series of events were about to begin that would bring fear, panic, and death to God's people. Jehoiakim's fourth year marks the end of one world and the beginning of a new one.

23

23. I know. This is poor grammar. My teachers drilled it into me. "Never start a sentence with a number!" They taught me to reword the sentence. Or, they said, if you break the rule, the offense may be mitigated by spelling the number—in this case, "twenty-three." "Twenty-three," though, doesn't capture what I want to communicate. Presenting the number using letters diminishes the impact. I like 23. Digits appear in the first sentence of this paragraph because I want to emphasize a key idea in Jeremiah's life. I want to be unambiguous. 23.

Jeremiah writes, "For twenty-three years, from the thirteenth year of Josiah the son of Amon, king of Judah, to this day, the word of the LORD has come to me, and I have spoken persistently [*ashkame*] to you, but you have not listened" (Jeremiah 25:3). Thirteen years from Josiah's first year in 639 BC puts the beginning of Jeremiah's ministry in 626 BC. Twenty-three years later he sums things up with the word *persistently*—or, in Hebrew, *ashkame*.

Ashkame

The world's toughest ultramarathon is a grueling 544-mile race from Sydney to Melbourne, Australia. In 1983, 150 world-class runners were ready to run. So was a sixty-one-year-old farmer named Cliff Young. On the day of the race, Cliff approached the registration table wearing overalls and galoshes over his work boots. Needless to say, Cliff wasn't a professional runner. He was a potato farmer who also had a few sheep on the side. When Cliff had to round up his sheep, he did so by running.

When the gun went off for the ultramarathon, bystanders mocked

Cliff as he ran in his galoshes and overalls. "What a joke!" The contrast between Cliff and the other runners was a sight to see.

Five days, fifteen hours, and four minutes later, Cliff Young came shuffling across the finish line in Melbourne, winning the ultramarathon! Cliff didn't win by a few seconds, or even a few minutes. The nearest runner was nine hours and fifty-six minutes behind him. How did that happen? Ultramarathon runners run for eighteen hours, then stop and sleep for six. No one told Cliff. He kept shuffling along, day and night, night and day, without stopping. Cliff Young became a national hero. His strategy? "I just run to the finish line."

That's what Jeremiah says as well. When interviewed, the prophet used one Hebrew word to summarize his approach: *ashkame*.

The difference between the right word and the almost right word, said Mark Twain, is the difference between lightning and a lightning bug. A single word, if it's the right word, can, like lightning, illuminate and strike fire all at once. In Jeremiah 25, at the center of the book, the prophet chooses the right word—*ashkame*. Jeremiah likes this word. He uses it eleven times. *Ashkame*. "Persistently." And the night sky lights up!

Keep Getting Up

Walter Payton—nicknamed "Sweetness"—played running back for the Chicago Bears for thirteen years (1975–1987). During his career, Payton rushed for 16,726 yards. That's more than nine miles. What makes that figure even more spectacular? Walter Payton achieved it with someone knocking him down every 4.4 yards.

Jeremiah kept getting knocked down. Jeremiah kept getting back up— mile after mile, day after day. "For twenty-three years . . . the word of the LORD has come to me, and I have spoken persistently [*ashkame*]" (Jeremiah 25:3).

Ashkame is related to the Hebrew word *shechem*. Shechem is an Israelite town in the hill country of Ephraim. *Shechem* also means "shoulder." Then, as words often do, *shechem* developed another meaning. When people embarked on journeys, they loaded their supplies on a donkey's shoulder. The noun *shoulder—shechem—*therefore evolved into a verb that meant "load a donkey's shoulders for the day's journey." In a hot country like Israel, it was important to get in as many miles as possible before sunrise. Eventually, therefore, *ashkame* described the activity of people setting out at dawn with a heavy burden for a long journey. They would only reach their destination if they continued persistently.

For twenty-three years, Jeremiah ran his ultramarathon—preaching and teaching God's Word. God's Word equipped him to overcome mockery, rejection, imprisonment, and many dark nights of the soul. Jeremiah wrestled with stretches of discouragement and thoughts about quitting. "What difference does it make, anyway? Why not adjust to the mediocrities of the age? Why sweat it? I GIVE UP!" Repeatedly, Jeremiah would return to *ashkame* and carry on persistently.

Ashkame has a sunrise in it. People got up early to begin their journey. "My heart is steadfast, O God! I will sing and make melody with all my being! Awake, O harp and lyre! I will awake the dawn!" (Psalm 108:1–2). God's promises, new every morning, empower us for our difficult journey ahead.

- "O LORD, in the morning You hear my voice; in the morning I prepare a sacrifice for You and watch." (Psalm 5:3)
- "I will sing of Your strength; I will sing aloud of Your steadfast love in the morning." (Psalm 59:16)
- "My soul waits for the Lord more than watchmen for the morning, more than watchmen for the morning." (Psalm 130:6)
- "Let me hear in the morning of Your steadfast love, for in You I trust." (Psalm 143:8)

I invite you to redouble your efforts to meet God in His Word every morning. Delight in His promises for you in Jesus Christ. Do this persistently. When you're knocked down, get back up. When people ask you why you keep on keeping on, teach them some Hebrew—*ashkame.*

Rosie Ruiz

In the spring of 1980, Rosie Ruiz won the woman's division of the Boston Marathon. With great acclaim, race officials placed the laurel wreath on her head. What an incredible feat! Rosie won the prestigious Boston marathon! Then the truth came out. Rosie had jumped into the race during the last mile.

We all want to win, but who wants to run? Who wants to keep believing in Christ when they're lonely, angry, and hurt? Who wants to keep praying, worshiping, and communing when they feel like they're on the dark side of the moon? Who really likes persisting for twenty-three years—or more?

I'm not advocating for a bland, dull existence that trudges from one joyless day to the next. We all know people who spend a lifetime in the same profession or the same relationship—and they're slowly diminished in the process. They persist in the sense that they keep doing the same thing over and over again. We don't admire them for it. If anything, we feel sorry for them.

Don't feel sorry for Jeremiah. He wasn't stuck in a rut. He was committed to God's calling. He sought out God's mercies. After twenty-three years, Jeremiah was still spiritually alive and growing because he chose "the one thing needful." Like Mary, Jeremiah sat at God's feet and listened (cf. Luke 10:39). God's Word filled Jeremiah with hope.

Persistent Hope

Jeremiah lived persistently toward God because God first lived persistently toward Jeremiah. "You have neither listened nor inclined your ears to hear, although the LORD persistently [*ashkame*] sent to you all His servants the prophets" (Jeremiah 25:4). The Lord repeatedly sent prophets with messages of hope. For his part, Jeremiah often directed people to place their hope in God.

- "O You hope of Israel, its savior in time of trouble" (Jeremiah 14:8)

- "Are You not He, O LORD our God? We set our hope on You." (Jeremiah 14:22)
- "O LORD, the hope of Israel" (Jeremiah 17:13)
- "Plans . . . to give you a future and a hope" (Jeremiah 29:11)
- "There is hope for your future, declares the LORD." (Jeremiah 31:17)
- "The LORD, the hope of their fathers" (Jeremiah 50:7)

Without hope we wither and die, we flag and finally fail. Biblical hope stays the course even when things appear hopeless. Jeremiah quotes God as saying, "Behold, I will send for all the tribes of the north, declares the LORD, and for Nebuchadnezzar the king of Babylon, My servant, and I will bring them against this land and its inhabitants, and against all these surrounding nations. I will devote them to destruction, and make them a horror, a hissing, and an everlasting desolation" (Jeremiah 25:9). Don't stop with this verse! God continues speaking: "This whole land shall become a ruin and a waste, and these nations shall serve the king of Babylon seventy years" (Jeremiah 25:11).

Do you see the tension between "everlasting" in verse 9 and "seventy years" in verse 11? Which is it? What may appear to look like everlasting isn't forever. "Seventy years" announces that all is not lost. Babylon has a statute of limitations. Babylon has an expiration date. The empire will not last forever. Neither will our pain and suffering. "Why are you cast down, O my soul, and why are you in turmoil within me? Hope in God; for I shall again praise Him, my salvation" (Psalm 42:5). Hope empowers us to persist—*ashkame*.

Stay the Course

I'm like you. I read a book. I hear a sermon. I sing a hymn. I attend a conference or seminar. Then I'm pumped up, fired up, ready to go. "Bring on the Goliaths!"

And then, life.

By reiterating much of Jeremiah 7, chapter 26 moves from the prophet's resolute persistence to life's harsh realities. Jeremiah 26 narrates the prophet's trial (Jeremiah 26:7–16), intervention (Jeremiah 26:17–19), and subsequent rescue—events we aren't privy to in Jeremiah 7. Put another way, chapter 7 records the prophet's sermon, while chapter 26 describes people's response.

Jeremiah 26 unfolds in an alarming way. Before we know it, the prophet has become a victim of mob violence. "The priests and the prophets and all the people laid hold of him, saying, 'You shall die!'" (Jeremiah 26:8). Then, out of the blue, some government leaders say, "This man does not deserve the sentence of death, for he has spoken to us in the name of the LORD our God" (Jeremiah 26:16). Several state officials, along with Ahikam son of Shaphan, stand by Jeremiah's side. An earlier text from Micah vindicates the prophet (Jeremiah 26:16–19) and, for the first time in the book, *and* strategically placed at the beginning of its second half, some people positively respond to Jeremiah's preaching. The tide is turning! Jeremiah is saved from the lynch mob and acquitted of all charges.

Uriah the prophet was not. King Jehoiakim silences Uriah—sending henchmen as far as Egypt to execute him (Jeremiah 26:20–23). The throne was not content to banish Uriah. It could settle for nothing less than execution.

The upshot for Jeremiah? When God is involved, what looks like the end isn't always the end. The prophet knew this—deep within his heart. How else can we describe his calm response to those who would kill him? "But as for me, behold, I am in your hands. Do with me as seems good and right to you" (Jeremiah 26:14).

How do we, like Jeremiah, remain so calm? Take a deep breath. Claim biblical promises. Believe the Gospel. Pray fervently. Remember your Baptism. Worship weekly and receive Christ's very body and blood.

I invite you to close your eyes now and pray. Know that you're a baptized and brave warrior—fighting for what is true and honorable. Trust that you're a decorated soldier in a horrific battle that has a victorious ending. Make this your watchword: *ashkame.*

17

OVERCOMING THROUGH SURRENDER

"In returning and rest you shall be saved;
in quietness and in trust shall be your strength."

(Isaiah 30:15)

A man was on a huge Harley-Davidson motorcycle, waiting for the light to change to green, when an elderly man on a red-and-white bicycle pulled up beside him. The man on the bike commented to the guy on the Harley, "Boy, that's some motorcycle you've got there. Mind if I take a look?" The biker gave him the once-over and snarled, "If it turns your crank, old-timer, go for it." The old man couldn't see very well so he leaned over to look at the Harley. Then he grinned and said, "I bet that motorcycle sure goes fast!"

Just then the light turned green. The biker hit it—hard. Within thirty seconds, he was going 100 miles an hour. Chuckling with satisfaction, he noticed a red-and-white dot in his rearview mirror. It flashed by him so fast he didn't know what it was. It disappeared over the horizon, whipped around, and came right back at him.

The red-and-white dot was the man on the bicycle! After being whip-sawed back and forth, the bike finally crashed into the Harley. Reeling from the collision, the motorcyclist knelt beside the old man and asked, "What can I do for you?" The old man coughed, collected himself, and said, "Please unhook my suspenders from your Harley."

We don't intentionally hook our suspenders to anything dangerous, but we do lean over to get a closer look. The world around us is littered with broken people who only wanted a closer look.

There's the high school basketball star who got his girlfriend pregnant. There's the businessman who cut ethical corners, then got fired. There's the woman who just wouldn't say no to another drink and lost almost everything. There's the busybody who couldn't get enough gossip and slander, and now his social life is in ruins. We've all wanted a closer look at forbidden things. Then what happened? We got hooked to a Harley. The subsequent wreckage and pain became unbearable.

Perhaps that explains your sadness. You hooked yourself to a Harley. Now you're looking up from the wreckage. And as strange as it may seem, you're thinking about doing it again. Getting back into that relationship. Dialing that number. Making that contact. Opening that bottle. Going to that website. How do we refuse getting too close and hooking again to a Harley?

Jeremiah says surrender. That's pretty blunt, I know. Yet that's what Jeremiah says. Surrender or die.

Jeremiah 27–28 describes prophets who would rather die than surrender. Both chapters are set in the same time—the beginning of King Zedekiah's reign in 597 BC. Pharaoh Psammetichus II had also recently ascended to Egypt's throne. A number of Judean officials put two and two together. What did they come up with? "Now is the time to rebel against Babylon and hope that Egypt will come to our rescue. If all goes according to plan, the Babylonians will leave us alone—permanently."

False Prophets

How do I avoid getting my suspenders hooked to a Harley? How do I stay sober? centered? solvent? How do I avoid getting angry and making a mess of everything—again?

Surrender to God's will.

In the context of Jeremiah 27–28, surrender means ignoring false prophets and their false promises. Their sermons sounded something like this: "Don't just sit there! Coax the Egyptians to muster their army against Babylon! If we do it now, we will have peace in our time!"

You may recall the words in that last sentence—"peace in our time." Neville Chamberlain, England's prime minister, said them on September 30, 1938. He had just met with Adolph Hitler. Less than a year later, the Nazis invaded Poland and World War II began.

Fake prophets were idealists, saying, "Peace! Peace!" (Jeremiah 6:14; 8:11). Jeremiah was a realist. The Babylonian menace wasn't going away quickly. A return to normal wasn't on the horizon. Healing wasn't around the next corner. Jeremiah basically said, "Peace will come, but it will come in God's time, not ours. Forget about Egypt."

The prophet's opponents disagreed—vehemently. As puppets of the Judean establishment, they spoke from the perspective of earthly power. Some even prophesied in Baal's name (Jeremiah 2:8; 23:13), while others engaged in adultery (Jeremiah 23:14; 29:23). The masses loved these pseudo-prophets (Jeremiah 5:31), even though they had no word from the Lord. They had not stood in God's council. "For who among them has stood in the council of the LORD to see and to hear His word, or who has paid attention to His word and listened?" (Jeremiah 23:18).

After the second Babylonian deportation, in 597 BC, and with so many looking to Egypt to save the day, Jeremiah puts yoke bars on his shoulders. Foreign envoys then come to Jerusalem—officials from Edom, Moab, Ammon, Tyre, and Sidon. They want Judah to join them, and Egypt, in a revolt against Babylon. Jeremiah points to his yoke bars and delivers God's message to the foreign emissaries.

- "I have given all these lands into the hand of Nebuchadnezzar, the king of Babylon, My servant." (Jeremiah 27:6)

- "To Zedekiah king of Judah I spoke in like manner: 'Bring your necks under the yoke of the king of Babylon, and serve him and his people and live.'" (Jeremiah 27:12)
- "Serve the king of Babylon and live." (Jeremiah 27:17)

Jeremiah wants the people to do nothing, surrender, abandon every form of force. His adversaries couldn't swallow such wimpy wisdom. They repeatedly vow that the Babylonian 597 BC deportation wouldn't last long. With Egypt's help, exiles will be on their way home in a matter of months.

While Jeremiah councils for surrender, he doesn't think Babylonian aggression will go on forever. Note the word "until." "All the nations shall serve [Nebuchadnezzar] and his son and his grandson, until the time of his own land comes" (Jeremiah 27:7). Suffering won't go on and on. There will be an end. "Until." Jeremiah affirms hope, but it won't be quick and it won't be easy.

Hananiah

Another false prophet, named Hananiah, appears in chapter 28. His message is also a call to arms. Judean leaders must form a coalition with Egypt and other nations. Babylon, then, will be wiped off the map. Hananiah's position might be likened to that of the Jewish Zealots during Roman occupation in the first century AD: Draw the sword! Armed resistance is the only way forward. A rebellious uprising will bring a speedy end to the exile.

Hananiah (whose name means "the Lord is gracious") believed God was about to show His grace—in the next two years. Hananiah believed it would soon be the best of times. Jeremiah says, "Add sixty-eight to two and you're in the ballpark. For seventy years, it will be the worst of times."

While false prophets named Ahab and Zedekiah also take an anti-Babylonian stance (Jeremiah 29:21–22), Hananiah is the group's ringleader. Blinded by unfounded optimism and false expectations, Hananiah invites people into his fictitious world. His first speech (Jeremiah 28:2–4) directly contradicts Jeremiah (Jeremiah 27:16–22). Hananiah not only denies a second, more massive dismantling in 587 BC, but glibly says that everything will soon return to normal—the temple's vessels will even be restored (Jeremiah 28:3) and Jehoiachin will again sit on the throne (Jeremiah 28:4). According to Hananiah, there is no need to let go of the old world. Judah's crisis is temporary and, in the long run, inconsequential. After a few more years, life will return to normal. With ringing authority, Hananiah even gives dates and places. "All's well that ends well."

Wouldn't it be great if sorrows could fit into such neat and tidy packages through quick fixes and makeshift measures? Alas, Jeremiah says it won't work. We can't live in La-la Land. The past isn't going to return. Judah won't be renewed anytime soon. "Do not let your prophets and your diviners who are among you deceive you, and do not listen to the dreams that they dream" (Jeremiah 29:8). Jeremiah addresses prophets like Hananiah throughout his book:

- "They have healed the wound of My people lightly, saying, 'Peace, peace,' when there is no peace." (Jeremiah 6:14; 8:11)
- "Where are your prophets who prophesied to you, saying, 'The king of Babylon will not come against you and against this land'?" (Jeremiah 37:19)
- "Do not let your prophets and your diviners who are among you deceive you, and do not listen to the dreams that they dream." (Jeremiah 29:8)

Fake News

I once received this in the mail: "Reed Lessing is the $1,578,000 winner!" I thought, "After all these years, finally! I've struck gold! No more fast-food dinners for me!" Then I looked at the fine print. "To collect, you must return the Grand Prize winning number."

That's deceptive. So were the false prophets of Jeremiah's day. "Do not listen to the words of the prophets who prophesy to you; they are deluding you. They speak visions of their own minds; they keep saying, 'It shall be well with you . . . no calamity shall come upon you'" (Jeremiah 23:16–17, author's translation). Purveyors of religious fantasy always attempt to seduce us into quick solutions. They never work.

The showdown between Jeremiah and Hananiah intensifies. Hananiah rips the yoke bar off Jeremiah's shoulders, then prophesies that that's what the Lord will do to Babylon—and then some. Jeremiah returns with a yoke of iron (Jeremiah 28:13). Imagine that! Iron is a ton heavier than wood—and a million times more difficult to break.

What gives with Hananiah? We all know. He embodies what we all want—a return to the "good old days." None of us wants angst and brokenness to stay. We just want to forget the trauma and pretend it didn't happen. That's why we try to create a more pleasant, comfortable world that conforms to our daydreams. Yet, fabricating a fictive world, no matter how appealing, won't bring healing. Hope involves telling the truth. Hope means letting go of the old. *Hope surrenders to God's plans and God's timing.*

Two Ways

Remember Yogi Berra and all of his Yogisms? "Baseball is 90 percent mental. The other half is physical." "No one goes there nowadays. It's too crowded." "When you come to a fork in the road, take it!" That's not what Robert Frost said. In his poem "The Road Not Taken," he describes two roads and tells us he took the one less traveled.

Jeremiah also invites us to take the road less traveled. It's called "surrender." Jeremiah describes this road. "Thus says the LORD: Behold, I set before you the way of life and the way of death. He who stays in this city shall die by the sword, by famine, and by pestilence, but he who goes out and surrenders to the Chaldeans who are besieging you shall live and shall have his life as a prize of war'" (Jeremiah 21:8–9). These verses invert God's promise through Moses: "See, I have set before you today life and good, death and evil" (Deuteronomy 30:15). For Moses, life is in the land. For Jeremiah, life is surrendering to Babylon and leaving the land. We're not masters of our destiny. We're not captains of our ship. Our best prayer? "Thy will be done."

Sometimes people say, "God won't give you more than you can handle." That's not true. They've misread Paul when he writes, "No temptation has overtaken you that is not common to man. God is faithful, and He will not let you be tempted beyond your ability, but with the temptation He will also provide the way of escape, that you may be able to endure it" (1 Corinthians 10:13). God helps us in times of temptation. That doesn't mean God will never give us more than we can handle. Sometimes He does.

Perhaps that describes you now—you've got more on your plate than you can manage. You've experienced the death of a spouse, then a favorite uncle died, and then you found out that the account is bankrupt. Your heart wasn't broken once but three times. You've survived one round of chemo, but now there are four more. Grief upon grief. It's just too much. The pain is too deep.

Paul knows. "For we do not want you to be unaware, brothers, of the affliction we experienced in Asia. For we were so utterly burdened beyond our strength that we despaired of life itself. Indeed, we felt that we had received the sentence of death. But that was to make us rely not on ourselves but on God who raises the dead" (2 Corinthians 1:8–9). Our Father in heaven gives us more than we can bear so we "rely not on ourselves but on God." Do you see the two ways? Rely on ourselves or on God. It's time to surrender. Give up your need to control. Surrender to the God "who raises the dead."

The Temple Vessels

What we wanted didn't come. What came, we didn't want. We've lost something of great value. The greater the value, the more acute our pain. What was it for you? Did you bury a child? a grandchild? a dream? the love of your life?

Much of the debate between Jeremiah and the false prophets in chapters 27–28 focuses on what Judah lost—the nation's most valuable treasure, her temple's vessels. Nebuchadnezzar confiscated the liturgical accoutrements and carted them off to Babylon in 597 BC. We can't blame people for wanting them back. The sooner the better.

In the tenth century BC, Solomon hired Hiram, king of Tyre, to oversee the creation of these cups, pots, shovels, and basins for God's house. In 705 BC, King Hezekiah displayed the vessels to Babylonian officials. Isaiah's response was swift. The vessels would be taken to Babylon (Isaiah 39). The prophet's words came to pass. Nebuchadnezzar "carried off all the treasures of the house of the Lord and the treasures of the king's house, and cut in pieces all the vessels of gold in the temple of the Lord, which Solomon king of Israel had made, as the Lord had foretold" (2 Kings 24:13). Babylon's king then placed the vessels in his temple in Babylon (2 Kings 25:13–17; Jeremiah 52:17–23). In the ancient Near East, taking a god's liturgical treasures and placing them in another temple was to declare that god's defeat. From Babylon's perspective, Israel's God was a has-been, a loser—never to be seen or heard from again.

No wonder Hananiah and the others pined for the past. They wanted the temple vessels restored. And the Lord, the maker of heaven and earth, was going to do it. Now.

Our Choices

We have three choices when we lose something or someone of great value. First, we can let it *destroy* us. "A tsunami has crushed me and ruined my life. Every day is worse than the day before. All is lost! There is no hope! There is no future!"

Second, we can let it *define* us. For the rest of our lives we relive our heartache—every day. Over time, it defines us. It's who we are, totally, completely, eternally, everlastingly.

Third, we can let it *develop* us. How does that happen? Surrender. Jeremiah doesn't try to solve suffering, explain life's pain, or answer all our questions. Jeremiah does, however, offer this word. *Surrender.* What does that look like?

Surrender with acceptance. Usually, when we communicate bad news to someone, they start shouting, "No! No! It can't be true! I don't believe it!

It can't be! That's impossible!" The first reaction to loss is often "This really isn't happening!"

God helps us surrender. He's almighty. We're not. No matter what the loss is, we need to say, "It's over. It's done." We surrender to what can't be changed. We surrender, however, not as victims. And not with a grudge. We don't surrender with a hard heart. We surrender with acceptance.

Acceptance doesn't mean we stop caring. We still care. *We will always care!* Acceptance doesn't mean we think what happened was good. It wasn't good. It was a nightmare! Acceptance means we can't change it.

What do you need to accept that's over? Maybe it's a relationship. You keep hoping she's going to call. She's not. It's over. Some of us had a dream. It hasn't happened. It's not going to happen. It's over. For some, it's health. It's not coming back. Pain is the new normal. The only way to keep from going crazy in all of this is to surrender with acceptance to our almighty and compassionate God.

Surrender in hope. When we experience a catastrophic loss, it's normal to feel like it's the end. "I'm done. I'm toast. I'm ruined forever." We disappear into sadness. We know—we just *know*—we'll never be happy again. Then, over time, we become numb. We lose our sense of feeling. Suffering turns us into bricks and rocks and stones. We commit emotional suicide. Either that or we self-medicate so our heart won't feel like a million knives are cutting it up.

Legend has it that when someone challenged Ernest Hemingway to write a story in six words, he came up with this: "For sale: Baby shoes, never worn." Isn't that tragic? It's a story about so much hope—"Baby shoes." It's a story about crushed hope—"never worn."

Jeremiah offers something better. While he discourages hope for a quick return of the vessels that Babylon seized when King Jehoiachin was deported (Jeremiah 27:16–22), he does promise that in His time, God will bring the treasures back (Jeremiah 27:22).

God made good on His Word! In 538 BC, the Persian king Cyrus II entrusted his treasurer, Mithredath, to give the vessels to "Sheshbazzar the prince of Judah" (Ezra 1:8). The precious temple vessels are subsequently given to twelve priests—Sherebiah, Hashabiah, and ten of their relatives (Ezra 8:24). Priests ministering in the second temple, dedicated on March 12, 515 BC, would use Solomon's plates, cups, bowls, and the like!

Losing the accoutrements to Babylon, then, was a hiccup. It wasn't a defining moment. "Thus says the LORD of hosts, the God of Israel, concerning the vessels that are left in the house of the LORD, in the house of the king of Judah, and in Jerusalem: They shall be carried to Babylon and remain there until the day when I visit them, declares the LORD. Then I will bring them back and restore them to this place'" (Jeremiah 27:21–22). Restoration!

Like Jeremiah, we can surrender to our present circumstances in hope that they aren't set in stone. Sadness, sorrow, sickness, and suffering will never, ever be the last word. Not for us. Not for the baptized. For us the last word is always restoration!

Raise the White Flag

My happy place is sitting in the stadium of my favorite baseball team— the St. Louis Cardinals. It's a day game in late September. The sun is out, splashing the field with brilliant light. I'm sitting right behind home plate with a root beer in one hand and hot dog in the other. The early autumn air is crisp and clear. The game is about to begin. The crowd is electric. Everything is on the line as we face our archenemy—the North Siders, the Chicago Cubs. I get lost in sights and sounds that take me back to my childhood—the summer of 1969. That was the first time I saw the Cardinals play. It was against the Cincinnati Reds, who had a lineup of all-stars, including future Hall of Fame catcher Johnny Bench.

I was ten years old with my whole life in front of me. I envisioned playing second base someday for the Cards, getting the game-winning hit in the seventh game of the World Series, being cheered on by the crowd and overwhelmed by the media who wanted me to describe it all. Everything would fall into place. Every dream would be realized. Every relationship perfect. Every day splashed with brilliant sunshine and light.

Then what happened? Life! Some events have hurt; other events have crushed us completely. We've become disillusioned and wonder about God's goodness. Should we continue to believe? trust? pray? Wouldn't it be better to take the bull by the horns? forge our own way? take matters into our own hands?

Not if Jeremiah has anything to say about it. His message is consistently clear: Submit and live. Peace comes through surrender. To resist is to die by suicide.

The situation was so dire that Jeremiah actually puts it this way: If the attacking Babylonian army is reduced to the walking wounded, even then they would triumph and end up burning Jerusalem to the ground (Jeremiah 37:10). Some followed Jeremiah's counsel. They raised the white flag. They survived (Jeremiah 38:19–20; 39:9).

The only other option? Fight! Resist! Defy! If you stubbornly refuse to let go and let God, it will lead you to a dead end called stress.

Stress

Stress kills. Literally. Sixty percent of all illnesses and diseases are related to stress. Seventy-five percent of all doctor visits are connected to stress. Thirteen percent of all Americans between ages 18 and 54 suffer from acute stress. That's 19 million people. Forty-four percent of all Americans lose sleep every night because of stress. If you're age 65 or older, your number one health issue is stress. We have a greater chance of having a heart attack, heart disease, or stroke because of stress.

Why are we so stressed? Because we walk around with the world's weight on our shoulders, convinced that if we just work more, exercise more, party more, and make more money, life will work out.

No one likes the word *surrender*. Hananiah didn't. Surrender meant giving in to Babylon. Surrender meant saying, "We lose. You win." Let me ask you this. In a contest between us and God, who's going to win? It makes imminent sense—and it greatly reduces stress—to surrender.

We can't change who our parents are. We can't change what we look like. We can't change when we were born or where were born. We can't change the amount of intellect and skill God gave us. We certainly can't change the past.

Paul knows. He writes, "I have learned the secret of being content in any and every situation, whether well fed or hungry, whether living in plenty or in want. I can do everything through Him who gives me strength" (Philippians 4:12–13, author's translation). Paul didn't write these words while he was on vacation on the French Riviera. Paul was a prisoner in Rome. Through Christ, Paul learned to accept things he couldn't change.

We can also learn how to surrender to God's plans—here it comes, brace yourself—even when we don't understand them. Have you noticed that God doesn't always explain His plans? It only adds to our stress when we start asking, "God, why is this happening? God, why did You allow this?"

Paul should know. He says, "I heard a voice saying to me in Aramaic, 'Saul, Saul, why do you persecute Me? It is hard for you to kick against the goads'" (Acts 26:14, author's translation). Before Saul/Paul met Jesus, his mantra was "I did it my way!" Paul knew exactly how his life should go. He refused to surrender. Paul kicked against the goads.

I know what you're thinking. "What in the world are goads?" Goads were made from wood—blunt on one end and pointed on the other. Farmers used the pointed end to get a stubborn ox to move. When the ox kicked back, the goads would stab his leg. So why kick against the goads? Why fight God's plans? It only hurts us and it hurts the people around us. That increases stress!

The prophet Elisha once met a woman whose husband had died. She had no money and her creditors were knocking on the door, demanding she pay her debts. The widow said to Elisha, "Your servant has nothing" (2 Kings 4:2). When we have nothing, we frantically run around trying to acquire something, anything. Elisha said, "Go outside, borrow vessels from all your neighbors, empty vessels and not too few" (2 Kings 4:3). What kind of financial advice is this? "Empty vessels and not too few"?

The widow doesn't have enough of nothing so Elisha tells her to collect *more* of nothing? Is the prophet insane?

No, he's not. He knows divine math. Nothing plus God equals everything! "As she poured they brought the vessels to her" (2 Kings 4:5). The widow's sons kept bringing empty jars and she kept pouring from her small jar of oil. The oil kept flowing. The widow who had nothing soon had enough oil to pay her debt.

God wants to bring us to nothing. Elisha teaches that. So does Paul. So does Jeremiah. And so does Augustus Toplady. In his hymn "Rock of Ages, Cleft for Me," Toplady includes these words: "Nothing in my hand I bring; Simply to Thy cross I cling" (*LSB* 761:3). When we have nothing we are much more likely to cling to the cross. To trust Jesus. To follow Jesus. To receive and believe in Jesus who surrendered to God's plan perfectly for us. We call that plan Calvary.

When we're stressed out, frantically trying to fix our broken lives, we wonder, "Is Jesus really for someone like me? Does Jesus really love me? Not just on Easter Sunday when my shoes are shined and my clothes are new? How does Jesus feel about me when I snap at anything that moves? when my thoughts are in the gutter? Then how does Jesus feel about me?" I'll let Him tell you. "My grace is sufficient for you, for My power is made perfect in weakness" (2 Corinthians 12:9). What's another word for weakness? Surrender.

Life is like a big aircraft carrier and problems are like circling planes, lining up and waiting to land. We all have at least thirty planes waiting to land right now. Just when one plane lands, number two moves up to the number one position and number three moves up to number two. On and on it goes. You know the drill.

It's high time—in fact, it's past time—for us to give up running the control tower. Instead, let's pray, "Jesus, if it's going to be, it's up to *Thee*!"

18

OVERCOMING THROUGH SHALOM

"Peace I leave with you; My peace I give to you."

(John 14:27)

Have you ever been in a conversation when someone asks, "If you were shipwrecked on a desert island, what book would you most like to have?" The best response to this question is surprising but obvious: "I'd like a book describing how to build a boat." This makes sense, doesn't it? If you're shipwrecked on a desert island, a guide to boat building would help you get back home.

In chapter 29, Jeremiah sends a letter to Judeans who might as well be shipwrecked on a desert island. They were forced to travel seven hundred miles across the Fertile Crescent, leaving their home, temple, and familiar landscape of hills, mountains, and valleys. In Babylon, their new residence, customs were strange, the language was incomprehensible, and the countryside was flat and featureless. All the familiar landmarks were gone. Even the weather was different. It was a whole lot hotter.

Exile is being stuck in a place we didn't choose and a place we don't like.

The Judean exile in Babylon is a dramatic instance of what we all

Overcoming Life's Sorrows

experience. We're in a job, a marriage, a house, a city, and/or a family, and we feel far from home—far away from what we prefer. Often, when the first wave of exilic pain recedes, another one comes, more powerful than the first. It leaves us stuck in the depths of despair. Our settled ways of finding worth and significance have completely vanished. They've gone with the wind.

Judah's Exile

Israel's beginnings in Genesis and Exodus include stories about barren women, landless patriarchs, state slaves, and wandering nomads. Barrenness, homelessness, bondage, and marginality didn't last forever. Under Joshua, Israel entered the Promised Land with great fanfare. Fast-forward almost eight hundred years later and many of God's people left their land shattered, refusing to be comforted—just like Mother Rachel (Jeremiah 31:15).

Exiles were back where their ancestors started—the land of the Tigris and Euphrates Rivers. Judean deportees were slaves, trapped in a prison with no way out. They felt as barren as Sarah, as hopeless as Abraham, and as oppressed as Moses. Abundance and prosperity had turned into departure and displacement. Golden Jerusalem had been exchanged for Babylonian brutality. Optimism was a rare commodity in Babylonian refugee camps. Judeans were desperate for anything that looked like hope.

Jeremiah's Letter

In 2018, a Brooklyn mail carrier was fired because he failed to deliver over seventeen thousand pieces of mail. The carrier, Aleksey Germash, told investigators he "made sure to deliver the important mail." Thank God Jeremiah's letter was delivered to exiles in Babylon! It was certainly important!

Jeremiah 29 begins as follows: "These are the words of the letter that Jeremiah the prophet sent from Jerusalem to the surviving elders of the exiles, and to the priests, the prophets, and all the people, whom

Nebuchadnezzar had taken into exile from Jerusalem to Babylon" (Jeremiah 29:1).

The prophet's letter doesn't promise a quick return to Judah. Instead, it empowers exiles to embrace life where they are—Babylon. Jeremiah saw that during their time of displacement, refugees would be tempted to sit back and do nothing. It would be easy to sit back and watch life happen. That's why Jeremiah's letter urges exiles to unpack their bags, put down roots, affirm the bonds of family, and work toward peace and community building in Babylon. "Seek the peace [shalom] of the city where I have sent you into exile, and pray to the LORD on its behalf, for in its shalom you will find your shalom" (Jeremiah 29:7, author's translation).

God's peace—shalom—doesn't happen when we withdraw. It happens when we embrace life in our place of exile. To have a relationship with God is to have a relationship with where He puts us. We are called to invest in our communities—to build and to plant (cf. Jeremiah 1:10).

Jeremiah sounds like he's got money invested in Babylonian real estate! "Really?" the exiles probably wondered. "We should purchase property and settle down—in Babylon? Jeremiah? Come on!"

Realtors tend to fabricate. "Cozy," the ad will say. It means the house is roughly the size of a one-bedroom apartment. "Needs some touch-up" translates into "bring the bulldozer." But when Jeremiah quotes God as saying "this is your home," we'd best take Him at His word. It's time to stop renting and buy. How important is this? The expression "thus said the LORD" occurs nine times in Jeremiah 29—more frequently than in any other part of the book.

While the new world of exile in Babylon pulsates with anxiety and fear, it also presents unique opportunities. Jeremiah encourages deportees to seize the moment, put down roots, and throw themselves into their new land. Babylon's shalom is their shalom.

Our Exile

Our first exile happened when we exited our mother's womb. Talk about strange and harsh surroundings! Soon after that, we landed in the terrifying and demanding world of school. Once we graduated, we made our way in the world of college, military, or work. After that, some of us moved from our hometown and had to manage life in a new city and state. And we all know the feeling of being used to one set of circumstances when suddenly everything is turned upside down by this sentence: "We're going to move!"

All of these losses trigger an identity crisis. When we're no longer in a relationship, who are we? When we're no longer part of a group, where do we go? When a different season of life descends on us, how do we embrace a new role? When we're thrown a cruel curve, how is it possible to still be ourselves?

It's easy to think that if we were in a different place, with different people, at a different time, things would be better. The thought of going back to more familiar surroundings is compelling. But false dreams interfere with real living. Living in a land of make-believe stymies our healing. We need to give up fantasizing and instead engage in the world as it is.

God Delivers the Mail

We, like Judah's exiles, need Jeremiah's letter. Upon opening and reading it, we realize that it's connected to Jeremiah 27–28, where the prophet warns that the exile will go on for seventy years. The truth begins to sink in. It's time for us to settle in for the long haul. We need to exchange our pipedreams and rose-colored glasses for something better—reality.

Jeremiah describes an alternative to escapism on the one hand and hopelessness on the other. He charts a course that holds to the theme of his book in Jeremiah 1:10—uproot, tear down, destroy, overthrow, build, and plant. Displacement will be long and unavoidable, but not permanent. It's time, therefore, to engage and connect with the community, as isolation only deepens despair.

The prophet sends his letter to a traumatized community who had lost everything—loved ones, homes, and culture. The issue addressed by

Jeremiah's letter is universal: How do we go on after a devastating setback? How should we live when we're where we don't want to be?

For Judean exiles, seventy years in Babylon meant the rest of their lives. The seventy began with Babylon's rise after the Battle of Carchemish in 605 BC and would end with the return of the first exiles in 536 BC. The wise thing to do was to accept the situation for what it was and seek to live a meaningful life in the land of the Tigris and Euphrates Rivers.

It's as though Jeremiah says, "Don't sit around and feel sorry for yourself. The aim of the person of faith is not to be as comfortable as possible, but to live as joyfully as possible. Deal with the reality of life. Discover truth. Create beauty. Live with zest. The only opportunity you have to live by faith is in your present circumstances—this house you live in, this family you find yourself in, this job you have, the weather conditions that prevail at this moment."

No matter how much we want things to be different, things are the way they are. Now the question is, how do we, in these circumstances, live the best possible life? Where do we find spine to seize the day? Where do we find strength to build and plant?

Shalom Comes through Community

When we're where we don't want to be, it's tempting to do nothing and wait it out. Jeremiah counsels against this. He wants us to get involved. "Build houses and live in them; plant gardens and eat their produce. Take wives and have sons and daughters; take wives for your sons, and give your daughters in marriage, that they may bear sons and daughters; multiply there, and do not decrease" (Jeremiah 29:5–6). The exiles weren't camping out in Babylon. This was their home—their permanent home. It was time to dig foundations. Construct walls. Shingle the roof. Decorate the kitchen. Hang pictures. Meet the neighbors. If all we do is pine for the day when things change, we will melt into nothing. Life right now is every bit as valuable as it used to be. Assimilate is the order of the day. *The status quo is the status quo.*

Plant gardens and eat their produce. Enter into the rhythm of the seasons. Become a productive part of society. Get your hands dirty in the soil. Cultivate fruits and vegetables. Discover the local landscape. Walk down to the corner drugstore. Get some new recipes and cook them. Cheer on the local teams. We won't heal if we remain aloof from others.

The fact that Jeremiah references children and one's children's children (Jeremiah 29:6) suggests that exiles had better prepare for the long haul and make the best of their current situation. They're also advised to actively work for the well-being or peace of their newly adopted city—even praying to God for the city to prosper. As immigrant communities throughout the ages have known, if the city prospers, they will prosper. The future hope isn't *out of* Babylon. It's *in* Babylon.

Jeremiah insists we need community. Solomon agrees. "There was a man all alone; he had neither son nor brother and no one from his generation. There was no end to his toil, yet his eyes were not content with his wealth. 'For whom am I toiling,' he asked, 'and why am I depriving myself of enjoyment?' This too is meaningless, a miserable business!" (Ecclesiastes 4:8, author's translation). When we isolate ourselves, life becomes meaningless, a totally miserable business.

Together we have greater success. Solomon continues, "Two are better than one because they have a good return for their work" (Ecclesiastes 4:9, author's translation). We can accomplish much more together than we can alone. Take, for instance, American prisoners during the war in Vietnam. POWs developed what they called a "tap code." They communicated with one another by assigning numbers to words. For example, a tap then a pause and another tap equaled *A*. A tap then a pause and another two taps meant *B*—and so on. POWs who used the tap code to connect with one another had a much higher survival rate than those who didn't.

Together we have greater stamina. Solomon goes on to say, "If one falls down, his friend can help him up" (Ecclesiastes 4:10, author's translation). None of us is made of steel. We all get tired and discouraged. We all fall down. Another person beside us keeps us going when we want to quit. They encourage us when we want to throw in the towel.

Two reporters from *The Wall Street Journal* went on a mission to find the happiest people in America. They found that the most joyful aren't those who spend time, money, and energy getting stuff. Stuff loses its luster. The happiest people in America are people who spend their time, energy, and money increasing their relational capacity. Happy people have friends who help them up when they fall down—and when they get cold.

"If two lie down together, they keep warm" (Ecclesiastes 4:11, author's translation). Several years ago, as they hurried down a Himalayan peak at Mount Everest, a group of American climbers discovered a Sadhu—a holy man from India—lying in the snow, half-frozen and barely alive. The weather was deteriorating rapidly, so two of the climbers wanted to leave the Sadhu and continue down the mountain. The third climber, instead, lifted the Sadhu onto his back and began carrying him. Hours later, the climber carrying the Sadhu came across the frozen corpses of the other two climbers. The combined body heat of the third climber *and* the Sadhu kept them both alive until they arrived at the base camp.

Why are two better than one? We can't keep physically warm by ourselves. We also can't keep spiritually warm by ourselves. When our heart grows cold toward Jesus, when our heart grows cold toward our job or our family, others warm us up. Their presence stokes the fire of our faith.

Why do we think we can overcome sorrow by going it alone? I'll tell you why. Society tells us we are happiest when we're staring at TV screens, computer screens, movie screens, tablet and cell phone screens. Everyone around us says, "Stare at screens! Stay away from people!" Don't believe them. Instead, go to your mailbox. There's a letter in it for you. It's from Jeremiah.

Shalom Comes through Prayer

At the heart of Jeremiah's letter is the encouragement for exiles to pray for the shalom—peace—of the city (Jeremiah 29:7). The key to surviving displacement is to ask God to make Babylon prosperous? This had to be a hard pill to swallow. Ask God to give our enemies success? for their armies to conquer on the battlefield? for their reach to extend farther? for their administrative structure to expand? to forego, for seventy years, aspirations to return to Jerusalem? This was a hard prayer to pray.

Recall what Christ's disciples requested: "Lord, teach us to pray" (Luke 11:1). This is the only time the disciples ask Jesus to teach them anything. They could have asked for instructions on how to multiply bread, still a storm, raise the dead, write a sermon. They didn't. Instead they asked, "Lord, teach us to pray."

Let's face it. Prayer for Babylon—prayer for anything—is difficult. Sometimes when we're praying, our thoughts go hither, then yon, then hither again. Distractions swarm upon us like mosquitoes on a summer night in Minnesota—the land of ten thousand lakes and a bazillion bugs. When praying, we think of a thousand things we need to do, even as we forget the one thing we set out to do—*pray*.

I've got a checkered history with prayer. You probably do as well. We pray hard and petitions aren't granted. We pray long and requests go unanswered. God breaks our hearts. "Why keep knocking on this door? God has ignored me one time too many. I won't let Him do it again!" Would you like to pray more? better? deeper? stronger? with more fire, faith, fervency?

Have you ever had a one-way conversation with someone—you know, one when the other person didn't listen to a single word you said? Let me rephrase that. Have you ever had teenagers in your house? We all know what it feels like to be slighted, ignored, or tuned out.

Just imagine how frustrating it must be for God when He tells us to pray for the shalom of the city and we start asking for stuff that has absolutely no connection to that. We also ignore what the Bible says about God's character. Then we don't ask Him to develop that character in us. We ignore His blessings, so we fail to thank Him. We gloss over sin, so we fail to confess it and repent. We leapfrog over God's commands, so we don't ask Him to help us apply them in our lives. "O God! Teach us to pray!"

Pray like this: "God, I'm pouring out my soul to You. I've been hurt before and don't want to be hurt again. I'm so tempted to become a hermit and isolate myself. But I reject that. I ask You to pour out Your shalom on my new home, my new city, my new relationships. Marshal all your Gospel power to make me a conduit and channel of Your saving shalom. You've done it in my life before. Mercifully, do it again. I ask this in Jesus' name. Amen."

Check out God's answer! "I will be found by you, declares the LORD, and I will restore your fortunes and gather you from all the nations and all the places where I have driven you, declares the LORD, and I will bring you back to the place from which I sent you into exile" (Jeremiah 29:14). Note the dominant use of first-person verbs: "I will be found . . . I will restore . . . I have driven . . . I will bring back . . . I sent." Shalom is anchored in God's promises connected to prayer.

Prayer helps us to face reality head on with resolve and courage, with fortitude and faithfulness. The God who wields all power in heaven and earth marshals that same power for us when we are utterly powerless. He is not absent but findable, faithful, and approachable through prayer.

God's Plans

Shalom doesn't happen through our ingenuity, grit, know-how, toughness, or virtue. It's part of God's plan. "For I know the plans I have for you, declares the LORD, plans for welfare [shalom] and not for evil, to give you a future and a hope" (Jeremiah 29:11). This is Jeremiah's most famous statement. In the first part God literally says, "I Myself know the plans." God knows. We don't. God's in charge. We aren't.

God knows the plan. There's no happenstance in heaven. God doesn't make things up as history unfolds. "Stuff" doesn't happen. Providence happens. And it happens from the God who plans for deep sighs to turn into exuberant singing. Jeremiah 29–33 pulsates with promises of shalom:

- Restored land (Jeremiah 29:14)
- A rebuilt city (Jeremiah 30:18–21)
- A renewed covenant (Jeremiah 31:31–34)
- The gift of forgiveness (Jeremiah 31:34)

- Divine mercy and power (Jeremiah 32:18)
- Health and healing, prosperity and security (Jeremiah 33:6)

Shalom doesn't mean the absence of warfare. It means God's power to renew our lives. The verbal form of shalom appears in Joel 2:25 where God pledges to heal what has been ravaged and broken.

Healing Shalom

When I lived in St. Louis, our attic was filled with a bunch of bent, broken, and busted stuff. My son, Jonathan, asked me to fix GI Joe's head. After years, Joe was still headless. My daughter Abi asked me to fix her bookshelf. Years later, the shelf was still bookless. My other daughter asked me to repair her bike. Little Lori Beth Lessing remained bikeless. What was my strategy? Hide all the torn, tattered, and twisted stuff in the attic. Out of sight, out of mind. Then, presto, after a few years, the whole family would be clueless!

There was one slight, tiny problem with my plan. Occasionally my children went up into the attic. They reminded me again of my inability to be "Mr. Fix-It Dad." In the face of their inquisitions, I was speechless.

Who's behind the mess in our lives? Whose plan is it to clutter the attic of our hearts? Satan. Satan orchestrates much of our brokenness. His lies strip away the Father's baptismal promises, Christ's eucharistic joy, and the Spirit's Gospel power. Satan's deceptions lead us to whisper wicked words, lunge for lustful looks, hate with hard hearts, and go on in godless gossip. The end result is a disheveled life that we hide so everyone remains clueless. In the end, it makes us feel completely hopeless.

Remember the short little ditty about Humpty Dumpty? "Humpty Dumpty sat on a wall. Humpty Dumpty had a great fall. All the king's horses and all the king's men Couldn't put Humpty together again." When was the last time you felt like that? What shattered into a million pieces? Your marriage? Your career? Your health? Your finances? Sometimes the hurt seems bottomless. We feel so hopeless.

God has a gift for you. It's His gift of healing shalom that puts Humpty Dumpty back together again. Jesus, the Prince of Shalom/Peace (Isaiah 9:6), isn't afraid of littered attics. At Jacob's well, He talked with a Samaritan woman who had been married and divorced five times. In Jericho, Jesus met Zacchaeus, whose life was empty in spite of his great power and wealth. Countless other times Jesus fixed torn and tattered people. His goal was singular: put Humpty Dumpty back together again.

To heal us, Jesus had to be paraded outside of Jerusalem to a hill called Calvary, where people were intentionally bent and broken, maimed and mauled, then systematically thrown away. There Satan stalked Jesus, took aim, shot straight, and had Him killed.

Alive on the third day, what did Jesus do? He entered an upper room that was a lot like a messy attic. His disciples were hiding behind locked doors. Peter had denied the Savior. Judas had killed himself. Thomas was so disillusioned that he didn't even show up. What did Jesus say to this ragtag mess? "Where were you when I needed you most? Why did you turn on Me after three years? How could you?" John 20:19 records what Jesus said. In His native Aramaic, it was like this: "*Salam lachem.*" In English, it's "Peace to you."

This peace/shalom is delivered to you in the Holy Supper. That's when Jesus enters our littered attic with His real body and blood to put our Humpty Dumpty lives back together again. After consecrating the bread and wine, the pastor says, "The peace of the Lord be with you." Then we sing, "O Christ, the Lamb of God, who takes away the sins of the world, grant us Your peace." Often pastors dismiss people with the words "Depart in peace." When all have communed, we frequently sing Simeon's Song, "Lord, now let Your servant depart in peace." At the end, we hear these words from the Aaronic Benediction: "The LORD bless you and keep you; the LORD make His face shine upon you and be gracious to you; the LORD turn His face toward you and give you peace [shalom]" (Numbers 6:24–26, author's translation).

Why, then, do we hide all our ugly stuff in our attic? Why do we lock the doors and refuse to let Christ in? Are we too proud? too cynical? too unbelieving? A part of me is too ashamed. Another part is too embarrassed. And still another part of me doesn't think Jesus can really fix my mess.

Even so, Jesus doesn't stop knocking. "I stand at the door and knock" (Revelation 3:20). Open the door. Let Jesus take what is faithless, hopeless, and lifeless and fix you with a shalom that is absolutely fathomless.

All Things New

Exile forces us to make a decision. Will we focus on what is wrong and be overwhelmed? Will we scream, "I want to live where I lived ten years ago! I want to feel like I felt ten years ago! I want to look the way I looked ten years ago!"? We can choose a better way. "God, I'll do my best with what's here. Far more important than the climate of this place, the economy of this place, the people of this place, is the Savior of this place. And the Savior of this place is the Savior of the world."

All of us endure moments, days, months, years of exile. What will we do with them? Complain? Escape into fantasies? Drug ourselves into oblivion? Or build and plant and seek the shalom of the city? Babylon isn't the end. Babylon is a time of waiting. Babylon is an interim. Babylon isn't permanent. Full and final shalom is coming when Christ returns to make all things new. On that day, everything will be restored. He will transform this entire littered attic into a new heavens and new earth. We will live in a shalom that is deathless and categorically endless.

That's God's plan—His great and awesome plan—for people in exile. I can live with that. So can you.

19

OVERCOMING THROUGH THE NEW DAVID

*"Weep no more; behold, the Lion of the tribe of Judah,
the Root of David, has conquered."*

(Revelation 5:5)

Judah's trip over the Babylonian waterfall was certain. Unrepentant idolatry brought the nation to the point of no return. Things came to a head during Manasseh's long reign of terror. "I will make them a horror to all the kingdoms of the earth because of what Manasseh the son of Hezekiah, king of Judah, did in Jerusalem" (Jeremiah 15:4). Who, of all people, announces this judgment? Nebuzaradan, the commander of the Babylonian imperial guard! He says, "The LORD your God decreed this disaster for this place. And now the LORD has brought it about; He has done just as He said He would. All this happened because you people sinned against the LORD and did not listen to Him" (Jeremiah 40:2–3). Nebuzaradan doesn't stop with that. He frees Jeremiah from prison and offers the prophet life in either Babylon or Judah. Better days are on the horizon—for Jeremiah and Judah.

Chapters 30–31 explode with divine deliverance. Jeremiah paints a montage—a piece of art with different perspectives that creates a unified whole. Judah's time of captivity is not the nation's concluding episode. Even though everything is reduced to rubble, demolition and devastation are never God's last words. There will be a second springtime of love, exceeding all expectations! It's almost too good to be true. But this is most certainly true!

What will bring this glorious future to pass? God's dogged fidelity. He plans, promises, initiates, and intends for new life to come from the old. Freedom from Babylon won't happen because of the exiles' determination, resolve, or strength. God does it all.

God Begins Where We Are

Jeremiah 30–31 moves from pain to promise, from exile to homecoming, from captivity to glorious freedom. How strange, then, to see this verse: "For thus says the LORD: 'Your hurt is incurable, and your wound is grievous'" (Jeremiah 30:12).

What's going on? God always begins where we are—full of despair, certain that we're not going to make it. Suddenly and miraculously, though, God says, "For I will restore health to you, and your wounds I will heal, declares the LORD, because they have called you an outcast: 'It is Zion, for whom no one cares!'" (Jeremiah 30:17).

When we think that no one cares, someone cares. God cares! When we think we're utterly beyond healing, there is healing! There is an end—but not a full end! Nothing in the Judahites brings about this change. God decides to restore. God reverses His people's status. Exiles go from crushed and weak to cherished and strong.

God's land promise stands at the beginning of Jeremiah 30–31. "I will bring them back to the land that I gave to their fathers, and they shall take possession of it" (Jeremiah 30:3). The land! The land of promise and the land flowing with milk and honey. The new exodus from Babylon includes restoration to the land of Israel (Jeremiah 24:6; 27:22; 29:10; 30:3), where people will securely dwell (Jeremiah 23:8; 30:3; 32:37).

Yet Jeremiah doesn't promise utopia. He doesn't offer perfect healing or absolute peace and happiness. There will still be the blind and the lame (Jeremiah 31:8) and people who cry (Jeremiah 31:9). The prophet is realistic. Life will get better, but exiles who come home won't experience heaven on earth.

King David

There's a hallway in Florence, Italy, in the Galleria dell'Accademia di Firenze. The corridor is part of a museum and, as you stand in it, you're flanked by four unfinished pieces of stone. An artist was working but stopped in the middle of his work, leaving four undeveloped pieces of marble. The rocks look like they've been cut from the quarry. Yet, emerging from these blocks of stone are the beginnings of people. Some have no faces. Others are missing arms, hands, and feet. People are stuck in stone.

What they once were, rough blocks of marble, is gone. What they will become, beautiful people, has not yet happened. The past is gone and not yet gone. The future is here and not yet here. Things are taking shape, yet the past is still painfully present.

Michelangelo sculpted these marble blocks. He gave them names. The young slave, the bearded slave, the awakening slave, and the old slave. They're prisoners aching for freedom.

Can you picture yourself as one of Michelangelo's marble figures? Can you see the past, painfully present? Some of us have lost our hands; that is, we can no longer hold our children—they've grown up and moved on. Others have lost their mouths; there's no praise of God on their lips—just empty ritual and bland recitation. Still others have lost ears; they can't hear the truth and joy of the Gospel. All they hear is a tape playing in their mind that incessantly reminds them of pain and sorrow. Some have lost eyes; they no longer see God's beauty and promises in Christ. Some have lost faces; their countenance is flat. They feel listless, lifeless, and dead. To some degree, we're all like Michelangelo's slaves—stuck and stranded in stone.

The Galleria dell'Accademia doesn't leave us with these sculptures.

Remember? They're displayed in a hallway, not a closed room. At the end of the hallway stands a work of remarkable beauty—Michelangelo's most famous piece, David.

Michelangelo's David stands, looking fully alive, in perfect freedom. That's God's promise to us. Sure, we still see our past, sorely with us. But the future! It's taking shape. We will stand—just like David—fully alive, in glorious freedom! "They shall serve the LORD their God and David their king, whom I will raise up for them" (Jeremiah 30:9). The Davidic dynasty will rise from the ashes. So shall we.

- "There shall enter by the gates of this city kings and princes who sit on the throne of David." (Jeremiah 17:25)
- "There shall enter the gates of this house kings who sit on the throne of David." (Jeremiah 22:4)
- "Days are coming, declares the LORD, when I will raise up for David a righteous Shoot.'" (Jeremiah 23:5, author's translation)
- "David shall never lack a man to sit on the throne of the house of Israel." (Jeremiah 33:17)

Creation's permanence testifies to God's promises to David. "Thus says the LORD: If you can break My covenant with the day and My covenant with the night, so that day and night will not come at their appointed time, then also My covenant with David My servant may be broken, so that he shall not have a son to reign on his throne" (Jeremiah 33:20–21). The "if" in verse 20 may appear to sound a note of conditionality. Nothing could be further from the truth. The cessation of the heavens and the earth is impossible—it will never happen. Just so, God's promises to David will never cease. The covenant with David is completely reliable. It's fixed. It's irrevocable. It's forever.

- "Your house and your kingdom shall be made sure forever before Me. Your throne shall be established forever." (2 Samuel 7:16)
- "Your name will be magnified forever, saying, 'The LORD of hosts is God over Israel,' and the house of Your servant David will be established before You." (2 Samuel 7:26)

- "For You, O Lord GOD, have spoken, and with Your blessing shall the house of Your servant be blessed forever." (2 Samuel 7:29)
- "Once for all I have sworn by My holiness; I will not lie to David. His offspring shall endure forever." (Psalm 89:35–36)

These promises spoke life into Babylonian exiles whose hearts were haunted by memories of defeat and death for the house of David. In 597 BC, Nebuchadnezzar imprisoned Jehoiachin (2 Kings 24:10–12). Zedekiah, Judah's last king, was captured in 587 BC. Then at Riblah, where Nebuchadnezzar slaughtered his sons, Zedekiah was blinded (2 Kings 25:6–7; Jeremiah 52:10–11). It appeared as though God's promises to David's house were null and void. Yet now God makes an almost-too-good-to-be-true pledge. He will renew His covenant with David to include exiles—weak, weary, and worn-down refugees in Babylon.

David's Son and David's Lord

With high delight we confess that the final and perfect King has arrived—Jesus, David's Son and David's Lord. While Judah's last four kings—Jehoahaz, Jehoiakim, Jehoiachin, and Zedekiah—fizzled and faded, Jesus lives and reigns forever. You do understand, don't you? After Christ's crucifixion, Satan's plan was to keep Jesus, and us, permanently stuck and stranded in stone.

Yet the stone (!) was no match for Jesus! Mary saw Him. As did Peter and John. Even Paul, on the road to Damascus, saw the risen Christ. What God begins, He completes. What looks like death ends in life. What begins with captivity ends in perfect freedom.

While it looks like Michelangelo carved four figures *into* stone, his commentary indicates he was freeing people *from* stone. *This is Jesus.* Using the chisel of His Word, Jesus frees us from despair. Jesus hammers away our rough edges. He reconstructs our hands, ears, eyes, and faces. Jesus brings a brilliant glow through the beauty and power of the Gospel. Exile doesn't signal final defeat and failure. It's where God reshapes us. And one day we will stand before God, like Michelangelo's David, in perfect freedom. How can I be so sure?

I invite you to another place. It's not a museum. It's an altar. It's not a testimony to frustration. It's a meal of salvation. It's where the Master Artist is present to give you His true body and blood. In Holy Communion, God gives us a foretaste of what's coming. He will give back everything He took away.

Jeremiah puts it this way: God will "restore the fortunes of [His] people" (Jeremiah 30:3). God is faithful to the promises He made to the house of David. Exiles will live in the land. They will have more than they need. Their cups will overflow. Do you doubt this? Jeremiah repeats the promise. "Thus says the LORD: Behold, I will restore the fortunes" (Jeremiah 30:18). After bondage, God gives freedom. "Then fear not, O Jacob My servant, declares the LORD, nor be dismayed, O Israel; for behold, I will save you from far away, and your offspring from the land of their captivity. Jacob shall return and have quiet and ease, and none shall make him afraid" (Jeremiah 30:10).

God's freedom is favor and protection (Jeremiah 30:10–11), deliverance from captivity (Jeremiah 30:10–11, 18–21; 31:7–14, 23–25), and a life of abounding joy (Jeremiah 30:18–19). God helps the helpless. God comforts the downtrodden. The promises of Judean kings failed. Babylon's promises failed. God's promises will never fail—ever. They are "Yes" and "Amen" in Christ (2 Corinthians 1:20).

Grace in the Wilderness

"Thus says the LORD: 'The people who survived the sword found grace in the wilderness'" (Jeremiah 31:2). The wilderness is a foreboding place. It's where Sarah banishes Hagar and Ishmael. It's where Israelites wander for forty years. It's where Satan tempts Jesus for forty days.

I once got lost in the wilderness of Joshua Tree National Park. I was hiking with my son, Jonathan. Before I knew it, he turned left and I turned right—and Jonathan had our water. Ugh! For five hours in 100-degree heat, I forged my way through the wilderness. Like Israel, I found grace in the wilderness. My son-in-law, AJ, found me. He not only had an air-conditioned vehicle, but it was full of cool, thirst-quenching water!

Isn't that just like our God? To deliver us from life's deserts and dry places? "Their life shall be like a watered garden, and they shall languish no more" (Jeremiah 31:12). God provides for His people in the wilderness, again.

Again

We've all seen Olympic gymnasts who stumble, lose their balance, and fall. What do they do? Mope? Quit? Throw in the towel? No. They hop back up and get on with their routine. Before we can blink, they're back at it again.

The adverb *again* epitomizes God's resolve. "Again" appears three times in Jeremiah 31:4–5. God says, "Again I will build you. . . . Again you shall adorn yourself. . . . Again you shall plant vineyards." "Again" implies resilience and buoyancy. Rather than quit, God does—*again*. God puts right what has gone wrong. God repairs what has become broken. The joyful sounds gone silent (Jeremiah 7:34; 16:9; 25:10; 33:11) will be heard "again."

The adverb *again* lies at the heart of Holy Baptism. Consider, for instance, when Jesus is talking with Nicodemus about being born again (John 3:3, 7). Just imagine what Nicodemus must have thought. "Born? Again? Say what?" The Savior is saying that we were all passive when we were born. Our mothers did all the work. The same is true for spiritual birth. God does all the work through water and the Spirit (John 3:5).

Water and the Spirit first appear together in Genesis 1:2: "The Spirit of God was hovering over the face of the water." In like manner, the Holy Spirit is present in water when we are baptized in the name of the Father, Son, and Holy Spirit. The Holy Spirit creates life, again.

"Nicodemus said to Him, 'How can these things be?'" (John 3:9). "Start again? Bounce back because you're baptized? Nonsense!" Nicodemus was living in the darkness of rules and regulations. "'You are Israel's teacher,' said Jesus, 'and do you not understand these things?'" (John 3:10, author's translation).

Nicodemus should have understood that the Old Testament is all about starting again. Abraham worshiped the moon. God called him to bless the world. Moses killed a man. God called him to lead His people out of Egypt. Aaron built a golden calf. God called him to be Israel's first high priest. Jeremiah 31:31 promises a new covenant. Ezekiel 36:26 promises a new heart. Lamentations 3:23 says God's mercies are new every morning.

Can God really be that generous? that loving? that giving? Yes. Yes. And yes! In John 3:16, Jesus doesn't say, "Everyone who achieves" or "everyone who succeeds." Jesus says, "Everyone who believes."

Did Nicodemus believe? Did Nicodemus embrace grace? Did he begin, again? John 19:39 tells us that Nicodemus and Joseph of Arimathea prepared Jesus to be buried. *Amazing!* The one who came in the dark finally lived in the light. The one who crept through the shadows came to the cross. The one caught in the clutches of legalism lived in the freedom of God's grace. Nicodemus? He was born—again!

With "again" tucked deeply into his heart, Jeremiah quotes God as saying, "Then shall the young women rejoice in the dance, and the young men and the old shall be merry. I will turn their mourning into joy; I will comfort them, and give them gladness for sorrow" (Jeremiah 31:13). It's time to dance with exuberant joy, again!

Yet

The baptized don't engage in naivete or wishful thinking. We trust a different voice, from a different book—Holy Scripture. The liturgy shapes our language. The creeds provide our reference points. We defy the rulers of this present age as we sing, "The Lamb who was slain has begun His reign" ("This Is the Feast," *LSB*, pp. 155, 172). Life's losses look different to us. Through Holy Baptism, we've been crucified, buried, raised, and seated with Jesus in the heavenly places. And the day is coming, at Christ's second coming, when we will be glorified with Him forever.

Yet we continue to have moments of deep grief and doubt. Time doesn't heal all wounds. Jeremiah says that in this life, we will never completely get over our hurt. "Thus says the LORD: 'A voice is heard in Ramah, lamentation and bitter weeping. Rachel is weeping for her children; she refuses to be comforted for her children, because they are no more'" (Jeremiah 31:15). Rachel is utterly broken. All her children are dead and buried. Overwhelmed with unspeakable sorrow, she's crying her eyes out. Rachel, standing for Judeans, saw Babylon fragment her world into a million pieces.

Why use Rachel as a representative of God's people?

In the Book of Genesis, all three matriarchs were barren at some point in time. Sarah, Rebekah, and Rachel lived through shame and disgrace. For Rachel, though, it was worse. Her sister, Leah, had multiple children. At the end of her rope, Rachel demands of Jacob, her husband, "Give me children, or I shall die!" (Genesis 30:1). She finally gives birth to Joseph. Later Rachel tragically dies giving birth to her second son, Benjamin. Through Jeremiah, we still hear her haunting screams of horror.

This includes the crying in Bethlehem. Sure, Christmas includes singing angels, bewildered shepherds, and humble Magi. But there's also a dark side to Christmas—a monster named Herod the Great. Born into a politically well-connected family in 73 BC, Herod was destined for a life of political hardball. He married ten times and ordered the executions of two wives and three sons. When Herod's father was poisoned by a political opponent, he formed an ingenious plan. Seething with revenge, he invited his father's killers over for a dinner party. As they arrived, Herod ordered them to be slaughtered.

It comes as no surprise, then, that when Jesus was born, Herod ordered the execution of all boys under age 2 in and around Bethlehem. Can you see army boots marching across the manger scene? Rachel is crying again. To describe the lament of these little boys' mothers, Matthew 2:18 quotes from Jeremiah 31:15.

God acknowledges Rachel's unspeakable grief. But He doesn't leave it at that. How could He? "There is hope for your future, declares the LORD, and your children shall come back to their own country" (Jeremiah 31:17). The children, long since considered dead, are very much alive! The inconceivable becomes conceivable. Rachel's deep pain will be replaced with deep joy. Can you imagine? The dead will live again (there's that adverb "again"!) and come home! What a compelling portrait of God's restoring love for all inconsolable Rachels.

None of this depends upon our grit and determination. It all depends upon God's resolute faithfulness and solidarity with His people. Just as Rachel remembers the past with angst, so does God. Two times Jeremiah 31:20 employs intensifying verbal modifiers. God literally says, "I will utterly remember . . . I will utterly have compassion" (author's translation). We don't deny grief, but neither will we allow it to destroy us. "Utterly." It's God's resolve and our certain hope!

Mercy

What about Ephraim—another name Jeremiah employs for the exiles? God disciplined Ephraim because he was like an untrained calf who felt shame and disgrace (Jeremiah 31:18). End of story? Not on your life. God calls Ephraim His "dear son" and His "darling child" and continues, "Therefore My heart yearns for him; I will surely have mercy on him, declares the LORD" (Jeremiah 31:20). The prodigal returns to his loving Father. The dysfunctional family of chapters 2–4 is healed. God who scatters in wrath gathers in love. God doesn't forget His everlasting covenant with creation (Genesis 9:8–17), the patriarchs (Genesis 17:7), or with David (2 Samuel 23:5). The zealous, "jealous God" (Deuteronomy 4:24) is also the God abounding in mercy (Deuteronomy 4:31).

Moses reminds us that mercy is one of God's chief characteristics. "The LORD passed before him and proclaimed, 'The LORD, the LORD, a God merciful and gracious'" (Exodus 34:6). God says this right after Israelites build a golden calf and worship it. We might expect God to throw down the gauntlet, execute justice, and lock Israel in the slammer with no opportunity for parole.

God leads, instead, with mercy. Justice gives us what we deserve. Mercy gives us grace. Justice keeps score. Mercy keeps no record of wrongs. Justice demands full and complete payment. Mercy is kind, tender-hearted, and forgiving. "Mercy triumphs over judgment" (James 2:13).

The Hebrew word for "mercy," *rachum*, is related to the Hebrew word for "womb," *rechem*. Normally a mother's womb is the place where a helpless and utterly dependent child receives deep compassion. That's mercy!

There's more. Mercy allows Judas to betray Him with a kiss. Mercy allows the soldiers to slap Him and spit on Him. Mercy allows Pontius Pilate to sentence Him to the cross. Mercy hangs between heaven and earth for six God-forsaken hours. Mercy has a name. *Jesus!*

God will never cease showing mercy. Even when He wants to end the relationship—to erase Israel from His memory—He can't and He won't. "I have loved you with an everlasting love; therefore I have continued My faithfulness to you" (Jeremiah 31:3).

In the depths of our despair, we see the depths of God's mercy. "Behold, I will bring them from the north country and gather them from the farthest parts of the earth, among them the blind and the lame, the pregnant woman and she who is in labor, together; a great company, they shall return here. With weeping they shall come, and with pleas for mercy I will lead them back, I will make them walk by brooks of water" (Jeremiah 31:8–9). Broken people are made whole. The weak become strong. The joyless are filled with inexpressible gladness. While exile implies displacement, return means the Promise Keeper makes good on all His promises.

There are other voices. You know. You hear them. So do I. What do they say? "Don't you get it? Life is a cosmic accident. It has no meaning. So have fun! And do it now, before you die, because when you die, that's it, forever!" Can this be true? Is this all there is? Not when we know Jesus.

Jesus is more loving, more kind, and more merciful than we ever thought possible. That's because every last bit of God's mercy is packaged and delivered to us in Holy Baptism, the Holy Supper, and the Holy Gospel. We are stuck in stone no more.

20

OVERCOMING THROUGH
THE RENEWED COVENANT

"In speaking of a new covenant, He makes the first one obsolete."

(Hebrews 8:13)

Remodeling an old house presents us with a whole host of challenges—even before you can think about what color to paint the walls or what kind of floor tile to use. Is the foundation in good order? Does the roof leak? Is the wiring up to code? Are the fixtures antiquated, and do they need to be updated?

When people consider these and a boatload of other challenges, I'll tell you what many of them are doing. Instead of investing time and money to remodel, they're choosing to tear down the old and build something new.

Is that what God does when He looks at the mess of our lives? Does He get out dynamite, call in the bulldozers, and blast away? No. God could have said, "I'll make all new things; the old won't do." Instead He says, "I'll make all things new." Our God is a renewing God!

God's Promise

In the most famous section in his book—Jeremiah 31:31–34—the prophet announces that God is a remodeler, not a destroyer. These four verses are the longest Old Testament quote in the New Testament. They appear in Hebrews 8:8–12. The author partially repeats them in Hebrews 10:16–17. Four times, New Testament writers link the "new covenant" with Christ's Holy Supper (Matthew 26:28; Mark 14:24; Luke 22:20; 1 Corinthians 11:25). Although Jeremiah 31:31 is the only place in the Old Testament where the expression "new covenant" appears, synonymous terms include "new heart" and "new spirit" (Ezekiel 11:19; 18:31; 36:26), as well as the word "covenant" when it appears as a promise for the future (Isaiah 42:6; 49:8; 59:21; Hosea 2:18–20).

The Hebrew adjective for *new* can mean something created new, from scratch, or something refreshed and restored that is good as new. The context of Jeremiah 31 suggests that "new covenant" denotes "renewed covenant." We have been baptized into a story of redemption, not replacement. God, the master remodeler, is working to fix what is broken. Mend what is torn. Heal what is sick. Make all things new. Not all new things.

Like prophets before him, Jeremiah envisions the future in terms of the past. Take note of the following features in Jeremiah 31:31–34 (in italics) that relate to earlier parts of the Old Testament:

- *Promise*—God makes a covenant; also with Noah, Abraham, Moses and David.
- *Divine revelation*—God's Word on our hearts; Moses (Deuteronomy 6:6–7; 10:12; 30:6) and David (Psalm 37:31; 40:8) likewise describe this.
- *Fellowship*—"I will be your God." (Exodus 6:7)
- *People*—"I will take you to be My people." (Exodus 6:7)
- *Relationship*—"Know that I am the LORD." (Exodus 6:7)
- *Forgiveness*—Given to Adam and Eve, Cain, Moses, David, and many others.

God doesn't send a wrecking ball. God sends the remodeling crew. God renews earlier promises. He also amplifies and intensifies them. The renewed covenant is the old one, reborn, reaffirmed, and re-inaugurated— in a more profound and intimate way. It may be likened to a marriage.

One of Jeremiah's primary metaphors depicting God's relationship with Israel is that of a husband and a wife: "though I was their husband" (Jeremiah 31:32). The marriage began well (Jeremiah 2:2–3), then deteriorated (Jeremiah 2:5–13), leading God to judge His bride (Jeremiah 13:22–26). The marriage didn't end. There was, however, a separation—we call that the Babylonian exile—for seventy years. Now the relationship is miraculously renewed.

The Renewed Covenant

The United States' "Mothball Fleet" is made up of approximately eighty-nine US Navy ships anchored in various American harbors. In an emergency, these vessels can be readied for action; yet in most cases, over time these ships become useless and out of date. Then they are either dismantled or their parts sold, or they are submerged during weapon testing.

That's what happens when we descend into despair and shame. We place God's promises in mothballs. We put biblical truth on hold. "One of these days, I'll get back to God. One of these days, I'll get back to worship and the Word." Even then, God speaks. God speaks into our deadness— with kindness and compassion—to awaken our faith. The prophet accents God's speaking in Jeremiah 31:31–34. Four times in four verses Jeremiah employs the expression "declares the LORD."

God bases the renewed covenant on His words, not ours. Gospel promises flow from Him, not us. Nowhere in these verses does Jeremiah mention what we do. The plan comes from God's resolution to restore. The renewed covenant begins with God saying, "I will," not "If you."

While most English translations then read "make a new covenant," this is misleading. The Hebrew isn't "make." It's "cut." In the Old Testament, covenants weren't made. People didn't sign their names to paper.

There were no attorneys or notaries public with stamps and seals. There was, however, blood. In the Old Testament, people cut covenants. They killed animals, slit throats, and poured blood. It was a messy business. A more accurate way to render the Hebrew, then, is "I will cut with them a renewed covenant."

A covenant isn't a contract. A contract is legally binding. Break a contract and you could get fined, fired, flogged—or worse. Neither is a covenant a consumer relationship where each side says, "I'm in this as long as you're meeting my needs." In a consumer relationship we say, "I'll be what I should be as long as you are what you should be. And if you aren't? I'm out!" On the other hand, a covenant is an intimate relationship God establishes through blood. God says, "I'll be what I should be, even if you're not what you should be." God goes so far as to say, "Even if I must die, even if I must be cut to pieces, I will still bless you."

How long is God's renewed covenant in place? Let me spell it out for you. F-O-R-E-V-E-R. "I will make with them an everlasting covenant, that I will not turn away from doing good to them" (Jeremiah 32:40). There's no fine print, no factory recall, no revoking the warranty, no bait and switch. The renewed covenant is guaranteed. *Forever.*

The Heart of the Problem

Jeremiah says that Judah's hearts haven't been circumcised (Jeremiah 4:4), that the people have a stubborn heart (Jeremiah 5:23).

The heart of our problem isn't our job, or marriage, or children, or our health. If all our financial problems vanished today, we would still be unfulfilled. If all our political problems went away, we would still be restless. If all our emotional problems, family problems, and health problems were gone, we would still be holding an empty bucket. Every financial, political, social, and psychological problem is the result of our fallen, sinful condition. That's why Jeremiah doesn't promise a renewed economy, a renewed government, or a renewed social plan. He promises a renewed heart—a heart filled with God's Word. "I will put My Torah [law] within them, and

I will write it on their hearts" (Jeremiah 31:33, author's translation).

It happened on a Friday. That's when Jeremiah's renewed covenant was cut. With a lacerated back and open wounds from His head to His feet, Jesus takes a deep breath and speaks these words: "It is finished" (John 19:30). The veil was rent. The blood was poured. The curse was removed. The sacrifice was complete. Death was defeated. Paradise was restored. Now we receive the Father's welcome, a Shepherd's embrace, a Friend's infinite love—and we receive full forgiveness for all our sin.

With this Gospel in our hearts, listening to and following Christ's directions is as natural as breathing. We simply do it. It's our delight. Our sinful inclinations to turn inward, retreat, resist, and recoil evaporate when divine revelation floods our heart. This inward change happens through God's forgiveness. We, the godless, now have godly hearts.

God Forgives Us

The renewed covenant is everlasting because God forgives sin—all our sin. "For I will forgive their iniquity, and I will remember their sin no more" (Jeremiah 31:34). The reason God unleashed the Babylonian Empire on Judah was because the people—and especially the nation's last four kings—lived in unrepentant idolatry. This pushed God to the limit. His response was to unleash Sinaitic covenant curses like those described in Leviticus 26 and Deuteronomy 28.

God's gift of forgiveness, however, will restore His people, take away shame, and enable them to begin anew. Curses do not have the final say. Exile does not have the final say. "I will remember their sin no more." This has the final say! The Hebrew word translated "forgive" only has God as its subject. God alone has the authority to wipe our slate completely clean.

Think about it. Noah got drunk. Abraham lied about Sarah—two times. Jacob was a deceiver. Moses was a murderer. Aaron was an idolater. Rahab was a prostitute. Gideon didn't have a spine. Sampson was a womanizer—remember Delilah? David had an affair and was a murderer. Elijah was suicidal. Jonah ran from God. Job became impatient. And the list goes on.

God forgives people throughout the Old Testament. How? Through the blood of goats and lambs, red heifers and rams. The problem with all these sacrifices is that Israelites had to keep offering them—every day, every week, every year.

Now, in Christ, forgiveness is achieved once and for all—at a hill called Calvary. Jesus says, "I don't remember your sins. You don't have to either. You don't have to live in the past, rehash the past, or be bound to the past." Christ's forgiveness means we don't need more effort, more work, or more sweat and blood. The sweat and blood have already been poured out—by the Savior, on the cross, for you. "He has no need, like those high priests, to offer sacrifices daily, first for His own sins and then for those of the people, since He did this once for all when He offered up Himself" (Hebrews 7:27).

Let's suppose we're driving along a highway and we see a sign that says "Free Pizza!" We look at each other and say, "We've struck Italian gold! Pizza! It's free! And we're famished!" Then we begin asking questions like these:

- Who is the pizza for? Adults? Children? Arm wrestlers from Bulgaria over age 60?

- How long does this offer last? Through the week? month? year? Or is it just on the fifth Friday of every month when a full moon appears on the second Wednesday?

- Where do we get the pizza? Is it delivered? Do we pick it up? Is there a phone number? Where is the restaurant? In the next town? county? city? state? universe?

It's one thing to offer free forgiveness. It's something else to make it available for all people, until the end of time, and deliver it right where they are. Yet that's what Jesus does. His body and blood were broken and shed for everyone. These gifts are available all our days. He delivers the forgiveness of sin through Holy Communion—directly into our mouths. This clear biblical teaching is worth fighting for.

Martin Luther Did

The place was Marburg, Germany. The year was 1529. The event was the Marburg Colloquy, and the debaters were Martin Luther and the Swiss reformer Ulrich Zwingli. The topic? The Lord's Supper. Luther believed in real presence. Zwingli believed in real absence. Then, on October 4, 1529, Luther dramatically stripped the tablecloth from the table where they were sitting and pointed to the Latin words he had earlier written on it. *Hoc est corpus meam.* "This is My body!" Free forgiveness! It's for you, for a lifetime, and it's distributed through Christ's true body and true blood.

Sometimes we say, "I don't feel forgiven." We're emotional creatures. We have feelings. Feelings are fine. Feelings are good. But feelings aren't facts. Do you want the facts? "The Son of Man has authority on earth to forgive sins" (Mark 2:10). All sin. Every kind of sin. Small sin and big sin. Your sin. My sin. Everyone's sin. F-O-R-E-V-E-R.

We Forgive Others

When someone takes our seat at the airport or sings out of tune right behind us in church, it's easy to allow it to fester. With larger disappointments and hurts, though, the pain can go on for months or years. Our entire life can be destroyed by angry memories. Let me write that again. *Our entire life can be destroyed by angry memories.* "How could *he* have done that to *me*?" We respond like Peter. Peter asked Jesus how many times we need to forgive those who wrong us—"As many as seven times?" Jesus corrected Peter. "Seventy-seven times" (Matthew 18:22). Christ's forgiveness extends to all, "from the least of them to the greatest" (Jeremiah 31:34).

So why do we hold on to the hurt? Why do we want people to pay? What is it about getting even, settling the score, and wanting those who crushed us to get a taste of their own medicine? Does it work? bring peace? help us sleep better at night?

Rehearsing resentment is like drinking poison and waiting for the other person to die. It's like shooting yourself and hoping your enemy is hurt by the recoil. Resentment always hurts us more than it hurts the other person. Always.

God has forgiven us *through Jesus.* We forgive others *through Jesus.*

There are five myths when it comes to forgiveness. Here's the first one. "Forgiveness is the result of my emotional healing." In other words, "Once I'm emotionally healed, once I'm on the other side of the hurt—then I'll forgive." That's a myth. Forgiveness is the *beginning* of emotional healing. Do you want to be healed from your hurt? Forgive. Let it go. When I forgive someone who hurt me, I decide I'm not the judge and I'm not the jury. I decide that I'm not going to repay evil for evil. When I forgive someone, I decide I'm going to repay evil with good. It's called taking the high road.

The second myth is this: "Forgiveness means I forget that the pain ever happened. If I haven't forgotten, I haven't forgiven." That's not true. If the hurt is deep enough, in this life, I'll always remember it. When I forgive, though, I don't seek revenge. I don't make her pay. I stop rubbing it in. I refuse to let the pain control the rest of my life.

Ready for the third myth? "If I have a difficult time forgiving, then I haven't really forgiven." Not true. There's a huge difference between finding it hard to forgive and being unwilling to forgive. There's a great divide between trying to forgive someone and looking at them straight in the eye and saying, "I'm going to make you suffer for the rest of your life!"

The fourth myth confuses forgiveness with analysis. Analysis looks back to learn. Forgiveness looks back to leave. Analysis asks, "Why?" Forgiveness releases the "Why?"

Here's the fifth and final myth. "I'll forgive them when they ask for forgiveness." Don't let the offender hold the key to your freedom. Jesus holds that key. He's given it to you. That key is forgiveness.

I need to warn you. Forgiveness isn't an instant solution—not even close. Forgiveness, though, is the only solution. Forgiveness is the door that leads to living again. And forgiveness isn't a matter of ability. It's a matter of faith, trusting that God is the Judge and we're not.

Be on guard! Most of the ground Satan gains is because of our unwillingness to forgive. Once you forgive someone, expect an onslaught of second thoughts. Brace yourself for the need to keep on forgiving, perhaps for the rest of your life.

Knowing God

Jeremiah's renewed covenant includes this gift: "No longer shall each one teach his neighbor and each his brother, saying, 'Know the LORD,' for they shall all know Me, from the least of them to the greatest" (Jeremiah 31:34). There are different kinds of knowing. "I know you on Facebook." "I know you, sort of." "I know you intimately." "I know you inside and out." What's our goal in knowing God? To know God inside and out. This is an ongoing motif in the Book of Jeremiah.

- "Thus says the LORD: 'Let not the wise man boast in his wisdom, let not the mighty man boast in his might, let not the rich man boast in his riches, but let him who boasts boast in this, that he understands and knows Me, that I am the LORD who practices steadfast love, justice, and righteousness in the earth. For in these things I delight, declares the LORD.'" (Jeremiah 9:23–24)
- "[King Josiah] judged the cause of the poor and needy; then it was well. Is not this to know Me? declares the LORD." (Jeremiah 22:16)
- "I will give them a heart to know that I am the LORD, and they shall be My people and I will be their God, for they shall return to Me with their whole heart." (Jeremiah 24:7)

In Jeremiah's pre–587 BC world, priests and the people didn't know God (Jeremiah 2:8; 4:22; 9:3) and the rich and poor didn't understand God's ways (Jeremiah 5:4–5). This lack of knowledge led the nation down the road to destruction. But in the post–587 BC world, people will know—inside and out—the God of Abraham, Isaac, and Jacob.

Jeremiah's promise of intimately knowing God has arrived in Jesus—*now*. Paul puts it this way: "I count everything as loss because of the surpassing worth of knowing Christ Jesus my Lord" (Philippians 3:8). This knowing, though, is only in part. When Jesus reappears, our knowledge will be perfect. "Then I shall know fully, even as I have been fully known" (1 Corinthians 13:12). What a day that will be!

The Renewed Jerusalem

Jeremiah watched the Babylonian army decimate his hometown of Anathoth, his country of Judah, and his nation's capital city, Jerusalem. The whole world crumbled before his very eyes. We know what that looks like. We know what that feels like.

It's painful to see your city break down and collapse. Because my three children live in Fort Collins, Colorado, I go back to my hometown of Denver two or three times a year. Buildings that were new when I was a child are now boarded up or torn down. My teachers are either retired or buried in a cemetery. The old Aladdin Theater on East Colfax, where I first saw *The Sound of Music*, was destroyed in 1984. High school sweethearts are divorced. Our fastest halfback died of cancer. My elementary and junior high schools both went the way of the wrecking ball decades ago.

I wish I could make it all new again. I wish I could go to Panorama Park and play Little League football and baseball again. I wish I could ride my bike to 38th and Wadsworth and buy 1974 Topps baseball cards again. I wish I could walk through the old neighborhood and see the familiar faces. I wish I could walk the halls of Jefferson High School and be eighteen years old again and a senior, with my whole life in front of me. I wish I could make it all new again. But I can't.

God can. And God does. Jeremiah's vision of a renewed covenant is incomplete without a renewed Jerusalem. "Behold, the days are coming, declares the LORD, when the city shall be rebuilt for the LORD" (Jeremiah 31:38). Note the geographical specificity:

- "From the Tower of Hananel to the Corner Gate. And the measuring line shall go out farther, straight to the hill Gareb, and shall then turn to Goah. The whole valley of the dead bodies and the ashes, and all the fields as far as the brook Kidron, to the corner of the Horse Gate toward the east, shall be sacred to the LORD." (Jeremiah 31:38–40)

Here's Jeremiah's bottom line. Our future is more important than our past. Our past? The landscape isn't pretty. Recall the hallways where we shouted and raged; bedrooms where we were blamed and shamed; houses, schools, churches, and offices that hold bitter memories. Our future is infinitely more important than this past. What's our future hold? A perfect city with perfect streets, roads, buildings, and parks. Perfect relationships. Perfect bodies. Perfect bliss and perfect joy—forever.

Six hundred years ago, European sailors feared the western horizon. If ships sailed too far west, they would fall off the edge of the world—and that would be that. On the Pillars of Hercules at the Strait of Gibraltar, Spaniards inscribed three Latin words: *Ne plus ultra*—"Nothing more beyond." Then came Christopher Columbus who sailed the ocean blue in 1492. His discovery of the New World changed everything. Spain acknowledged this on its coins. They came to bear the slogan *plus ultra*—"more beyond."

Plus ultra—"more beyond." A renewed Jerusalem is on the horizon. When Christ comes again, He will finish His remodeling job. We'll walk into the heavenly city. We'll see people waiting for us. We'll hear our name spoken by those who know us. And we'll see the face of the One who would rather die than live without us—*Jesus*. Jesus, who could have said, "I'll make all new things; the old won't do." Instead He says, "I'll make all things new"—even, and especially, you.

21

OVERCOMING THROUGH TAKING RISKS

"I will most gladly spend and be spent."

(2 Corinthians 12:15)

The Book of Jeremiah not only gives us the most thorough account of any Old Testament prophet—in all of his agony—it's also a survivor's guide for exiles living in despair. Jeremiah is for people who realize that sorrows disrupt sleep, eating habits, vacations—everything. The book is for those overwhelmed with shame and disgrace, for those who are trying to reengage in life as best they can. Jeremiah is a road map for people whose lives have been utterly undone.

The prophet puts Babylonian exiles between a death that has already happened and a resurrection in full view. We, too, are in between—living in the "not yet" of God's final victory. In a sense, we live between Good Friday and Easter—a Saturday that has become the longest of all days.

While we wait, what should we do? Relive old hurts? Bide our time? Watch the clock? Hope to die? Binge-watch Netflix? God says invest, take risks, get back in the game. Jeremiah 32 gives us an example of what that looks like. The chapter unfolds as follows:

- Jeremiah 32:1–5—The historical setting.
- Jeremiah 32:6–15—The prophet buys land.
- Jeremiah 32:16–25—The prophet's prayer.
- Jeremiah 32:26–44—God's response to Jeremiah's prayer.

The Setting

Years ago, when two of my children were still at car-seat age, I drove my family home after church. Usually the route was predictable, but that day I chose a different way home. Children love routine so I soon heard them lament, "Daddy, we're going the wrong way." They looked out the minivan windows and, since the roads weren't familiar, it seemed like I didn't know where I was going. It didn't help that I already had established myself as "the lost dad." I had a record of getting lost—at least once a month!

The children's laments grew more intense. I assured them that I knew the way home, but they just cried louder, "DADDY! We're going the wrong way!" Did I know where I was going? This time, I really did! Did my children enjoy the ride home? Not one single bit.

In the first thirty-one chapters of his book, Jeremiah laments that everyone is lost—kings, priests, prophets, and people. He even accuses God of not knowing the right way. All of this changes in Jeremiah 32. We finally see the prophet step up.

The events in Jeremiah 32 are set in Judah's darkest hour, just months before the Babylonians ransacked, pillaged, and destroyed Jerusalem. Nebuchadnezzar, the great Babylonian king, had established his headquarters at Riblah in modern-day Syria. Having destroyed the Judean fortresses at Lachish and Azekah, Nebuchadnezzar's troops began to lay siege to the prize, the jewel, the crown of his military campaign—Jerusalem.

Commercial enterprises were collapsing. Epidemics and diseases were sweeping through the city. Property values were plummeting. Worst of all, God's prediction was horrifically and apocalyptically coming true: "I will make them eat the flesh of their sons and their daughters, and everyone shall eat the flesh of his neighbor in the siege and in the distress" (Jeremiah 19:9).

It's zero hour. Jeremiah is in prison, having been accused of being a Babylonian spy. In the midst of the chaos, God says to Jeremiah, "Buy the field . . . and get witnesses" (Jeremiah 32:25). God wants Jeremiah to persuade a bank to give him a loan when his city is surrounded by the most powerful army on the planet. Will he do it?

Jeremiah is willing to bet the farm. He's willing to go on record as a hoper against hope. He puts his money where his mouth is. Jeremiah trusts God when everything is turning to nothing. The prophet's gamble comes down to these words in verse 25: "Nevertheless, You, You said, Lord God" (author's translation).

Faith lives by adversatives. "However." "But." "On the other hand." "Yet." "In spite of." "Nonetheless." Jeremiah goes against the flow. He acts against the facts. He dares to say "nevertheless." The prophet will buy the field.

The field belongs to Jeremiah's cousin Hanamel, who must have been quite the wheeler-dealer! We can almost hear him say to Jeremiah, "Cousin! Have I got a sweetheart deal for you! This is a once-in-a-lifetime opportunity!" Hanamel wanted to make a shady shekel before Babylon decimated everything.

The field Hanamel is trying to unload is in Jeremiah's hometown of Anathoth, just three miles north of Jerusalem. I'm from Denver and I would leap at the opportunity to have some Mile-High turf, but hometown or not, who wants to invest in this field when the Babylonians are knocking at the door?

I don't have a degree in real estate, but I know there are three things that matter when deciding whether or not to buy property: location, location, location. Hanamel offers Jeremiah land in a war zone. The bottom has fallen out of the housing market. This is hardly the time to purchase property—or purchase anything!

Hanamel's proposed business transaction comports with these words of Moses: "If your brother becomes poor and sells part of his property, then his nearest redeemer shall come and redeem what his brother has sold" (Leviticus 25:25). It was just a matter of days before Judah came under foreign rule. Who *wasn't* poor and downtrodden? Even so, Jeremiah was still obligated to buy the family property.

But it's 588 BC! Every financial investment in Judah's future is hopeless. The Jerusalem stock market is roaring like a bear. Jeremiah had better get some better financial advice or a different real estate agent, or he'll lose his shirt.

"My," we gasp, clutching our bankbooks and billfolds. "I sure wouldn't buy that field in Anathoth. Why, it's not worth a plugged nickel! Get lost, Hanamel! I could lose my shirt!"

When we lose a loved one, a job, our health—whatever—we become paralyzed. We don't want to do anything, think about anything, risk anything. Our response is to play it safe. Don't invest. Don't roll the dice and bet on the slow horse. And whatever we do, don't ever again get involved. It will end in heartbreak, again.

When we have opportunities to invest in new relationships, we say, "I'll remain aloof, disconnected, uninvolved." And so it goes. We might lay down a penny here and a dime there. But we've already been hurt. "Fool me once, shame on you. Fool me twice, shame on me." We've been burned once. Why should we try again?

Buy the field? In Anathoth? When Nebuzaradan—the Babylonian butcher—is ready to enact Nebuchadnezzar's scorched-earth policy? "Jeremiah!" we cry out. "Play it safe! Cousin Hanamel is about to make out like a bandit! Jeremiah! You could lose your shirt!"

The Sale

"I knew that this was the word of the LORD. And I bought the field at Anathoth from Hanamel my cousin, and weighed out the money to him, seventeen shekels of silver" (Jeremiah 32:8–9). What? Jeremiah went through with it? He really bought the field? Well, what else would you expect from someone who buries his underwear and digs it up years later? From someone whose nickname is "Terror on Every Side"? From an unmarried social outcast and an inmate serving time? What else would you expect from someone who is so depressed that he says, "Cursed be the day I was born"? Hanamel probably laughed himself silly all the way to the bank. Take note, though. Jeremiah didn't buy the field on the advice of his broker. He bought his cousin's property by the leading of almighty God.

There's a cash transfer, documents are signed, witnesses are gathered, and the deed is publicly filed. Who shows up to help him? His buddy Baruch.

This is the first mention of Baruch in Jeremiah's book. Baruch's actions here closely resemble those of his brother Seraiah in Jeremiah 51:59–64. Jeremiah connects the brothers to documents that testify to God's promises. Baruch, however, is more than a mere scribal functionary like Seraiah. Baruch publicly aligns himself with Jeremiah and the prophet's message.

As Jeremiah prepares to buy the field, Baruch creates two copies of the purchase documents. God tells him, "Take these deeds, both this sealed deed of purchase and this open deed, and put them in an earthenware vessel, that they may last for a long time" (Jeremiah 32:14). The prophetic sign-act announces that "houses and fields and vineyards shall again be bought in this land" (Jeremiah 32:15). Someday life will return to normal. Why would someone believe that? I'll let Jeremiah answer for you.

- "'The days are coming,' says the LORD, 'when I will raise up to David a righteous Shoot, a King who will reign wisely and do what is just and right in the land. In His days Judah will be saved and Israel will live in safety. This is the name by which He will be called: The LORD is our Righteousness.'" (Jeremiah 23:5–6, author's translation)
- "'For I know the plans I have for you,' says the LORD, 'plans to shalom you and not to harm you, plans to give you hope and a future.'" (Jeremiah 29:11, author's translation)

- "Oh Sovereign LORD, You have made the heavens and earth by Your great power and outstretched arm. Nothing is too hard for You." (Jeremiah 32:17, author's translation)

Buy the field? Invest in the future? Jeremiah says, "You bet." He places all his trust in God's Word. "What You spoke has come to pass" (Jeremiah 32:24). The entire book points to this unmistakable fact. What God has spoken happens—*always.* Recall what God says in the vision of the almond tree: "I am watching over My word to perform it" (Jeremiah 1:12).

One Greater than Jeremiah

Israel's greatest Prophet once made similar outrageous investments. He offered living water to the Samaritan woman, healing to blind Bartimaeus, and resurrection to Lazarus, who was dead. Skeptics said, "What else would you expect from someone reared in Nazareth whose nickname is "Beelzebub" (Lord of the Flies); who is so fixated on His death that He says, 'We are going up to Jerusalem. And the Son of Man will be delivered over to the chief priests and scribes, and they will condemn Him to death' [Matthew 20:18]?" No wonder some equated Jesus with Jeremiah (Matthew 16:14).

Because of His investments, Jesus lost His shirt—literally. "When they had crucified Him, they divided His garments among them by casting lots" (Matthew 27:35). Jesus lost more than just His shirt. He lost His friends in Gethsemane. He lost the skin and muscle off His back at Gabbatha. He lost the presence of His Father at a hill called Golgotha.

Look. Blood and spit are caked on His cheeks. His lips are cracked and swollen. His lungs scream with pain. Stretched nerves threaten to snap as death twangs her morbid melody. Why would someone make an investment and intentionally lose it all? I'll let Jeremiah answer that for you.

- "The LORD appeared to him from far away. I have loved you with an everlasting love." (Jeremiah 31:3)

- "I will cleanse them from all the guilt of their sin against Me, and I will forgive all the guilt of their sin and rebellion against Me." (Jeremiah 33:8)

- "Then shall the young women rejoice in the dance, and the young men and the old shall be merry. I will turn their mourning into joy; I will comfort them, and give them gladness for sorrow." (Jeremiah 31:13)

Let the world know that three days later, what was uprooted and torn down, destroyed and overthrown, was built and planted. There was an open tomb. People saw Jesus alive in Jerusalem, Emmaus, and Galilee. There is life not only beyond Babylon. There is life beyond divorce, beyond relocation, and beyond disease. There is even life beyond death!

We're risky investments—to a person. Yet we've been purchased and won from all sin, from death, and from the power of the devil. God did this, not with gold or Jeremiah's seventeen pieces of silver, but with Christ's holy, precious blood, and with His innocent suffering and death—so we may be His own forever.

Here is a pivotal point in chapter 32. Jeremiah prays, "Ah, Lord God! It is You who have made the heavens and the earth by Your great power and by Your outstretched arm! Nothing is too hard for You" (Jeremiah 32:17). This statement of faith alludes back to Genesis 18:14: "Is anything too hard for the LORD? At the appointed time I will return to you, about this time next year, and Sarah shall have a son" (Genesis 18:14). The God who gave a child to elderly Abraham and barren Sarah is the same God who will finally triumph over Babylon. *Impossible* isn't in God's vocabulary. It need not be in ours.

The Smart Money

Jeremiah 33:10 describes life immediately after Babylon's destruction of Judah in 587 BC. The land is without people, "without man or inhabitant or beast." This sounds like a song that we can't get out of our head. "Without, without, without, without, without."

Even in this bleak situation, the Gospel empowers us to find time and energy for new relationships, to reengage in worship and prayer, to invest again in God's work in the world. Jeremiah says bondage and barrenness—to say nothing of Babylon—will never override divine purposes. The prophet testifies that God's mighty power isn't confined to yesteryear. It continues "to this day" (Jeremiah 32:20, author's translation). Indeed, to our day—today!

"Yet You, O Lord GOD, have said to me, 'Buy the field'" (Jeremiah 32:25). Jeremiah did. He invested. So will we.

22

OVERCOMING THROUGH TENACITY

"I have fought the good fight,
I have finished the race, I have kept the faith."

(2 Timothy 4:7)

The movie *Chariots of Fire* depicts English runner Harold Abrams as he runs against the Scottish champion Eric Liddell. Abrams loses for the first time in his life. The pain of failure is so great that he decides never to run again, stating that if he can't win, there is no sense in running. His girlfriend, Sybil, counters that if he never runs, he will never win.

Failure isn't running and losing. Failure is refusing to run.

We open our eyes in the morning. One thing is certain. We don't feel like running again. Our sleep was too short. We tossed and turned for most of the night, again. Something snaps. Today we give up. We don't want to fight the battle anymore. Our thoughts are spiraling out of control. We hurt. We just hurt so bad because of what we've lost, what we've experienced, what we've been through. The storm passes. We get up and begin the day.

Why even try? We can't turn back the clock. We can't recapture bygone days. Everything's over. Done. Finished. It's all permanent and chiseled in stone.

If you want to stay distressed, look within. If you want to stay defeated, look back. If you want to be distracted, look around. But if you want to get up and run again, look to the scroll. Fix your eyes as Jeremiah did, on God revealed in the words of the enduring scroll.

King Jehoiakim and the Scroll

Paper shredders range in size and price from small and inexpensive units, meant for a few pages, to large machines used by commercial shredding services that cost thousands of dollars. Companies offer all kinds of sizes, makes, and models.

In Jeremiah 36, we meet Mr. Paper Shredder himself—King Jehoiakim. "As Jehudi read three or four columns, [King Jehoiakim] would cut them off with a knife" (Jeremiah 36:23). *J*s are wild. Jehudi is in Judah of Jerusalem in 604 BC, reading the Book of Jeremiah while Jehoiakim shreds it with a knife.

Our paper shredders destroy bills, credit cards, bank statements, and other sensitive documents. Jehudi's knife shreds God's Word. Who in their right mind would cut up and shred God's Word?

Jeremiah 36 begins with a king shredding God's Word. It ends with the Word's resurrection. The chapter starts with these words: "In the fourth year of Jehoiakim" (Jeremiah 36:1). Remember? That's how Jeremiah 25:1 begins. In fact, when we step back and get a bird's-eye view of the book, three major sections—chapters 1–25, 26–36, and 37–45—each end by referencing the fourth year of Jehoiakim. Jehoiakim's fourth year was the first year of King Nebuchadnezzar. It was the year the ancient Near East began to hemorrhage and convulse. The Fertile Crescent was about to experience massive political upheaval. There was a new bully on the block—Babylon.

In Jehoiakim's fourth year—a time of great anxiety—God said to Jeremiah, "Take a scroll and write on it all the words that I have spoken to you against Israel and Judah and all the nations, from the day I spoke to you, from the days of Josiah until today" (Jeremiah 36:2). God wanted His people to listen to the scroll and return to Him. "It may be that the house of Judah will hear all the disaster that I intend to do to them, so that every one may turn from his evil way, and that I may forgive their iniquity and their sin" (Jeremiah 36:3).

Do you see the hope? God says, "It may be . . ." Judahites might repent. They might turn and be forgiven. "It may be . . ." The window isn't shut. The door isn't closed. God welcomes a new beginning. The scroll is God's gift of grace.

Problem. Jeremiah can't read the scroll in Jerusalem's temple. He's been banned from Solomon's house of worship (Jeremiah 36:5). A number of priests and prophets, along with the masses, took Jeremiah to be a Babylonian traitor, worthy of death (Jeremiah 26:8–9). Does that stop Jeremiah? Does anything stop Jeremiah?

Perish the thought! The prophet throws a "Hail Mary." Jeremiah gives his scroll to Baruch, then instructs his scribe to read it in the temple on a day of fasting. "It may be" that people will believe.

About a year later, everything is set. The plan is ready to launch (Jeremiah 36:9). Baruch publicly reveals God's Word. It calls into question Judah's political and military strategies. Leaders are alarmed. Scribes and royal officials request a second reading (Jeremiah 36:15). As the truth begins to sink in, the next step is clear. Jeremiah and Baruch had better hightail it out of the temple and go into hiding (Jeremiah 36:19).

Meanwhile, the unsettling scroll makes its way into the court of Jehoiakim.

The scroll shredder does his work. "As Jehudi read three or four columns, the king would cut them off with a knife and throw them into the fire in the fire pot, until the entire scroll was consumed in the fire that was in the fire pot" (Jeremiah 36:23). Jehoiakim sets in motion an inferno that will engulf Judah and Jerusalem. Jeremiah describes it all, with painful detail, in chapters 37–45.

Some of the government officials named in Jeremiah 36:10–19, 25 are members of the same family that brought a biblical scroll to King Josiah in 622 BC (2 Kings 22–23). Shaphan is the most prominent leader to appear in both narratives. During Josiah's reign, Shaphan takes a scroll that was found during the temple's restoration and gives it to the king. Josiah repents and leads others to turn to God. Shaphan is again present during Jehoiakim's destruction of the scroll. What are we to make of these connections between Shaphan, the two kings, and their scrolls? Josiah is humble. Jehoiakim is proud. Josiah hears. Jehoiakim destroys. Josiah believes. Jehoiakim would rather burn than turn.

In Jeremiah 36:23, Jehoiakim *cuts* the scroll. With this verb, Jeremiah further contrasts Josiah with Jehoiakim. When Josiah heard God's scroll, he *cut* his garments in an act of repentance (2 Kings 22:11). Meanwhile, Jehoiakim *cuts* the scroll with great arrogance.

Whatever the cost, whatever the compromise, Jehoiakim orders the scroll's message to be muted, its dreams deadened, its promises explained away. The contrast between Jehoiakim and Josiah couldn't be any sharper.

It appears as though Jehoiakim has won the day. Appears. That's the key word. Jehoiakim appears to be autonomous. He appears to be the one calling the shots. Without the scroll, Jehoiakim can order life any way he wants. There is, however, a concluding scene in the narrative (Jeremiah 36:27–32). God continues to make scrolls.

More Paper Shredders

What got into Jehoiakim that he shredded God's Word? You know. So do I. This is the work of *the* paper shredder. We don't know him by that name, though. Instead, we know him by names like liar, deceiver, destroyer, serpent, and Satan. The devil.

The Greek word for "devil" is *diabolos*. *Diabolos* comes from the Greek verb *diaballein*, which means "to split." The devil is a splitter, a divider, a wedge driver. The *diabolos* divided Adam from Eve, Jacob from Esau, Absalom from David. And the *diabolos* divided Judas from Jesus. The *diabolos* divides spouses, families, friends, and churches. He isn't a comic book character with horns, a tail, and a pitchfork. The devil isn't a figment of our imagination or a throwback to more ignorant and unenlightened times.

Satan is real and his strategy is singular. He doesn't want us to have delight in God's Word, power in God's Word, hope in God's Word, life in God's Word, or forgiveness in God's Word. Satan shreds God's Word every chance he gets. Want some proof? A George Barna survey of *Christians* found these stunning results:

- 58 percent didn't know who preached the Sermon on the Mount.
- 52 percent didn't know that the Book of Jonah *is* in the Bible.
- 70 percent didn't know that "God helps those who help themselves" is *not* in the Bible.
- 15 percent agreed that the Gospels are Matthew, Mark, *Luther*, and John.

Why does Satan shred God's Word? So he can shred our lives. Satan meets us in the morning and says, "This day is hopeless. Go back to bed." He sees us in the bathroom and says, "You're ugly. How could anyone love you?" At the end of the day, he says, "You're a sorry excuse for a Christian. God is finished with you!" When we don't have God's Word in our head and heart, Satan chews us up and spits us out.

The devil has allies—more fallen angels called "demons." The Bible speaks about them more than a hundred times. It calls them evil and unclean spirits, rulers, authorities, powers, dominions, thrones, and leaders. This may sound like science fiction to you, but it's all very real.

Martin Luther knows. He writes in his hymn "A Mighty Fortress Is Our God," "The old evil foe Now means deadly woe; Deep guile and great might Are his dread arms in fight; On earth is not his equal" (*LSB* 656:1). To fight back, Luther embraced God's Word—full throttle.

Enter *another* paper shredder—the Medieval Roman Catholic Church. In 1517, an archbishop named Albert of Brandenburg set out to silence Luther. The archbishop was selling indulgences to pay his debt to the pope. The pope taught that indulgences—pieces of paper signed by the Church and purchased by people—lessened time in purgatory. Luther's Ninety-Five Theses taught that indulgences were wrong. And because people began believing Luther instead of the Church, Albert was out big bucks. God's Word must be shredded.

Then, in July 1519, a debate took place in Leipzig, Germany. John Eck upheld Rome's position—that people are saved in part by what they do. Luther wouldn't budge. Salvation was by grace alone, through faith alone, for Christ's sake alone. After the debate, Pope Leo X excommunicated the reformer. The document began with words from Psalm 80:13: "Arise, O Lord, a wild boar has invaded Your vineyard." God's Word must be silenced and shredded!

It came to a head at an imperial assembly in Worms, Germany. On April 17, 1521, the Roman Catholic Church ordered Luther to recant. He asked for an evening to pray about it. Then, on April 18, 1521, the reformer announced, "My conscience is captive to the Word of God. I cannot and will not recant. Here I stand."

Luther's tenacity came from the Bible's central teaching—Christ crucified for sinners. Christ's death on the cross means the Gospel promises given in Jeremiah are now freely yours. Christ is your substitute. Christ is your righteousness. Christ loves you with an everlasting love. He will never let you go.

The Scroll Shredder

On Good Friday, Pontius Pilate gave Jesus over to professional shredders. They ripped and removed skin from the Savior's back, preparing Him for the biggest, most industrial-grade shredder of the day. What was that called? *Mors turpissima crucis*—that's Latin for what Rome called its shredder: "the utterly vile death on a cross." Jesus was crucified, dead, and buried. Could this be the end? Take a look at this: "Then Jeremiah took another scroll and gave it to Baruch . . . who wrote on it at the dictation of Jeremiah all the words of the scroll that Jehoiakim king of Judah had [shredded and] burned in the fire. And many similar words were added to them" (Jeremiah 36:32).

Jeremiah's resurrected scroll previews another resurrected Scroll— and then some. Christ Jesus, the Word made flesh, rose again. Death has no more dominion over Him! Silent for three days, the Scroll speaks! "Do not be afraid; go and tell My brothers to go to Galilee, and there they will see Me" (Matthew 28:10). Death has no power over Him. Christ is unshredable!

Those who heard the living Word were beside themselves. Mary cried out, "Rabboni!" The Emmaus disciples exclaimed, "Did not our hearts burn within us while He talked to us on the road?" Then Thomas confessed, "My Lord and my God!"

Let me repeat the last line from Jeremiah 36:32. "And many similar words were added to them." It's as though Jeremiah says, "Mess with my sermon and the next time I'll add to it!" The resurrected scroll puts Jehoiakim on the alert. His days are numbered. Divine judgment is imminent. Jeremiah will resurrect as many scrolls as it takes. Jehoiakim's gag order fails. God's Word prevails!

Alive with the life of Jesus and the breath of the Holy Spirit, the Holy Bible is the living voice of the Gospel. For you, right now, it announces forgiveness for every sin, showers you with grace, and instills in you tenacity to hold on and carry on. God's Word announces weakness is power, loss is gain, and servanthood is greatness. Wherever God's Word is preached, studied, read, and memorized, it is victorious over every satanic force.

"The word of the Lord remains forever" (1 Peter 1:25). The Latin of this verse is *Verbum Domini Manet in Aeternum*, which is summarized with the letters *VDMA*. Luther and his followers sewed "VDMA" on their coat sleeves and cloaks. Today we place "VDMA" deep in our hearts. To all paper shredders, we boldly confess, "*Verbum Domini Manet in Aeternum.* The Word of the Lord endures forever!"

Throughout chapter 36, leaders and officials ignore and reject Jeremiah. They hate him and despise him. Through it all, Jeremiah endures. "And the king commanded Jerahmeel the king's son and Seraiah the son of Azriel and Shelemiah the son of Abdeel to seize Baruch the secretary and Jeremiah the prophet, but the LORD hid them" (Jeremiah 36:26). Jeremiah and Baruch survive. With the same God and same divine Word, so shall we.

Whoever

I smell a beautiful fragrance coming from my mother's kitchen. It's chocolate chip cookies! I follow the smell until I'm standing over a pan of pure chocolate pleasure. I have learned to wait until my mom gives the green light. Salivating on my shirt, I ask, "Who are they for?" My mom might break my heart and say, "Reed, they're for someone down the block. Don't touch them!" Or "They're for a friend. Stay away!" Or, or, she just might say, "Reed, they're for whoever!" And since I qualify as a whoever, I dig in! Whoevers are always welcome!

Whoever implies *whenever*. Whenever! It's never too late to trust and follow God's Word. *Whoever* also means *however*. However broken you are, however messed-up you feel, God loves you. *Whoever* also means *wherever*. Wherever you are—in a pit, in a pinch, or in a pickle—wherever you are, you're not too far from God's redeeming love.

We lose so much, don't we? We lose jobs and opportunities. We lose friendship and love. We lose hopes and dreams. We lose so much in life, but we will never, ever lose our place on God's "whoever" list. "I am the light of the world. *Whoever* follows Me will not walk in darkness, but will have the light of life" (John 8:12, emphasis added).

No shame is too deep. No hour is too late. No place is too far away. However. Whenever. Wherever. Whoever. That includes you, delighting in God's loving Word—*forever*!

23

OVERCOMING THROUGH THE STORM

"He made the storm be still, and
the waves of the sea were hushed."

(Psalm 107:29)

When sailors describe a storm no one can escape, they call it a perfect storm. Not perfect in the sense of ideal, but perfect in the sense of its combining factors. Combining factors like hurricane-force winds with a cold front, rain, and a high tide. The hurricane-force winds alone would be impossible. But hurricane-force winds and a cold front and rain and a high tide? It's a perfect storm.

We don't need to be sailors to experience a perfect storm. All we need is a layoff and a recession with a child going away to college, a disease and a divorce and a parent with dementia, a breakup with a sweetheart and a college rejection letter. We can usually handle one storm, but two or three or four at a time? A bomb cyclone and a polar vortex? Gale-force winds with thunderstorms and hail?

Judah's Last Days

Judah's last days are a perfect storm. The nation is caught in the crossfire between two great ancient Near Eastern empires—Babylon and Egypt. Add to that the inept Judean king Zedekiah. All was lost.

Zedekiah didn't have the evil resolve of Jehoiakim; neither was he like his father, Josiah. One minute, Zedekiah saves Jeremiah. The next minute, he shows no mercy. The king vacillates between listening to the prophet and listening to government officials. Zedekiah possessed neither the faith nor the resolve to rescue Judah. One word describes him—ambivalent.

Then, a light! In 587 BC, when Pharaoh Hophra led the Egyptians against the Babylonians, it looked like the tide might turn. No one wanted to admit, though, that betting on Egypt was always betting on the wrong horse. The faithful had known that since the days of Moses. Pharaohs never win. Pharaohs always lose. "Thus says the LORD, Behold, I will give Pharaoh Hophra king of Egypt into the hand of his enemies and into the hand of those who seek his life" (Jeremiah 44:30).

Egypt helped, but only for a moment. "Thus says the LORD, God of Israel: Thus shall you say to the king of Judah who sent you to Me to inquire of Me, 'Behold, Pharaoh's army that came to help you is about to return to Egypt, to its own land. And the Chaldeans shall come back and fight against this city. They shall capture it and burn it with fire'" (Jeremiah 37:7–8). The Babylonian army would crush Judah's resistance forces once and for all.

Jeremiah's Storms

During Babylon's final assault, Jerusalem authorities imprison Jeremiah—not once, but twice. The vocabulary and location are similar in both imprisonments (Jeremiah 37:11–21; 38:1–12). The two scenes move from imprisonment to pardon, from death to resurrection. The prophet is momentarily muted, then miraculously restored.

In the first episode, government officials accuse Jeremiah of being a Benedict Arnold, that he had been aiding and abetting Babylon. Jeremiah experiences police brutality, and then he's thrown into prison. But the prophet is released. Later Jeremiah pleads with Zedekiah not to send him back to jail where he would inevitably die. The king not only grants the request, he also provides food for the prophet (Jeremiah 37:17–21).

In the second prison episode, Jeremiah is mired in mud, in the cistern of Malchiah, the king's son. This time the prophet faces certain demise— or so it would seem. Out of the blue, a previously unknown man enters the scene—an African court official named Ebed-melech. This kind soul, along with thirty others, rescues Jeremiah from deep in the pit. God then grants life to Ebed-melech, the prophet's Ethiopian helper, because of his fidelity to the prophet. "'For I will surely save you, and you shall not fall by the sword, but you shall have your life as a prize of war, because you have put your trust in Me,' declares the LORD" (Jeremiah 39:18).

Jeremiah is two for two. Twice at the end of his rope. Twice rescued and restored.

Stuck in a Pit

Imagine being stuck a pit. In the Old Testament, synonyms for "mud" include "hole," "cistern," and "Sheol." *Sheol* literally means "the place of no return." That's where Jeremiah was—the place of no return.

He didn't see it coming. Jeremiah didn't get out of bed that morning and say, "I'd better pack some extra food and water and put on padded clothing because today I'm going to get thrown into a muddy pit." The attack came as a complete surprise.

So did ours. That's the way the enemy works. Maybe your pit came when Satan reminded you of a misdeed long ago or of a commandment broken just yesterday. Perhaps you find yourself in the pit of shame and despair because of Satan's constant lies—lies that you've fallen for times without number. People then often add insult to our injury with their snide remarks and cutting criticisms.

Then there's Christmas. Christmas can be a deep emotional pit—a living hell. The Yuletide can be a time when we become painfully aware of what we don't have—of who isn't with us. It can be a season of dark despair.

We all want Christmas to be the best of times. That's why we decorate and donate and shop until we drop. We put up trees, hang tinsel, cook turkeys, and put together all kinds of toys. We all want a holly, jolly Christmas. But let's be honest. As much as we want Christmas to be the best of times, sometimes it's the worst of times. There are old hurts that won't heal and new wounds that won't go away. We miss loved ones at Christmas—terribly. This happens because of distance, death, or cruel, insidious design.

Who hasn't experienced some form of a pit on Christmas?

Several years ago, I was teaching in Moscow, Russia. After that, I boarded a train for St. Petersburg to teach there for two more weeks. It all looked good on paper. Let me emphasize the words *on paper.* My Russian friends failed to tell me that it was an all-night train. They also failed to tell me that this all-night train would be full of Russians who would be up all night. And for the record, they failed to tell me that these late-night-loving Russians would sing and carouse as they drank vodka all night long. I was stuck with no way out, save jumping off the train!

When we're stuck in a pit, sometimes we think there's no way out. That's not what the Book of Psalms says.

- "O LORD, You have brought up my soul from Sheol; You restored me to life from among those who go down to the pit." (Psalm 30:3)
- "He drew me up from the pit of destruction, out of the miry bog, and set my feet upon a rock, making my steps secure." (Psalm 40:2)
- "Bless the LORD, oh my soul . . . who redeems your life from the pit." (Psalm 103:2, 4)

God is not the great terminator. God is not the cosmic Ebenezer Scrooge. God is not a vengeful judge, a nitpicky tax accountant, or a police officer waiting to give us a ticket. God sets us free from the condemnation of our sin, free from the pain of our past, free from worry about our future, free from every muddy pit.

Zedekiah's Last Stand

You've heard of Custer's Last Stand at the Battle of Little Bighorn in 1876? Let me tell you about King Zedekiah's last stand at the Battle of Jerusalem in 588 BC. The siege of the capital city is underway. Babylon's hordes are standing at the gates. Zedekiah—Judah's last and most inept king—is on the throne, a Babylonian puppet who risked everything when he revolted against the empire.

Jerusalem's days are coming to an end. Its citizens will either die or be displaced. There's no third option. Jeremiah has repeatedly encouraged Judahites to surrender and live. If they rebel, they will die. No one listened. Self-assertion always leads to self-destruction. The expression "You have neither listened nor inclined your ears to hear" (Jeremiah 25:4) recurs in Jeremiah 34:14; 35:15; 44:5.

The Babylonian siege lasted eighteen months (Jeremiah 39:1–2). The walls finally succumbed to the empire's battering rams. "Then all the officials of the king of Babylon came and sat in the middle gate: Nergal-sar-ezer of Samgar, Nebu-sar-sekim the Rab-saris, Nergal-sar-ezer the Rab-mag, with all the rest of the officers of the king of Babylon" (Jeremiah 39:3). Babylonian leaders take their seats in the middle gate to assert their control over Jerusalem. Then they prepare to raze the city. Up next? King Zedekiah.

Zedekiah is a case study of what happens when we don't listen to God's Word, when we just know we have all the answers, when we opt for a "go it alone" strategy. Everything comes to a horrific end. "The king of Babylon slaughtered the sons of Zedekiah at Riblah before his eyes, and the king of Babylon slaughtered all the nobles of Judah. He put out the eyes of Zedekiah and bound him in chains to take him to Babylon" (Jeremiah 39:6–7). After this nightmare, Nebuzaradan, a leading Babylonian official, frees Jeremiah and gives him the choice to live in Babylon or in Judah. Babylon treats Jeremiah better than his countrymen ever treated him.

Do you see the irony? Zedekiah is brutalized. Jeremiah is vindicated. Zedekiah is enslaved. Jeremiah goes free. The strong becomes weak while the weak becomes strong. Jeremiah persists and prevails. Jeremiah overcomes the perfect storm. "So [Jeremiah] lived among the people" (Jeremiah 39:14).

Buried

It didn't seem like it could happen, but it did. Everything turned to ashes. It all became dust in the wind. "The Chaldeans burned the king's house and the house of the people, and broke down the walls of Jerusalem" (Jeremiah 39:8). In the Book of Lamentations, Jeremiah replays the ordeal:

- "She weeps bitterly in the night, with tears on her cheeks; among all her lovers she has none to comfort her." (Lamentations 1:2)
- "Her fall is terrible; she has no comforter." (Lamentations 1:9)
- "For these things I weep; my eyes flow with tears; for a comforter is far from me." (Lamentations 1:16)
- "Zion stretches out her hands, but there is none to comfort her." (Lamentations 1:17)
- "They heard my groaning, yet there is no one to comfort me." (Lamentations 1:21)

What do we call all this? *Buried.*

An episode of the old *Alfred Hitchcock Presents* TV show is about a woman prisoner who became good friends with the prison caretaker. When a prisoner died, the caretaker would ring the death bell, get the body, put it in a casket, and nail the lid shut. Then, placing the casket on a wagon, he would take it to the graveyard outside the prison walls and bury the corpse.

Knowing this routine, the woman prisoner devised an escape plan. She shared it with the caretaker. "The next time the death bell rings," she whispered, "I'll leave my cell and sneak into the coffin with the dead body. Nail the lid shut. Take the coffin outside the prison with me in it. Bury the coffin," she continued, "and because there will be enough air for me to breathe for some time, come back to the graveyard under the cover of night, dig up the coffin, and set me free." The caretaker agreed to the plan.

One day, the woman prisoner heard the ringing of the death bell. She got up, walked down the hallway, found the coffin containing the dead body, and climbed in. Soon she heard the pounding of the hammer and nails. The coffin was lifted onto the wagon and taken outside to the grave-yard. After the dirt was poured on the coffin she began to giggle softly, "I'm free, free!"

Feeling curious she lit a match to identify the prisoner beside her. In the glimmer of light, she discovered that she was lying next to the dead caretaker! In classic Alfred Hitchcock fashion, the final scene fades as we hear the woman screaming, screaming, screaming—then silence.

Have you ever been buried like that before? Sure you have. So have I. We've been buried in questions. "If God is so good, why do I hurt so bad?" "If Jesus is the light, why am I in the dark?" "If Jesus is alive, why do I feel so dead?"

We've been buried in disappointment. "You're fired!" "Your disease is terminal." "I don't love you anymore!"

We've been buried in the past. The minute we lost our temper. The hour we lost our purity. The day we lost control. The years we lost our priorities.

Then they nailed the lid shut.

Buried, boxed in, and six feet under, it's dark, frightening, and claus-trophobic. If there isn't screaming, there are heavy sighs, lifeless looks, and broken hearts.

Buried. That's how things felt after the Babylonians destroyed Solo-mon's temple.

It all prefigured another temple that was toppled and torn apart. That temple would be Jesus. The Savior once promised, "Destroy this temple, and in three days I will raise it" (John 2:19). Because of your sin and mine, the enemy marshaled every weapon of mass destruction. Judas, Herod, Pilate, thorns, nails, and darkness. And there was screaming, screaming, and more screaming. Then silence. It ended crucified, dead, and buried. Nothing is as lifeless as a grave, as hopeless as a tomb. Smell the mildew, the odor of blood, the of stench death. See the confines, the darkness, the sealed stone. Where does that leave us when we're buried?

I guess we can light a match and see who we're buried with. Do you see? Do you see it? You're buried with Jesus!

- "We were buried therefore with Him by baptism into death, in order that, just as Christ was raised from the dead by the glory of the Father, we too might walk in newness of life." (Romans 6:4)
- "[You were] buried with Him in baptism, in which you were also raised with Him through faith in the powerful working of God, who raised Him from the dead." (Colossians 2:12)

Through the waters of Baptism, you're buried with a triumphant Savior whose resurrection raises you to new life—forgiven life, joyful life, abundant life, eternal life. You're not alone when your world caves and you feel buried. You're with Jesus.

The Tornado

Following Jerusalem's demise, Nebuzaradan—a Babylonian official—takes center stage. He gives land to the poor, releases Jeremiah, and validates the prophet's message. "The LORD has brought it about, and has done as He said. Because you sinned against the LORD and did not obey His voice, this thing has come upon you" (Jeremiah 40:3). This outsider is more in line with God's will than most Judean insiders. A Babylonian tells Judeans about their lack of faith. Jeremiah is vindicated! "The captain of the guard gave him an allowance of food and a present, and let him go" (Jeremiah 40:5). Freedom and a government severance package to boot!

Following this kindness to Jeremiah, the Babylonians appoint Gedaliah to serve as Judah's governor. They choose Mizpah to be the provincial capital. Finally! Everything seemed to be settling down. After all, Gedaliah came from a family that was politically well connected. His grandfather Shaphan served as Josiah's secretary (2 Kings 22:3), while his father, Ahikam, had enough bureaucratic muscle to step into a riotous mob and save Jeremiah (Jeremiah 26:24). Things started well under Gedaliah.

They quickly deteriorated—in a horrific series of events. Jeremiah 40:7–41:18 describes unspeakable violence, bloodshed, and duplicity. Leading the bloodbath was a certain Ishmael whose grandfather Elishama was one of Zedekiah's chief officers (Jeremiah 41:1). With political connections of his own, Ishmael, along with ten others, murdered Gedaliah. Prominent Judeans and Babylonians were also massacred. When eighty men arrived from Shechem, Shiloh, and Samaria to mourn the deceased, Ishmael proceeded to slaughter seventy of them and throw their bodies into a pit. Ishmael escaped unpunished. It was another perfect storm.

So was the Joplin tornado.

The Joplin, Missouri, tornado hit on Sunday, May 22, 2011. Sustained winds reached 200 miles per hour; 158 people died; 1,150 people were injured; the total damage was $3.1 billion.

The next day, Monday, May 23, 2011, my son Jonathan and I began riding our bikes across the state of Missouri. Let me underscore the obvious. *This was not a very good idea!* Storms resulting from the Joplin tornado chased us all the way from Kansas City to St. Louis. On Tuesday night, May 24, we camped along the Missouri River, near McBaine, Missouri—about twenty miles west of Jefferson City. The sky grew dark and cloudy. Winds began to howl. And the rain came down in buckets. I thought of Don McLean and his song "American Pie": "This will be the day that I die!"

There we were, in a two-man tent, in the middle of nowhere. And it wasn't as though we could just get in the car and drive home. Let me again underscore the obvious. *We had no car.* We were on bikes. All night long one storm after another rolled in. We were stuck in a storm—a very, very bad storm.

You know what it feels like to be stuck in a vulnerable, exposed place when a storm hits. Are you raising teenagers? Did you get cut from the team? Did you lose the love of your life? Are finances tight? What about your health? Is old age getting the best of you?

The sky is dark and cloudy. Winds are howling. The rain is coming down like holy buckets. Add to that the lightning and thunder. "This will be the day that I die!"

Are you stuck in a bad place? Jesus was stuck in a bad place. Are you hurting? Jesus hurt. Are you bleeding? Jesus bled. Do you feel like you're gasping for air? Jesus gasped for air. Are you crying? Jesus cried. Is your heart breaking? Jesus' heart was absolutely broken. What's it all mean? It means we're not alone in the storm.

To the father haunted by his angry outbursts, Jesus speaks. To the husband and wife who barely talk to each other, Jesus speaks. To all of us exposed to the constant storm of sin, Jesus speaks. Listen. Can you hear Him? What does He say? "I love you more than you will ever know!"

What should we do when we're stuck in a bad place—a massive, life-threatening, Category 5 kind of storm? When it looks as though everything is going to get wiped off the map? Should we panic? pout? pretend?

God knows how to get His people safely through the storm. Isn't that Jeremiah's message? God doing whatever it takes to get His dear people safely through their unpredictable, ferocious, and hellish storms?

Are you bouncing up and down in a perfect storm? Are you doing everything you can to survive? Have you battened down the hatches? lowered the anchor? consulted the bank? changed your diet? called an attorney? tightened your budget? gone into counseling or rehab or therapy? Yet the sea still is churning? And the waves are still coming?

When parents send their children to camp, they have to sign a form that asks, Who is the responsible party? If Joey breaks his arm or Suzie breaks out with measles, who is the responsible party? So a parent signs his or her name.

Christ signed His name for us—and He wrote it in blood. When we were baptized, Jesus took full responsibility for us. When the perfect storm hits, Jesus is the responsible party—not us. It's His job to see us through. And He will—every single time.

Exiled to Egypt

Jeremiah overcomes prison, a pit, and Babylon's conquest of Jerusalem, only to be forcibly taken to Egypt by his own countrymen. Fearing Babylonian reprisal after Ishmael's attempted coup, Johanan steps up and convinces a group of Judeans to escape to Egypt. They drag Jeremiah and Baruch with them (Jeremiah 42–43). Just like the exiles in Babylon, Jeremiah must now live in a foreign land against his will. The prophet's life mirrors the lives of those for whom he writes his book. Like them, he faces loneliness, captivity, beatings, imprisonments, threats of death, and even, in the end, forced deportation.

We understand. We live in a world of put-downs, cold shoulders, and brush-offs. Phone calls aren't returned. Texts are ignored. Emails are neglected. We get unfriended on Facebook. Put it all together and we feel like one huge, unwanted, unnoticed nobody.

The pain of rejection is more powerful than physical pain. Did you know that? Try recalling an experience when you felt significant physical pain and your brain will say, "Ho-hum! No big deal." Then try reliving a painful rejection—actually, don't try, just take my word for it—and you will be flooded with many of the same negative feelings you had when it happened. We respond to rejection by becoming obsessed with our inadequacies. What a killer tornado!

God knows how to get us safely through this storm too. Isn't that the message in Holy Communion? With His true body and blood, Jesus takes us from a stormy place to a safe place. The Sacrament of the Altar is a place of peace in His presence. It's a place to lay our burdens down to receive forgiveness and new life.

Jesus has reserved a place—a place at His table—just for you, in your perfect storm.

24

OVERCOMING THROUGH FAITH

"Now faith is the assurance of things
hoped for, the conviction of things not seen."

(Hebrews 11:1)

In 1960, an amazing event occurred in a tiny village in the Ukraine. Grisha Siklenko appeared, much to the shock of his friends and neighbors. Everyone thought Grisha died in World War II. Truth be told, the night Grisha Siklenko marched away to war, he abandoned his regiment and scurried home, where his mother had made a hiding place for him under a manure pile. For eighteen years, Grisha Siklenko lived in manure. In the winter, he nearly froze to death. In the summer, he almost suffocated to death. Finally, in 1960, Grisha walked out of the manure, expecting to be prosecuted and placed in prison. His fears were groundless. The statute of limitations had long since expired.

Fear does that. We end up living in manure. Then what happens? Life stinks!

Do you know what the most frequent command in the Bible turns out to be? What instruction, what order, is given repeatedly, by prophets, angels, and apostles? What do you think? "Be good"? "Be holy"? "Don't sleep during the sermon"? The most frequent command in the Bible is "Don't fear." Why is that? Living in fear is like living in manure. Everything stinks!

After a setback, our fear grabs hold of us and won't let us go. We fear the next day, and the day after that. And then the day after that. There are children to take care of—and they are so vulnerable. Or perhaps an aging parent is screaming for your attention. Or you're not eating or sleeping well so it's difficult to hold down your job.

As much as we try to deny it, fake it, and stuff it down, fear is a frequent companion. It seems as though a grizzly bear is behind every corner. It's just a matter of time until he leaps out of the shadows, bares his ugly fangs, and chews us up—along with our family, friends, and all our finances. Fear twists us into emotional pretzels; it makes our eyes twitch, our blood pressure rise, our head ache, and our armpits sweat. We numb our fear with six-packs and food binges and too much TV. We express our fear with volcanic anger and silent stares. We're experts at both.

Jeremiah was in a similar position. Try to imagine what he'd been through. The list is long—death threats, forced celibacy, rejection, imprisonments, depression, and a mud pit. Add to that Jerusalem's demise and Ishmael's murderous vendetta against Gedaliah.

The proverbial last straw is now on the horizon. In all likelihood, Nebuchadnezzar will return and make everyone pay—again. People are overwhelmed with fear. They want to run as far away as possible. Someone suggests Egypt. What is the prophet's counsel? "Do not fear the king of Babylon, of whom you are afraid. Do not fear him, declares the LORD, for I am with you, to save you and to deliver you from his hand" (Jeremiah 42:11).

Reasons to Fear

Before the Judeans run to Egypt, seeking to avoid Babylonian reprisals for Ishmael's coup, they go to Jeremiah for advice. Before 587 BC, the prophet doesn't intercede for Judah (Jeremiah 7:16; 11:14; 14:11–12;

15:1–2). After 587 BC, however, he prays for survivors. "Jeremiah the prophet said to them, 'I have heard you. Behold, I will pray to the LORD your God according to your request, and whatever the LORD answers you I will tell you. I will keep nothing back from you'" (Jeremiah 42:4). Before 587 BC, Jeremiah's message is direct and to the point: submit to Babylon. After 587 BC, his message again is crystal clear: "Do not go to Egypt" (Jeremiah 42:19). The prophet leaves no room for imagination or a different interpretation. Egypt is a deathly alternative to life in Judah under Babylonian control.

How do the people respond? "Azariah the son of Hoshaiah and Johanan the son of Kareah and all the insolent men said to Jeremiah, 'You are telling a lie. The LORD our God did not send you to say, "Do not go to Egypt to live there"'" (Jeremiah 43:2). It is ironic that Jeremiah marshaled the same accusation against false prophets (Jeremiah 23:14; 27:10; 28:15; 29:21). The tables have turned. Now Judeans call Jeremiah a false prophet. Can things get any worse? Yes. Rebelling against the prophetic word, those hell-bent on fleeing to Egypt force Jeremiah and Baruch to go with them. They end up where Israel's history began—in Egypt, thinking it was the Promised Land (cf. Numbers 16:13).

The nation's journey, then, is from Egypt to the Promised Land and back to Egypt. It's a tragic story of arrogance, resistance, and unbelief. Judahites even go so far as to say to Jeremiah, "As for the word that you have spoken to us in the name of the LORD, we will not listen to you" (Jeremiah 44:16). Listening leads to life. Lack of listening spells certain death. Why didn't the people listen to Jeremiah? One word. Fear. False Evidence Appearing Real.[1]

Back to Egypt

Egypt looked like the answer to the people's problems. Yet looking to the land of the Nile would only compound their pain. Egypt appeared to be a refuge, but from the beginning, it has been a place of suffering

---

1   The FEAR acronym is popularly attributed to Neale Donald Walsch.

and death. Remember the pharaoh in the Book of Exodus? Remember his bricks, whips, and bag of countless tricks? Egypt placed production over people and money over mercy. The prophetic word is clear—never trust in Egypt.

- "'Ah, stubborn children,' declares the LORD, 'who carry out a plan, but not Mine, and who make an alliance, but not of My Spirit, that they may add sin to sin; who set out to go down to Egypt, without asking for My direction, to take refuge in the protection of Pharaoh and to seek shelter in the shadow of Egypt!'" (Isaiah 30:1–2)

- "Woe to those who go down to Egypt for help and rely on horses, who trust in chariots because they are many and in horsemen because they are very strong, but do not look to the Holy One of Israel or consult the LORD!" (Isaiah 31:1)

- "Behold, you are trusting in Egypt, that broken reed of a staff, which will pierce the hand of any man who leans on it. Such is Pharaoh king of Egypt to all who trust in him." (Isaiah 36:6)

- "What do you gain by going to Egypt to drink the waters of the Nile?" (Jeremiah 2:18)

- "You shall be put to shame by Egypt." (Jeremiah 2:36)

Egypt is a place to run from. Egypt is never a place to go to. To go to Egypt is to jump from the fire into a frying pan. It looked like a sure bet, but looks can be deceiving. They always do in Egypt. Jeremiah offers an ominous word to all who journey to Egypt: "You shall see this place no more" (Jeremiah 42:18). Goodbye, Promised Land, forever.

Fear is behind the mad dash to Egypt. When our hearts are fearful, we treat God's Word lightly, ignore His promptings repeatedly, and disregard prayer and divine promises nonchalantly.

How About Trying This?

Come to Jesus, confessing your fear, your worry, and your anxiety. Tell

Him about your helplessness and emptiness. Be honest and humble. Kneel before the Lord your Maker.

Years ago, my beagle dog Howard chewed the tongue off of a very expensive running shoe. Looking to save my investment, I took the shoe to a shoe repair shop. I told the man, "My dog got hold of this." He picked up the shoe and looked it over. I asked, "Well, what do you think?" He looked at me and said, "Give your dog the other shoe!"

What do we do when things look like a total loss? Renounce fear (False Evidence Appearing Real) and embrace faith. Faith? Forsaking **All I T**ake **H**im.[2] Him? That would be Jesus. Jesus, whose perfect love casts out fear (1 John 4:18).

An Ending That Doesn't End

Jeremiah's book has three endings—chapters 45, 46–51, and 52. There's no neat and tidy conclusion. The prophet refuses to glibly announce, "They all lived happily ever after." In this life, sorrows rarely, if ever, come to a satisfying end. It's difficult to close the book on deep loss. We can't just turn the page one day and announce, "They lived happily ever after." When we've been traumatized, complete closure rarely happens. One thing is certain, though. Because of Jeremiah, the nation was reconstituted. His book brought hope. Beauty arose from dust and ashes.

Jeremiah 45 announces Baruch's future. Chapter 51 describes Babylon's future, while Jeremiah 52 narrates Jehoiachin's future—and ours as well.

Baruch's Future

We've heard stunned survivors of a tornado or earthquake say, "We lost everything! But at least we're still alive!" Losing everything is disastrous. Having our lives, though, is no small miracle. "At least we're still alive!" That's an obvious precondition to having a future in this world. That's God's pledge to Baruch, Jeremiah's faithful scribe. Jeremiah 45 offers Baruch a future and a hope.

---

2   The FAITH acronym is from "F.A.I.T.H.," a poem by Luke Easter on ozofe.com.

The prophet delivers this oracle in Jehoiakim's fourth year, or 605 BC, the same year given in Jeremiah 36:1. The king's fourth year serves as brackets around chapters 36–45—a part of the book often called "The Baruch Section."

In Jeremiah 45, God rebukes Baruch for seeking "great things." The scribe laments. He wants more. What does God promise him? His "life as a prize of war." Baruch won't be taken captive. He won't be exiled or executed by Babylon. He will, however, survive. The expression his/your "life as a prize of war" also appears in these verses:

- "He who stays in this city shall die by the sword, by famine, and by pestilence, but he who goes out and surrenders to the Chaldeans who are besieging you shall live and shall have his life as a prize of war." (Jeremiah 21:9)
- "Thus says the LORD: He who stays in this city shall die by the sword, by famine, and by pestilence, but he who goes out to the Chaldeans shall live. He shall have his life as a prize of war, and live." (Jeremiah 38:2)
- "For I will surely save you [Ebed-melech], and you shall not fall by the sword, but you shall have your life as a prize of war, because you have put your trust in Me, declares the LORD." (Jeremiah 39:18)

Baruch and Ebed-melech function like Joshua and Caleb—they risk their lives for a divine cause. They believe, against the majority, in the promises of God. Baruch and Ebed-melech escape with their lives. That's it. Nothing more, but nothing less. Isn't that the way things often turn out after a catastrophe? Survival.

Baruch wanted great things. So do we. Instead, though, God gives us our "life as a prize of war." Is that so bad? After a massive loss? Survival with my faith in Christ still intact? With the Holy Christian Church as my family? With baptismal promises still in play? With the certain hope of eternal life through Jesus Christ?

When we're reduced to living in survival mode, questions pound us like waves crashing on the shore. What went wrong? Who's to blame? How did this happen? What should I have done differently? It's time to stop scratching our heads about what we don't know and press into what we do know. What do we know?

- "We know that for those who love God all things work together for good." (Romans 8:28)
- "We know that if the tent that is our earthly home is destroyed, we have a building from God, a house not made with hands, eternal in the heavens." (2 Corinthians 5:1)
- "We know that a person is not justified by works of the law but through faith in Jesus Christ." (Galatians 2:16)
- "We know that He abides in us, by the Spirit whom He has given us." (1 John 3:24)

Please don't misunderstand. None of this is easy or tidy. It's difficult and messy. It calls for "longsuffering." Now there's a word you haven't heard in a while. "Longsuffering" appears in the 1611 King James Version seventeen times. Modern translations of the Bible frequently render the word "patient." There are times when God calls us to be patient. Then again, there are times when God calls us to suffer for months, years, or even decades. There's a word for that—"longsuffering."

Another Nobody

For most of his book, Jeremiah is ignored, misunderstood, belittled, persecuted, and imprisoned. Kings, false prophets, royal officials, countrymen, and hometown acquaintances band together to silence him. Jeremiah felt like a nobody who died in Egypt against his will. Tragedies do that to us. They reduce us to feeling like we're one huge, unnoticed nobody.

It points to another nobody—in fact, He was Mr. Nobody. Don't get me wrong, though. At one point Jesus had been somebody. Check that; Jesus had been Mr. Somebody. Angels worshiped Him from eternity past, singing, "Holy, holy, holy" (Isaiah 6:3). John says, "All things were made through Him" (John 1:3). Paul proclaims, "He is the image of the invisible God" (Colossians 1:15). The writer of Hebrews says of Jesus, "He is the radiance of the glory of God and the exact imprint of His nature" (Hebrews 1:3). We confess in the Nicene Creed that Jesus is "begotten not made, being of one substance with the Father." Now that's Mr. Somebody!

Jesus, Mr. Somebody, accepted nobodies. Nobodies like Peter, James, and John—fishermen! Nobodies like the Samaritan woman, Jarius's daughter, and the widow of Nain's son. Nobodies like little Zacchaeus, blind Bartimaeus, and unbelieving Thomas. But Pharisees plot with Sadducees. Detractors say he's demon possessed. Christ's brothers ride and ridicule Him. The final assault begins with thirty pieces of silver as Judas betrays the Master.

Blood-soaked and spiked to wood, Christ hangs, His lungs screaming for air. Passersby mock Him, saying, "You are one huge, unnoticed nobody!" Joseph places Christ in the tomb. See the confines, the darkness, the sealed stone.

And witness the charred marks of a divine explosion to life! There is nothing dead about Jesus! Jesus blew the rock open from the inside and rolled away the stone. Jesus surged out of the tomb and is still surging into the world, right to you—just now, speaking words straight from His heart to yours. "My dear, dear child. No matter what, I will always accept you. No matter what, I will always welcome you." This is no sentimental or syrupy love—but instead, it is a fierce love for you. Driven by nails, marked with scars, crowned with thorns, sealed in Holy Baptism, and delivered to you in the Holy Supper of His real body and real blood.

Our risen Lord emboldens faith. "God gave us a spirit not of fear" (2 Timothy 1:7). Satan seeks to paralyze us with "what ifs" and "how comes" and "why nows." He traffics in lies that maximize our insecurities and anxieties. Here's the truth: You are wonderfully made. You are baptized and forgiven. You are chosen, a treasure, and deeply loved.

And you aren't just anybody. You're more than just somebody. And Jesus says no one is an unwanted, unnoticed nobody. That's not us. Not now, not ever. Our response? No more fear. Instead? Forsaking All I Take Him.

25

OVERCOMING THROUGH SINGING

"He called out with a mighty voice, 'Fallen, fallen is Babylon the great!'"

(Revelation 18:2)

True confession. I'm not a very good singer. Strike that. I'm a rotten singer. I sing off-key and off-kilter. When the song goes sharp, I fall flat. Things get remarkably better when I sing along with a song on the radio. God help us, though, if I turn it down and pick up the beat.

Jeremiah composed songs for us to sing. Some call them "guerilla liturgy" because the prophet's oracles about nations in chapters 46–51 anticipate the fall of Judah's enemies but don't encourage physical violence.

Jeremiah invites us to celebrate along with him. He promises to keep us in rhythm and on key. So let's turn up the volume, carefully listen to the prophet's voice, and sing these songs of victory. Revelation 11:15 is an apt summary of this section in Jeremiah: "The kingdom of the world has become the kingdom of our Lord and of His Christ, and He shall reign forever and ever." It's time to sing!

Oracles about Nations

One day, when my older daughter Abi was a small child, I promised to take her to see the Ringling Bros. and Barnum & Bailey Circus. Days passed. The excitement built. Abi could hardly wait to see the lions, trapeze artists, elephants, magicians, and her favorite—the clowns in their funny little cars. Finally, the big show was one day away. That night, Abi said to me, "Daddy, thank you for tomorrow!"

Exiles singing Jeremiah's songs about foreign nations saw through oppressive social and political systems and celebrated God's victory over ruthless enemies. Jeremiah 48–51 didn't encourage Babylonian refugees to escape the fractured world or transform it through violence. Rather, their holy defiance empowered them to imagine a counterworld order where God is King. Through these songs, exiles praised God today for what He promised to do tomorrow. The oracles are part of a larger hymnbook that includes these lyrics:

- "Let the heavens be glad, and let the earth rejoice, and let them say among the nations, 'The LORD reigns!'" (1 Chronicles 16:31)
- "The LORD reigns; He is robed in majesty." (Psalm 93:1)
- "Say among the nations, 'The LORD reigns!'" (Psalm 96:10)
- "The LORD reigns, let the earth rejoice." (Psalm 97:1)
- "The LORD reigns; let the peoples tremble!" (Psalm 99:1)

Any nation, person, or ideology who oppresses and ravages God's people won't have the final say. The final tomorrow will dawn when God will defeat all evil, vindicate His people, and make right every wrong. The days of arrogance, autonomy, and multiple atrocities will end. Who says? God says, and He reigns!

Oracles addressing other nations constitute almost one-fourth of Israel's prophetic corpus. Although Jeremiah is the only prophet who is distinctly designated to be "a prophet to the nations" (Jeremiah 1:10), Isaiah (13–23), Ezekiel (25–32), and all of the Minor Prophets except Hosea address other nations. Joel, for instance, writes about a northern army

(Joel 2:20) and includes a statement that is to be proclaimed "among the nations" (Joel 3:9). Obadiah focuses exclusively upon Edom, while Jonah is called to Nineveh not once, but twice (Jonah 1:2; 3:1–2). Micah envisions nations streaming to Zion (Micah 4:1–5), and Nahum is "an oracle concerning Nineveh" (Nahum 1:1). Habakkuk's vision is international as well: "Look among the nations, and see. . . . I am raising up the Chaldeans" (Habakkuk 1:5–6). Even Haggai, focused on Jerusalem and the rebuilt temple, proclaims that the postexilic community's wealth comes from the Lord's cosmic action: "I am about to shake the heavens and the earth, and to overthrow the throne of kingdoms" (Haggai 2:21–22). In Zechariah's first vision, God's messengers report that they "have patrolled the earth" (Zechariah 1:11), and Malachi says that the Lord's name will be "great among the nations" (Malachi 1:11).

There is countergovernance in the world that would-be autonomous nations don't acknowledge but can't escape. Israel's prophets were heralds of this universal God who is the judge of all the earth. The Lord is on His throne. He reigns!

Who Is in Charge?

Chaos ensued when President Ronald Reagan was shot on March 30, 1981. In an attempt to keep everyone calm, Alexander Haig, Reagan's secretary of state, told the press that he was in charge. Not so. Although Vice President George H. W. Bush was flying to Hawaii, the Constitution stated that while Reagan was in surgery, Bush was in charge, not Haig.

When we feel incapacitated by life's sudden twists and turns, the Lord of heaven and earth is still in control. That's Jeremiah's message throughout chapters 46–51. Although the word *king* appears 223 times in Jeremiah, the prophet boldly asserts that there is finally only one everlasting King—the Lord God Almighty, Maker of heaven and earth.

Jeremiah 46–51 contains nine oracles about foreign nations (counting Kedar and Hazor as one). Here is the lineup:

Egypt	Jeremiah 46:2–28
Philistia	Jeremiah 47:1–7
Moab	Jeremiah 48
Ammon	Jeremiah 49:1–6
Edom	Jeremiah 49:7–22
Damascus	Jeremiah 49:23–27
Kedar and Hazor	Jeremiah 49:28–33
Elam	Jeremiah 49:34–39
Babylon	Jeremiah 50–51

Jeremiah's Babylonian oracle is the longest and also concludes the section. The land of the Tigris and Euphrates Rivers is Israel's "last enemy." "She has proudly defied the LORD, the Holy One of Israel" (Jeremiah 50:29). Babylon crushed people in the name of progress, order, profit, and "the common good." But the brazen Babylonians, Israel's archenemy, are going down. The empire's day of reckoning is coming. Babylon is mighty but not almighty. Babylon is exceptionally powerful but not ultimately powerful. The Lord is the only true and eternal King. This is the refrain throughout Jeremiah's oracles.

- "'As I live,' declares the King, whose name is the LORD of hosts." (Jeremiah 46:18)
- "The destroyer of Moab and his cities has come up, and the choicest of his young men have gone down to slaughter, declares the King, whose name is the LORD of hosts." (Jeremiah 48:15)
- "I will make drunk her officials and her wise men, her governors, her commanders, and her warriors; they shall sleep a perpetual sleep and not wake, declares the King, whose name is the LORD of hosts." (Jeremiah 51:57)

Christ is the "King of kings" (1 Timothy 6:15; Revelation 19:16). The construction "X of Xs" is a biblical way to form a superlative. "Holy of holies" means the holiest place. "Song of songs" denotes the best song. "Vanity of vanities" means the utmost of vanities. "King of kings" announces that Jesus is the ultimate King. He has all authority in heaven and on earth. He mercifully uses His power for us and for our salvation.

Nothing happens by accident. Nothing is random. It may appear that other people or forces are calling all the shots, but Christ is large and He's in charge. We can believe this. We can believe this in the hardest places. We can believe this in the most confusing times. We can believe this when it doesn't look like God is at work. We can believe this even when it looks as though raw evil will win the day.

Babylon's Demise

Jeremiah calls Nebuchadnezzar "the king of Sheshach"—although the ESV renders the term "Babylon" (Jeremiah 25:26; cf. 51:41). *Sheshach* is *Babylon* written in reverse. That is to say, the first letter in the Hebrew alphabet is replaced by the last, the second by the next to the last, and so on (i.e., *B-B-L = s-s-k*). What does it mean? Babylon is an agent of evil that inverts God's created order. The empire calls evil good and good evil, darkness light and light darkness. It calls death life and life death. Jeremiah also calls Babylon "Merathaim" and "Pekod" (Jeremiah 50:21). The terms respectively mean "double rebellion" and "punishment." The empire is more than a political player in the ancient Near East. It's aligned with demonic darkness and every form of deception.

The oracles in Jeremiah 46–49 reveal that God used Babylon as His agent of judgment. Chapters 50–51, however, do a complete about-face. The agent of judgment is now judged. Jeremiah had already made this clear. "Then after seventy years are completed, I will punish the king of Babylon and that nation, the land of the Chaldeans, for their iniquity, declares the LORD, making the land an everlasting waste" (Jeremiah 25:12). God will crush Babylon. The empire faces death without any hope of resurrection.

As Jeremiah 50–51 celebrates God's victory over Babylon, the chapters make an array of stunning claims regarding God's reign on earth. He reigns in and through the losses of life and will one day put everything right. Everyone who resorts to the politics of arrogance and exploitation will stand before the Judge of heaven and earth.

By singing about Babylon's demise, beaten-down exiles were able to see that political power isn't ultimate reality, that economic-military domination is not the final word, and that God advocates for those who have been devastated with sorrow. By affirming God's rule and reign, Judean deportees dared to sing, "only the LORD and no other!"

Worship, therefore, is a call to arms—spiritual arms. Liturgy isn't some motions we go through. It's a militant mustering of the people of God. Oh, for a thousand tongues to sing our great Redeemer's praise! The psalmist writes, "It is good to give thanks to the LORD, to sing praises to Your name, O Most High; to declare Your steadfast love in the morning, and Your faithfulness by night" (Psalm 92:1–2). It's no surprise, then, that Saul, when he was downcast with an evil spirit, was refreshed when David surrounded him with songs (1 Samuel 16:23). That same refreshment is also God's gift to us.

We won't be silenced. We won't be quiet. We are the baptized and we have a song to sing! With Moses, Miriam, and all Israel at the Red Sea, we celebrate, "The LORD will reign forever and ever" (Exodus 15:18).

Jeremiah also picked up on exodus imagery. It permeates Jeremiah 50:33–40.

- Like Egypt (Exodus 9:2, 17, 35), Babylonian captors refuse to let exiles go (Jeremiah 50:33).
- The LORD comes as Israel's Redeemer (Exodus 6:6; 15:13; Jeremiah 50:34).
- Additional exodus allusions include "wise men" (Exodus 7:11; Jeremiah 50:35), "horses and chariots" (Exodus 14:9, 23; 15:19; Jeremiah 50:37), and the miracle of drying-up water (Exodus 14:21–22; Jeremiah 50:38).

Jeremiah's message is clear: if God rescued His people once, He will do it again. "Therefore, behold, the days are coming, declares the LORD, when it shall no longer be said, 'As the LORD lives who brought up the people of Israel out of the land of Egypt,' but 'As the LORD lives who brought up the people of Israel out of the north country and out of all the countries where He had driven them'" (Jeremiah 16:14–15).

Exiles need not cringe before the empire. The fraudulent and fake Babylon—who dared to utter "I am" (Isaiah 47:8)—will soon be terminated. Savage captors are no match for the LORD. The Persian king Cyrus the Great defeated Babylon in October 539 BC. Here's how it happened.

Clichés

Have you ever wondered where clichés come from? You know, like where did we get this phrase: "Sleep tight. Don't let the bedbugs bite"? Where did "lock, stock, and barrel" come from? Or "The grass is always greener on the other side"? Or "Don't judge a book by its cover"?

Most of the time, we have no idea where clichés come from. But things are different with the cliché "The handwriting is on the wall." Check this out. "The fingers of a human hand appeared and wrote on the plaster of the wall of the king's palace, opposite the lampstand. And the king saw the hand as it wrote" (Daniel 5:5). Do you remember Thing in *The Addams Family*? It was a disembodied hand that appeared from a box—just like this hand!

"The handwriting is on the wall." The cliché means it's time to wake up. It's time to face the music. It's time to change course and switch directions. And if we delay? Failure and disaster are imminent.

Belshazzar's great feast took place on October 11, 539 BC. Two years earlier, in 541 BC, the Persian army, led by Cyrus the Great, began digging a canal to change the course of the Euphrates River, dumping the river's water into a swamp. And on October 11, 539 BC, Cyrus finished his massive project.

With the Euphrates River drained as low as it could go, Cyrus planned to march into Babylon the next day. To do what? Conquer Babylon. So Belshazzar says, "Let's throw a party!" All over the city, people got excited.

One thousand nobles—the cream of Babylon's society—were invited, along with their wives. Counting waiters, guards, and various onlookers, the total crowd numbers well over eight thousand. Belshazzar says, "I don't like reality, so I'm going to throw a party!"

Enter the hand! The hand crashes Belshazzar's party. There's no body, no face, no torso—just a hand writing on the plaster wall. The king grows faint, his knees buckle, and he almost collapses. Just as suddenly as the hand appears, the hand vanishes. The words remain. Four words. "MENE, MENE, TEKEL, PARSIN."

Daniel's explanation of these Aramaic words is short and to the point. *Mene* means "numbered." God has numbered the days of Belshazzar's reign and now his number is up. *Tekel* means "weighed." God has weighed Belshazzar's life in the scales of justice and he has come up short. *Parsin* means "divided." Belshazzar's reign is over, his life will end, and his kingdom will be divided and given to someone else.

What's the cliché for all this? The party's over! And so is Belshazzar. "That very night Belshazzar the Chaldean king was killed" (Daniel 5:30). "MENE, MENE, TEKEL, PARSIN." Here's my loose translation of this Aramaic phrase: "Belshazzar, you blew it and that's that!" Here is Jeremiah's: "Though Babylon should mount up to heaven, and though she should fortify her strong height, yet destroyers would come from Me against her, declares the LORD" (Jeremiah 51:53).

It Is Finished

Babylon's sudden demise was shocking. How could it have happened? Jeremiah knew it was coming. He envisions Babylon as a scroll thrown into the Euphrates River, never to rise again. The brothers Baruch and Seraiah are both connected to scrolls. Baruch assists Jeremiah with one in chapter 36, while Seraiah's scroll announces the empire's doom in Jeremiah 51:59–64.

Jeremiah commands Seraiah, who was earlier exiled to Babylon, to read the oracle against Babylon and then throw it into the water. True, the

Lord summoned the "boiling pot, facing away from the north" (Jeremiah 1:13). And Babylon functioned as the "hammer of the whole earth" (Jeremiah 50:23). Now the empire will get a taste of its own medicine. It will no longer be on the giving end but on the receiving end. What goes up must go down.

An angel in Revelation 18:21 repeats Seraiah's symbolic act. He takes a huge stone (representing Babylon) and throws it into the sea. Then the angel says, "So will Babylon the great city be thrown down with violence, and will be found no more." In the Book of Revelation, Babylon stands for the Roman Empire persecuting the Church. John also uses Babylon to stand for every person, movement, government, and ideology that stands opposed to God's kingdom.

God versus Babylon is a cosmic battle between light and darkness, good and evil, Christ and the ancient serpent, who is the devil, Satan. History isn't a closed process. "Might doesn't make right." Circumstances aren't ultimately in the hands of the elite who manage things for their own benefit. Babylon is finished. Done. Defeated. After two lengthy chapters depicting Babylon's fall, nothing more needs to be said. "Thus far are the words of Jeremiah" (Jeremiah 51:64).

Jeremiah's oracle against Babylon isn't escapist fantasy or a pie-in-the-sky hope. If Babylon is a superpower, the Lord is *the* Superpower in heaven and on earth. The oracle celebrates that imperial dictates don't have the final say. Greed, oppression, fear, abuse, and death—everything symbolized by Babylon—are not ultimate.

The prophet invites us to envision a different future, one in which Babylon loses while God is victorious. This hope doesn't rely upon the data—what can be seen, heard, analyzed, and codified. It rests upon the sure promises of God fulfilled in Jesus Christ. We are children of the heavenly Father. We sing to the beat of His promises and celebrate with chants and hymns.

The Lord is the God of Abraham and Sarah, Moses and Miriam, David and Jonathan, and Peter and Paul. He enters the most broken places of our lives to make things new. In the end—and there *will* be an end—we will sing with the heavenly choir, "Hallelujah! Salvation and glory and power belong to our God" (Revelation 19:1).

Babylon's demise signals a grand homecoming for God's people. The exiles will return to the Promised Land!

Come Home

In August 587 BC, Judah's world caved in. The temple collapsed, the monarchy lay in ruins, the land became a wasteland, and hope was dismantled and destroyed. Then a massive aftershock brought further wreckage and ruin. Seven hundred miles from home, Judah's exiles were trapped. *Babylon*—or *Babilu*, as the locals called it—meant "the gate of the gods." Here was heaven on earth. Not so! God says to His people, "It's time to come home!"

- "Flee from the midst of Babylon, and go out of the land of the Chaldeans, and be as male goats before the flock." (Jeremiah 50:8)
- "Flee from the midst of Babylon." (Jeremiah 51:6)
- "Forsake her, and let us go each to his own country." (Jeremiah 51:9)

Exiles were slow to respond. They began to acclimate to their new surroundings. Living comfortably in a place of destruction and death became the new way of life. It was the whole boiling frog syndrome. You know, it's said that if a frog is placed in hot water, it will jump out. Conversely, if it's placed in lukewarm water that's gradually heated up, it will never get out but slowly die. The exiles believed their Babylonian basement was the new normal. They were in hot water. If they didn't get out soon, they'd die!

It was like a thirsty person choosing to drink raw sewage instead of water from a mountain stream, or a bankrupt company rejecting a government bailout. Exiles were unmoved by Jeremiah's alarming narratives, stunning doxologies, and multiple commands to leave.

Our bondage began with just one more drink, one more lie, one more fling, one more glance. One more always longs for one more—then just one more. Soon a massive earthquake hits and we find ourselves trapped in a basement much like Babylon. What next? The boiling frog syndrome unleashes its hypnotic power. Sure, being stuck in the blame game, nursing our wounds, or feeling sorry for ourselves is a strange place to be—at first. It's crushing to be trapped beneath tons of collapsed hopes and shattered dreams. In time, though, we become accustomed to living in the darkness. With each passing month, we become stuck deeper and deeper in our sorrow. We're in hot water!

It's in God's heart to call people out of darkness and into His marvelous light. He called Abraham and Sarah to get out of Haran. He urged Lot and his family to get out of Sodom and Gomorrah. God called Israel to get out of Egypt. At the core of the Bible is God's ongoing call for people to get out of decay, decadence, and death.

God even gives exiles the words with which to respond. "In those days and in that time, declares the LORD, the people of Israel and the people of Judah shall come together, weeping as they come, and they shall seek the LORD their God. They shall ask the way to Zion, with faces turned toward it, saying, 'Come, let us join ourselves to the LORD in an everlasting covenant that will never be forgotten'" (Jeremiah 50:4–5).

Picture it as Rembrandt does. In his famous painting of the prodigal son (1668), Rembrandt depicts what it's like to come home. Everyone in the picture, whether standing or sitting, is gazing at two people. The father, leaning into his son. The son, leaning into his father. The two are locked in a loving embrace. Rembrandt captures the homecoming and paints it upon our hearts forever.

When we look at the son up close, he looks less like a son and more like a slave. His head is shaven, as if he were a prisoner. His eyes are closed because he's exhausted. His clothes are worn and tattered. He wears only one shoe, and that one is almost ruined. Slavery took away everything he had. It almost killed him. What he thought would bring life—turning away from his father—ended up dispensing only death.

We also look exhausted, torn, and tattered—that's what sorrow and sadness does to us. Many times we're just barely holding on. Slavery takes away so much. Slavery to what? You know. After a loss, we become slaves to the past—the broken, wretched, painful, haunting past. What can we do? We can come home to our heavenly Father and seek a renewed place in His family.

What does the father do? Rembrandt's primary light is upon the father's face. The father isn't upset, angry, mad, or bent out of shape. Instead, his face radiates calm and peace. Not only is the father's face full of love, but so are his hands. The two are very different. The left hand upon the son's shoulder is strong and muscular. The fingers are spread out and cover a large part of the son's shoulder and back. That hand not only touches; with its strength, it also holds.

The father's right hand is so different! It's refined, soft, and tender. The fingers have an elegant quality about them. The right hand lies gently upon the son's shoulder, giving consolation and comfort.

The right hand is that of a woman. How do we know? Rembrandt left us a clue. The exact same hand appears in one of his earlier paintings where it's the right hand of a Jewish woman—delicate, gentle, and tender. The hand of the man is whose hand? It is Rembrandt's. It shows us who he was as a father who loved his four children. These two hands tell us why the son brings his slavery to his father.

Paul invites us to do the same, crying, "Abba." This is an Aramaic term, used by Jesus in Mark 14:36 and only again in the New Testament in Romans 8:15 and Galatians 4:6. *Abba* expresses a close, intimate relationship. It is very short word, but it includes everything. Yes it does. Everything. "Abba, we bring you our slavery; all of our hurt, all of our pain, and all of our past."

Consider again Rembrandt's depiction of the father's hands. The left, bigger and stronger. The right, smaller, more tender. This is your Father in heaven. He is mighty and merciful. He is protecting and welcoming. He is sovereign and saving. He is tender and tough. These hands don't scold you or judge you. These hands welcome you and embrace you.

As we look at the entirety of Rembrandt's painting, we see that the artist has frozen the story just at the moment before the son receives all of the father's gifts. The son doesn't have a robe over his shoulders. He isn't wearing his father's ring on his finger. He doesn't have good shoes on his feet. There is no fattened calf. Neither is there a feast or a celebration. What does the son have in the painting? He has the father. And the father is enough.

Rembrandt knew. He lost his wife, his wealth, three of his four children, and his reputation. He then lost his last and only surviving son. After losing all that the world would say gives meaning, Rembrandt chose to focus upon the one thing that this world can't take away—the Father's love in Jesus.

Do you get the picture? When we come home to our Father, He silences our fear and secures our future. Falling into His arms, His firm yet gentle embrace assures us that He is enough. The Father is always enough. His loving embrace will forever be *enough*. It's time to come home singing a new song!

26

WHO OVERCOMES?

"For everyone who has been born of God overcomes the world."

(1 John 5:4)

If you buy a lottery ticket, what are the odds that you will win a multi-state Powerball sweepstakes? They're 185 million to 1. If you play baseball in high school, what are the odds of playing in the major leagues? Try 6,600 to 1. Those are the same odds of someone guessing your four-digit PIN on the first try. What are the odds that you will be struck by lightning? They're 3 million to 1. By the way, a man named Roy Sullivan holds the world record for being struck by lightning. Roy has been struck seven times.

Jehoiachin's Future

The Book of Jeremiah closes with another "what are the odds" story. It's in Jeremiah 52. The prophet reviews the tragedy of Jerusalem's destruction. It's devoid of the charged and powerful language that saturates his oracles about the nations in chapters 46–51. Instead, it has the sense of a news report told by a passionless observer. The account lacks emotion and comes across as grim and hopeless. But not for Jehoiachin.

Jehoiachin—Jehoiakim's son and Judah's second-to-last king—had been stuck in Babylon for decades. Everything looked impossible. Then, daybreak! In 561 BC, the Babylonian king Evil-merodach orders Jehoiachin to take off his prison clothes. The expression "put off his prison garments" (Jeremiah 52:33 = 2 Kings 25:29) elsewhere in the Old Testament indicates a change for the better (Genesis 45:22; Zechariah 3:4–5). How much better? Evil-merodach welcomes Jehoiachin at the royal table and even gives him daily financial assistance.

Though this short vignette at the end of Jeremiah's book isn't much to hold on to, it's a prelude to the restoration of the Davidic monarchy. The Judean king is given "a seat above the seats" of other captive kings (Jeremiah 52:32).

"Wait a minute," you say. "Hold on. Didn't I read something earlier in Jeremiah's book about God rejecting Jehoiachin?" You did. Here it is. "Write this man down as childless, a man who shall not succeed in his days, for none of his offspring shall succeed in sitting on the throne of David and ruling again in Judah" (Jeremiah 22:30).

Poor Jehoiachin. He not only spends most of his life in a Babylonian prison cell, but Jeremiah also calls him "childless." The same word describes Abraham and Sarah in Genesis 15:2. We know that story. Abraham was an old man and Sarah was an infertile postmenopausal woman. When it came to the ability to procreate, Abraham was "as good as dead" (Hebrews 11:12).

Do you see the link between Jehoiachin and Abraham? Just as Abraham's offspring were multiplied beyond imagination, so the house of David will rise from the dead. David's dynasty will continue. God will reverse the curse. Here's what that looks like:

- Jehoiachin finally had children. (1 Chronicles 3:17–18)
- Jehoiachin's grandson Zerubbabel became a Persian-appointed leader in Judah. (Haggai 1:1)

- Haggai 2:23 employs the same terms as those in Jeremiah 22:24, indicating God's judgment against Jehoiachin wasn't permanent.
- Jehoiachin is even a ancestor of Jesus. (Matthew 1:12–16)

Our Exile

Jehoiachin's long life in exile represents our exile. The Bible calls it "east of the garden of Eden" (Genesis 3:24). Just like our first parents, every son of Adam and daughter of Eve is east of where God wants us to be. Cain traveled farther east and the place was called "Nod," or "wandering" (Genesis 4:16). Everything is in bondage and decay. This is why we experience so much pain and loneliness in life.

Peter teaches that the Christian life is one long exile. It isn't geographical. Our exile is spiritual. Our real home is in the renewed heavens and renewed earth.

- "Peter, an apostle of Jesus Christ, To those who are elect exiles of the Dispersion in Pontus, Galatia, Cappadocia, Asia, and Bithynia." (1 Peter 1:1)
- "And if you call on Him as Father who judges impartially according to each one's deeds, conduct yourselves with fear throughout the time of your exile." (1 Peter 1:17)
- "Beloved, I urge you as sojourners and exiles to abstain from the passions of the flesh, which wage war against your soul." (1 Peter 2:11)

What makes you feel like an exile? Maybe you grew up in a family that didn't work. Sometimes I run into people and they're walking zombies because when they were children, something was broken inside. Now they're a third or halfway through life and they think that what's broken will never be fixed. What was lost will never be found.

I'm talking about the one in three people whose parents got divorced. Or the one in four women who were sexually abused as children. Or the one in seven people who grew up with an alcoholic parent. I'm talking about the people who grew up in families with absentee dads, controlling moms, screaming parents, and abusive siblings. You feel as though the odds are against you.

Add to that life's unspeakable sorrows. For some, a spouse died, a marriage died, a child died, or a father died. For others, it means your dream died. I'd venture to guess that for some of you, your will to live has died. Most days it feels as though Mount Everest is sitting on your chest, crushing what's left of your heart.

Maybe it's a destructive habit. Gambling? Drugs? Pornography? Work? I once heard a guy say, "I spent my entire childhood feeling invisible. There was no abuse or other stuff like that. I just felt invisible. I wanted to say, 'Hello! I'm here! I'm a little person with a love-starved heart. Would you please notice me and see me and convince me that I matter?'" It never happened. Now he's addicted to his boat and his booze. Can you relate? You feel as though the odds are against you.

All the odds were against a man named Lee Capps. You might have followed Lee's story a few years ago. Lee, who didn't know how to fly, took off in a private plane with a friend who was a pilot. When they got up to cruising altitude, Lee's friend, the pilot, had a heart attack and died.

Lee grabbed the radio and cried for help. An air traffic controller in Renton, Washington, heard Lee's cry. He said, "This is your lucky day. I'm not only an air traffic controller, I'm also a flight instructor. Would you be interested in a flying lesson?" Being otherwise unoccupied, Lee Capps said, "Sure! Why not?" The air traffic controller said, "Lee, you're going to have to take a shot at landing the plane. No practice, no dress rehearsal, no spring training!"

Lee Caps came in like a drunk duck. He was all over the place. He hit pretty hard. But Lee Capps walked away from it all with only a few minor cuts. Afterward, the air traffic controller was interviewed by several TV stations. "Did you really think he would walk away alive?" The air traffic controller responded, "Folks, Lee Capps made it against all odds!"

I know. Stuff is going on—a whole lot of stuff is going on in your life. You're circling the runway and trying to land. Even after coming to the last chapter of this book, your greatest fear is that you will crash and burn.

The hidden addictions. The affair. The breakup. You think, "Life should be better than this. Family should be better than this. Finances should be better than this." Do you know what? You're right. *Everything* should be far better than this. God placed eternity in our hearts (Ecclesiastes 3:11). We have "perfect" in our DNA. That's why we run after it, work our fingers to the bone for it, and give our souls to experience it. The problem, though, is that we can't have it—not while we're in exile, east of Eden. The new Jerusalem is coming. When Jesus returns we will finally be secure, whole, complete, healed, and victorious.

Safe and Secure

It was 1994. Abi was eight, Jonathan was six, and Lori—little Lori Beth Lessing—was all of two years old. The Lessing circus was at it again. I held the children upside down and swung them all around. They spread their arms and giggled. I threw them up and caught them as they came down.

The children never questioned my judgment. They never asked, "Dad, have you thought this through?" "Dad, do you know what you're doing?" "Dad, how about first practicing with a teddy bear?" Never once did they think I would drop them. "If Dad says he can, he can! If Dad says he will, he will!"

How safe and secure do you feel when things look like a three-ring circus? when you're upside down and swung all around?

"Our God turned the curse into a blessing." Those are words in Nehemiah 13:2. "No one is able to snatch them out of the Father's hand." Those are words in John 10:29. "I am sure that [nothing] in all creation will be able to separate us from the love of God in Christ Jesus our Lord." Those are words in Romans 8:39. "We are safe and secure from all alarms." Those are words in the 1887 hymn titled "Leaning on the Everlasting Arms." The refrain includes these lyrics: "Leaning, leaning, safe and secure from all alarms."

The alarm might be a snake in the grass; an Egyptian pharaoh; Balak, king of Moab; Sennacherib, king of Assyria; Nebuchadnezzar, king of Babylon; Darius, king of Persia; or Pontius Pilate, governor of Judea. The alarm might be a tortured childhood, a financial fiasco, a letter of rejection, a failed business, or the death of a dream—but because God turned the curse of the cross into the blessing of Easter, no one and nothing can take His blessings from you. *Ever!* This promise is signed, sealed, and delivered for you. Signed in the Savior's cleansing blood. Sealed by the Holy Spirit. Delivered in the Means of Grace—the Gospel, Holy Baptism, and the Holy Supper. If the heavenly Father says He can, He can. If the heavenly Father says He will, He will. We are safe and secure from all alarms! Why is that?

Against all odds, Jesus Christ is risen from the dead! This is the greatest "against all odds" story ever written! We *profess* Easter—no doubt. God invites us to *possess* Easter with every ounce of our being. Paul says we can. "If the Spirit of Him who raised Jesus from the dead dwells in you, He who raised Christ Jesus from the dead will also give life to your mortal bodies through His Spirit who dwells in you" (Romans 8:11). Through the presence and power of the Holy Spirit, resurrection life happens *in* us. Then we trust God. We trust His timing. We trust His way. We trust His plan. Who overcomes life's sorrows? We do—forevermore.

"I know the plans I have for you, declares the Lord, plans for shalom not for evil, to give you a hope and a future" (Jeremiah 29:11, author's translation).